The Second War of Coalition
Volume 2

The Second War of Coalition
Volume 2
The Campaigns of Marengo and Hohenlinden, 1800-1802

ILLUSTRATED

George Armand Furse

The Second War of Coalition
Volume 2
The Campaigns of Marengo and Hohenlinden 1800-1802
by George Armand Furse

ILLUSTRATED

FIRST EDITION

Leonaur is an imprint of Oakpast Ltd
Copyright in this form © 2021 Oakpast Ltd

ISBN: 978-1-915234-14-8 (hardcover)
ISBN: 978-1-915234-15-5 (softcover)

http://www.leonaur.com

Publisher's Notes

The views expressed in this book are not necessarily those of the publisher.

Contents

From Ivrea to Milan	7
Passage of the Po and Battle of Montebello	52
Desaix Joins the Army of Reserve	82
The Battlefield of Marengo	99
The Battle	124
Desaix Takes Part in the Battle	166
Observations	201
Hohenlinden	233

CHAPTER 1

From Ivrea to Milan

The small town of Ivrea, situated on the Dora Baltea, at its issue from the mountains, is, by the fertility of the soil, purposely made for an army to recover after the severe toil of crossing the Alps. In years gone by it was of considerable strength, but it had been gradually allowed to fall into decay. In 1800, the walls were in ruins, and the defences but partially armed. As the Austrians were far from believing that Italy could be invaded from that side, they had made no adequate preparation for its defence. Nor did they attempt a combat in front of the city, by reason of the ground being hilly and broken, which would have necessitated a great expansion of their forces, so that, had things not gone well, a complete rout would have speedily followed.

Watrin was ordered to march from his position at Montestrutto on the 22nd of May, and to carry Ivrea; for this city, situated as it is at the opening of the valley of Aosta, was a most important position to secure.

Ivrea is picturesquely situated on the edge of a hill crowned by an extensive old castle with three lofty towers. It was the ancient Eporedia, which the Romans colonised 100 b.c., in order to command the Alpine routes over the Great and Little Saint Bernard. For the last century it had not seen an enemy; that was since it had been captured by the Duc de Vendôme in 1704. The Austrians had only thought of re-victualling it when the French were at the gates. They held the town and citadel with some 6,000 men, infantry and cavalry. (General Watrin's report to General Lannes, Ivrea, 22nd of May, 1800.)

Such had been the result of the obstruction offered by Fort Bard, that when Lannes might justly have expected to meet with imposing forces, he had to attack a walled town without having a single cannon.

The attack was very brisk, and after two hours' fighting, notwithstanding a vigorous resistance, a battalion of the 22nd, led by Captain Cochet, escaladed the citadel and carried it by a bold dash with the bayonet. Its fall led to the capture of the town. Attacked in three points, the defences were soon broken down and the gates blown open. The 22nd and 40th Regiments rushed in *en masse* from all sides, and captured 300 prisoners. Lannes himself carried the gate on the right. All the Austrian guns, fourteen in number by their own account, remained in the hands of the French.

The operation lasted one day. Ivrea fell on the 22nd of May, in proof of which can be cited the fact that Hulin addressed a letter to the municipality of Ivrea that day, stating that the war commissary, Barmal, alone was authorised to serve requisitions.

The town of Ivrea was surrounded by a rampart and ditch. The citadel, situated on a height, defended the bridge over the Dora Baltea. The French found it in a tolerable state of repair. The Austrians had taken some slight steps towards placing Ivrea in a state of defence, for the loopholes showed that they had been repaired, and a large quantity of gabions and fascines were found in the citadel. There were fourteen cast guns, mounted on serviceable carriages, many rounds of gun ammunition, and a considerable quantity of powder and artillery materials. Dupont, in his report to the minister of war, states that the captured guns had been spiked by the Austrians previous to their retreat.

The citadel needed only provisions, and had Lannes arrived before the town one day later the enemy would have strongly occupied it, and nothing then but a regular siege would have put the French in possession of it.

It must naturally strike the reader with astonishment that no means were adopted by the Austrian commanders to obstruct the progress of the French and stop their issue from the valley of Aosta. To this supineness they owed their defeat; for it dispirited their soldiers, while it inspired the enemy with courage, and gave the French time to recover from their fatigues and complete the re-organisation of their forces.

The many complaints Lannes received from the inhabitants made him issue some very stringent orders against pillaging, as it only estranged the friendship of the people, which it was so desirable to cultivate. Every delinquent was to be brought before a drumhead court-martial and sentenced to death.

Subsequent to its capture, and as the French Army concentrated at Ivrea, the French detailed a field officer to command the place, to whom were attached a captain of engineers and a captain of artillery. On the 25th of May, Bonaparte named Brigadier Vignolles to assume the command of the town and district. The citadel was to be garrisoned by a battalion of Chabran's division; the 12th of the line occupied the town. A hospital for the sick and wounded was established in the citadel, where a fifteen-days' supply of provisions for 500 men was collected.

It was laid down that, should Ivrea be attacked by considerable forces, the troops in the town were to withdraw and fall back on Bard, after having placed the necessary reinforcements in the citadel.

When driven out of Ivrea, the Austrians retired on the Chiusella, where General Haddick, who had been ordered to cover Turin, met them. The general had a large force at his disposal, with a strong contingent of cavalry under the orders of Pilatti and Count Palfy. Haddick had hitherto shown himself particularly prudent; his patrols had been scouring the country, still taking great care not to be drawn into an engagement. Lannes was impatient to act, but he was restrained by the peremptory orders which he had received from Berthier.

In war, to make a good beginning is all-important. From the 22nd of May, the advanced guard of the Army of Reserve was in occupation of Ivrea, and the entry of the army into the plains of Piedmont was now secure. The First Consul was still at Aosta, and the little fort of Bard continued to offer an energetic resistance, and barred the way to the artillery.

On the morning of the 25th of May, an order was sent to Lannes to assume the offensive to the south of Ivrea, and to drive the enemy beyond Chivasso. The French troops at Ivrea were at the time disposed as follows: The advanced guard was beyond the bridge of Ivrea, its right holding the heights of Fiorano, and the left resting on the Dora. Boudet's division was on the left bank of the Dora Baltea on the road to Vercelli. All that Lannes had been able to gather about the enemy was that Haddick and De Briey were posted on the heights of Mersenasco, about two leagues beyond Ivrea, with some 5,000 infantry and 4,000 cavalry. Bonaparte calculated that the Austrians had at the most from 7,000 to 8,000 men in that direction. He hoped that by beating them it would be possible for Lannes to gather some precise news of Turreau.

Watrin's division—supported by Boudet's division with the 12th Hussars and 21st Chasseurs—set out at break of day on the 26th of May to attack the enemy strongly intrenched on the right bank of the Chiusella. To cover Turin, Haddick had occupied a very good position along the Chiusella; his right resting on the Dora, the left—passing by San Martino—went as far as Baldissero. He had established a battery

Passage of the Chiusella, May, 1800

of four guns to sweep the bridge, whilst other guns were placed here and there along the front. The position was also strengthened with redoubts. The Austrian troops were under De Briey, Pilatti, and Palfy, Haddick being in chief command. The regiments of Kinsky, Bannats, Tuscany, Wallis, and the King of Sardinia's guards were present in the field. The cavalry consisted of De la Tour's dragoons, several regiments of hussars, and some heavy cavalry.

The stone bridge over the Chiusella was very long and narrow; to obtain possession of it was no easy matter. Lannes ordered his bravest men to capture it. The 6th Light attacked it boldly, but the enemy defended it with the greatest determination. Their four guns plied the attacking column with shot, whilst a musketry fire belaboured it on the flanks. The 6th got possession of it, when the regiments of Franz-Kinsky and of the Bannats rushed on them and compelled the French to abandon the bridge for a short period.

In his corps Lannes had an officer, Pavetti, already mentioned in the previous chapter. His home was at Romano, and he was consequently intimately acquainted with the locality. This officer informed Lannes that to the left of the bridge there existed a very practicable ford, and offered to lead the troops across.

After having attempted several times, but in vain, to cross the bridge under the deadly fire of the enemy's guns, the French crossed by this ford. Macon's brigade with the 6th Light rushed into the river, the water reaching nearly up to their necks, and, notwithstanding the grape and musketry which poured thick on all sides, gained the opposite shore, attacked the right of the Austrian position, and opened a heavy fire. At the same time the 28th, led by General Gency, charged the bridge in close column and compelled the Austrians to give way- Palfy, who was close to the bridge charging with some squadrons of cavalry, received a mortal wound. He was carried to Romano, where he died.

Haddick possibly believed it dangerous to bring on a general action against what he imagined a superior enemy; so, he ordered a retreat. The French followed up their first advantage, and pursued the Austrians up to Romano, where the latter had taken post on the heights. The Austrians, who had found the ground close to the Chiusella very unsuited for cavalry, as it was covered with bushes and underwood, had withdrawn to a better position in the plain, which extends between Romano and the hills of Montalengo. It was there that 4,000 cavalry rushed at the French. The Austrians executed several brilliant charges, but all void of results. The 40th under Malher, and the 22nd directed by Brigadier-General Schreiber, having forded the river on the right of the original position and some way below the bridge, came up in time, and met the several charges with the bayonet, until the arrival of the 12th Hussars and the 21st Chasseurs, who rushed on the enemy and put an end to the combat.

Boudet, who with his division had supported Watrin, and had moved up to Romano, was ordered to pursue, which he did up to the top of the mountains near Foglizzo. The Austrians retired very speedily, and it was found impossible to come up with them.

A point worth noticing in this engagement is the diversity of statements regarding the losses sustained by the French. Watrin, who regrets that the troops suffered heavily, sets down the number of killed and wounded at 300. Hulin estimates the casualties in killed and wounded at 400. Berthier reduces the figures to 250, and Bonaparte to 200! The Austrian account makes out the loss on their side to have been 348 men and 216 horses, against a loss of 1,700 men on the French side. A staff officer of the Austrian Army, who simply signs himself W., in a narrative, *La Campagne des Français en Italie en 1800,* published at Leipzig in 1801, goes further. He gives 400 men as the losses of the Austrians, and makes the French casualties amount to 2,500 men, 300 prisoners, and 300 horses.

Troops which retire precipitately, as Boudet relates that the Austrians did, rarely inflict such a heavy loss on their opponents. On the other hand, had the Austrians so maltreated the French, they had no excuse for hurrying away from the battlefield. If we assume that their figures are correct, they show that the Austrians lacked that spirit of tenacity which is the highest quality in fighting men, whilst the French marched on to victory, entirely heedless of its cost.

An indirect proof that the French losses were nothing like the Austrian accounts would make us believe, is that Lannes, who made such a fuss about his losses at Montebello, was silent on this point. Surely, he would have said something had they been extraordinarily heavy.

Haddick could not be made to believe that he had had to contend only with Bonaparte's advanced guard. He thought he had before him at least 20,000 men, so he sent word to Melas that, if he did not come to his assistance, Piedmont and Lombardy would fall into the hands of the French. This was on the 26th of May, and on this very day Melas arrived in Turin, where he was greeted with the announcement of Haddick's defeat at Chiusella.

In the narratives of this memorable campaign, the dates are very contradictory. The extract of the *Œstreichische Militärische Zcitschrift*, quoted by De Cugnac, vol. ii, states that Bonaparte and Berthier had arrived at Ivrea, and that the Battle of the Chiusella commenced at four in the morning of the 26th of May. Gachot goes even further, for he states:—

> Behind the 40th, Bonaparte, Berthier, Duhesme, Boudet, and the staffs of these generals, at one moment threatened, drew their swords and prepared to charge the enemy, who, being fired upon at point blank, and sabred on the left by the *Chasseurs*, retired. (Edouard Gachot, *La Deuxième Campagne d'Italie*.)

He also states that:—

> The First Consul re-entered Ivrea at six in the evening, ... that an officer of La Tour's dragoons had recognised Bonaparte, having been very close to him in the neighbourhood of Romano.

In opposition to all this, we find Bonaparte writing a letter to the Consuls from Ivrea on the 27th of May, in which he informs them, "I arrived yesterday evening at Ivrea." Statements from other officers fix the same date. On the 26th of May, the day of the engagement on the Chiusella, an attempt was made to carry Fort Bard by assault, at which the First Consul and Berthier were present. It was after this attempt had failed that the two officers left for Ivrea, where the headquarters of the army were only established on the evening of the 26th. General Marescot, in his order-book, writes from d'Arnaz, under date of the 26th of May, "The Headquarters left this morning."

It appears very strange that Marmont, in his *Mémoires*, should pass over in silence the engagements at the Chiusella or at Turbigo. He states:—

> We entered Milan without striking a blow (*Et nous entrâmes à Milan sans coup férir*).—*Livre* v.

Bonaparte ordered Lannes to remain in observation in front of Chivasso. Lannes appears to have been keen to occupy Turin and to push on as far as Asti; the object of such a move being evidently to effect Massena's deliverance. It had, nevertheless, the great inconvenience of leaving the Austrians masters of Lombardy and of abandoning Moncey, Béthencourt, and Lechi, who might be attacked and overpowered by superior forces. This Bonaparte was loth to do. He had resolved first to occupy the left bank of the Po, to sweep the enemy out of the north of Italy, then to concentrate four or five divisions at Piacenza, and to hasten to Genova.

Lannes on the 27th heard the thunder of cannon in the rear of Turin; it was the combat at Avigliano.

Haddick had retired to the right bank of the Oreo, leaving Lobkowitz's regiment of dragoons on the left bank. Melas had given him orders to dispute every inch of ground, and to fall back on Turin as slowly as possible; always keeping up close communication with Field-Marshal Kaim.

On the 28th Lannes descended from Foglizzo and made for the banks of the Oreo; under a brisk cannonade, he approached closer and closer to the bridge on that river. The Austrian dragoons withdrew across the bridge, to which they set fire as they abandoned it. This move of the French added strength to the already-formed opinion that Bonaparte intended to advance in the direction of Turin, with a view of effecting a junction with Turreau. The Austrians expected to be attacked by the French the following day; but Lannes made no move on the 29th, and remained quietly at Chivasso. On the Po he found a very large number of boats loaded with rice and corn, and these he appropriated.

Bonaparte himself proceeded to Chivasso, where he held a review of the advanced guard, and praised the troops for all the services they had rendered. He told them how the French cavalry was about to be concentrated; how it would attack the Austrian cavalry, so as to wrench from it its pretended superiority in bravery and in manoeuvring. By his presence at Chivasso he evidently sought to lead Melas astray, and to strengthen more and more the idea that the French were bent on marching on Turin. The Austrians were to be mystified; the veritable project was to be concealed from them. Appearances were to lead them to believe that the French Army intended to act in the direction of Turin—a belief which gained strength from Turreau's operations on the 22nd and on the 24th of May.

According to the bulletin of the 30th of August, the Austrians were led to conceive that the French intended to cross the Po in the neighbourhood of Chivasso, so as to get to Asti and intercept the troops retiring from Nice. To frustrate this object their troops at Chivasso had been strongly reinforced from Turin. One can form a good idea of the embarrassment of the Austrian general, and also his astonishment when the impending attack was not delivered.

Melas, however, was not as easily led into error as Napoleon in his correspondence would wish us to believe. He had sent reconnaissances in various quarters, and made use of reliable spies, by which measures he had on the 28th come to learn of the evacuation of the country round Ivrea and the march of the French on Vercelli.

Whilst Lannes with the advanced guard was directed to threaten Turin, Murat was receiving orders to send reconnaissances in the direction of Biella and Santhia, being supported by Monnier, who was to take post on the main road to Santhia, at a point three leagues from Ivrea.

Berthier, when he was at Ivrea, looking at the many rivers which water the plains of Piedmont and Lombardy, and disturbed by the absence of a bridging equipage—for it had been considered impracticable to bring the pontoons over the Alps—devised the formation of a corps of pontoniers, to be under the command of the chief engineer. For this service every division was made to contribute fifty men, taken from those who in ordinary life had been accustomed to the navigation of rivers.

All Bonaparte's generals were contributing their share towards the success of the campaign. Turreau, advancing from Savoy by the Mont Cenis route, opened a way for his column to Susa.

✶✶✶✶✶✶

In his narrative of the Battle of Marengo, Berthier states that Turreau had 2,500 men, which he had gathered from the garrisons of the Dauphiné, and with whom he had gone in the direction of Susa, after having forced the pass of Cabrières.

✶✶✶✶✶✶

He attacked the Austrians under Lamarsaille at the village of Gravière on the 22nd of May. A very spirited combat ensued, and victory for a time was uncertain. Led by Adjutant-General Liebault, the French, after several attempts, at last turned in a very able manner the Fort Saint Francois, carried all the positions by assault, and remained masters of the village of Gravière. The same evening at ten o'clock the garrison of Fort la Brunette capitulated.

Bonaparte had sent to inform Turreau that be expected to be at Ivrea on the 18th of May; that should the Austrians concentrate their forces they would necessarily reduce the troops in his front; and that he should then gather as many men as possible and push on to Susa. Turreau was to place himself in communication with the Army of Reserve by way of Largo and Ponte, to which towns reconnaissances would be sent to seek news of his column.

The intention was to call up Turreau's column to Ivrea, and unite it with the rest of the army. Turreau was to march by his left, keeping as clear as possible of Turin, still selecting a road practicable for artillery. On the 22nd of May, Bonaparte, writing to Berthier, enjoins him to send country people forward to ascertain if there was any news of General Turreau.

The general had planted his column between Susa and Turin, watching the Austrians, who occupied that corner of Piedmont. On the 24th, he made a forward movement as far as Avigliano, but he had to contend against superior numbers, and was beaten. After this he took up a defensive position some few miles to the east of Susa.

Turreau's force by the nature of the country was separated from the main army throughout the campaign. Nevertheless, it rendered important services in leading the enemy to a false conclusion.

When, on the 22nd of May, the head of Turreau's column showed itself descending from the Mont Cenis, it was but natural that the Austrians would have considered it to be the advanced guard of the main French Army, which was advancing by one of the most practicable passes—that of Mont Cenis. Lannes's party they would regard only as a detachment intended for the purpose of effecting a diversion. In this they were naturally led by the fact that the Mont Cenis road was more direct for troops intended for the relief of Genova than the one which led over the Saint Bernard. Being more practicable for artillery, they believed it was the one Bonaparte would have selected above all others for the passage of his main army.

The Austrians had sufficient troops round Turin to check Turreau and crush Lannes, thus laying bare the rear of the French Army. It may, however, be even more than doubted if Bonaparte at any time intended to retire by the way of the Great Saint Bernard. He certainly left a small garrison at the Hospice, but that did not mean anything, for he had the Simplon and the Saint Gothard routes open to him, and occupied by Béthencourt and Moncey.

As to the future of Bard, the First Consul had written to Berthier:—

> When you will have mastered it, do not suffer the supplies to be wasted; they should be placed under guard with an able commander. You understand that should we change our line of operations, it will be extremely important to have this small fort, which closes the valley and assures us the means of resum-

ing when we like the line of communications by Aosta. When the campaign will have taken a different character, then we may get rid of it by having it razed.

What Bonaparte had most to fear was a rapid concentration of the Austrian Army. The danger, however, was not great. The Austrians were pretty well scattered, and, Genova being at the last gasps, the Austrians were evidently loth to raise the siege. The orders for the concentration were issued on the 31st of May. Ott probably received his on the 2nd of June, and had he obeyed at once without waiting for the capitulation, he might have been at Montebello on the 7th, instead of on the 9th. On the latter day Lannes was already across the Po. Ott's delay was disastrous.

The Austrian staff at Turin had shown little enterprise in gathering information, and had readily come to believe that the strength of the French in the valley of Aosta did not exceed 6,000 men. When Melas returned from Nice he was dissatisfied with their sluggishness, and it is stated that he reprimanded them severely.

The French Army was at Ivrea, the Alps had been surmounted, and Bonaparte had left behind him only the fort of Bard, which Chabran, with his 5,000 men, was directed to blockade and reduce. It remained now for Bonaparte to decide as to his future movements. Three plans were open to him. The first was to move to his right, to form a junction with Turreau and attack the Austrians. The second plan was to cross the Po by means of the boats which Lannes had secured, and to advance to the relief of Massena, who was still holding out at Genova. The third was to march eastward across the Ticino, to form a junction with Moncey, and to capture Milan and all the stores and reserve parks of the Austrians.

The first plan was rejected because Bonaparte had somehow or other come to the conclusion that he was not strong enough to cope with Melas, and that it was hazardous to expose himself to a defeat with no safe line of retreat as long as Fort Bard continued to hold out. Bonaparte knew, nevertheless, that a large Austrian force was blockading Genova, and that another was in front of Suchet, on the Var; consequently, that if he made a junction with Turreau he would be stronger than Melas, having besides a line of retreat by the Mont Cenis open to him; a line easier by far than that of the Saint Bernard.

On the 24th of May, Bonaparte wrote a letter to General Brune, who was then at Dijon, which shows how utterly unfounded was the opinion that Melas could bring larger numbers against him, and how by rapid movements, of which no one was a greater master than himself, he could have beaten in detail the various parties of the Austrian Army as they retired from Genova and the Var.

You will find enclosed, the bulletin of the army.
The enemy appears surprised by our progress. He barely believes it. He hardly knows where he is. You can judge for yourself. Look at the enemy's situation on the 18th of May: 12,000 men at Nice; 6,000 at Savona and along the Genovese Riviera; 25,000 in front of Genova; 8,000 at Susa, Pinerolo, etc.; 8,000 in the valley of Aosta; 8,000 opposite the Simplon and the Saint Gothard—all that are infantry; two regiments of hussars at Genova and at Nice; four regiments close to Turin; the remainder cantoned at Acqui and in the interior of Lombardy. He has remained thus up to the moment when we arrived at Ivrea.

The 3,000 men who were in the valley have been beaten and scattered. All the corps which were on the side of Susa and of Pinerolo have moved to between Turin and Ivrea. Nice, therefore, has in all probability been evacuated at the present moment. They even write to me that Melas must have arrived at Turin; but that is not certain.

✶✶✶✶✶✶

Bonaparte was well informed. On the 21th of May, from Aosta, we find him writing to the Consuls, "A despatch which I have received from Nice and the news which comes to me from Ivrea show me that on the 19th Melas was at Nice, not alarmed by anything. . . . I am assured that he arrived by diligence at Turin yesterday in all haste."

✶✶✶✶✶✶

I calculate on having all the army concentrated at Ivrea by the 26th or the 27th, forming altogether about 33,000 men. I shall be master of the whole country from the Dora Baltea up to the Sesia.

The same day Moncey will cross the Saint Gothard with 15,000 men.

Suchet and Massena, who have been apprised of the movement, will follow the enemy as soon as they see him getting weak in front of them.

The castle and the town of Ivrea are ours, as much as the outer fort of Bard. The Hungarian captain, with his 400 Croats, has retired into a keep, where he has a dozen guns which defend the road; we are going to bombard him.

Should we have some success, this will only be a beginning. You are going to organise an efficient army corps, with which at the beginning of July you will have to play a fine role.

Push forward without remissness the arming and clothing of the conscripts as they arrive.

You will find yourself commanding the Army of Reserve the moment it effects its junction with the Army of Italy.

It is well to look at Melas's movements in consequence of an intercepted despatch of Massena's, which spoke of expecting to be delivered by Berthier's army. On this information Melas, who was on the Var, ordered three brigades to reascend the Col di Tenda and march on Turin—an order which was cancelled the following day on the receipt of a contradictory letter, which stated that Berthier was marching on the Var with the object of reinforcing Suchet. On the 18th, however, all doubt was removed by reason of a report sent by Kaim. This announced the approach of a considerable corps coming from the Valais. On the receipt of this news, Melas returned to his original project; he sent Knesevich's brigade to reinforce Kaim, and directed Zach to repair to Turin. He himself quitted Nice for Turin, and was to be followed there by Auersberg's brigade. O'Reilly's cavalry division, composed of Palfy's and Nobile's brigades, was also attached to Kaim.

It would be hard to explain why Bonaparte, who was so quick to discern the right move in a campaign, neglected to take advantage of his initiative and abstained from falling on the Austrians whilst they were occupied in effecting their concentration. Of the state of dispersion of the enemy he must have been fully aware, and the best proof is the above letter to Brune. Without counting Turreau's forces, he would have had 33,000 men with whom to meet about 11,000 of the enemy.

In what Napoleon wrote at Saint Helena, he argues that, of the three alternatives open to him, the first was contrary to the real principles of war because it amounted to attacking Melas, who had with him considerable forces. But by his own showing, by his letter to General Brune, Melas had no more than from 11,000 to 15,000 men, who could have been easily dealt with by Bonaparte's army before they had time to be reinforced by any troops coming up from Nice or Genova.

When making a study of the alternative roads leading from Switzerland into Italy, Bonaparte had given up the Simplon and Saint Gothard routes simply with the object of shortening his line of operations. This was because the dire condition of Massena's forces called for a speedy arrival of the Army of Reserve. The great parade made to hasten to Massena's assistance seems to have been all of a sudden forgotten; possibly owing to the risk of dipping into Piedmontese territory, where all the strong places were held by Austrian garrisons, without having any safe line of communications. This may have been deemed a risk hardly worth incurring, considering Bonaparte's uncertainty whether Massena could hold out for a sufficient time or not.

Massena agreed to evacuate Genova on the 4th of June. So, as it eventually turned out, Bonaparte would have had plenty of time had he adopted the second alternative open to him, and might have saved his lieutenant from the humiliation of an evacuation. Seeing that, as it was, Melas, though not imminently threatened, sent orders to Ott to raise the siege, it is fair to believe that the order would have been despatched sooner had the French made any move in the direction of the Maritime Alps.

The second alternative was dangerous because of the uncertainty whether Massena still held out at Genova, and of the ignorance of the enemy's movements.

The two first projects having been rejected, the third remained. This Bonaparte evidently considered the most promising—the junction of his army with the corps Moncey was bringing from the Rhine, which was calculated to raise the Army of Reserve to over 50,000 effective men. It was on this that he had so much calculated from the very beginning of the campaign.

Bonaparte's aim was more vast than the simple raising of the blockade of Genova—the rescue of a few thousand starving troops—it was to make the Army of Reserve strong by uniting the two main forces—those he had brought over the Great Saint Bernard and those that Moncey was bringing from the Army of the Rhine; to capture the enemy's magazines and sources of supply, and to cut off Melas entirely from his base and the Austrian empire.

The strategic aim of Bonaparte's operations was to gain possession of the enemy's line of communications. The great danger in such a manoeuvre, generally speaking, is that the assailant lays himself open to lose his own. It was this consideration, possibly, which prevented

Bonaparte from operating against Melas when he got to Chivasso. He has been reproached for having gone to Milan, and thus deserted Massena and left Genova to its fate. But he may have calculated that he would have effected the raising of the blockade indirectly by threatening the rear of the Austrians, and that Melas would have withdrawn his troops from Genova the moment the Army of Reserve appeared in Lombardy and threatened his line of communications. This withdrawal would have enabled Massena to gather together all his disposable forces, and pass from the defensive to the offensive.

The First Consul's great aim was to sever the Austrian communications with the Mincio. This he was resolved to do, and then to compel his adversary to fight at a disadvantage when he had no longer a secure line of retreat. He thought there was little to be gained by saving Genova, whereas by beating Melas he could at one single stroke recover the greater portion of his former conquests in Italy.

Up to the 24th of May, it was fair to imagine that Bonaparte intended to concentrate his army at Ivrea; and that, having effected this, he would assail the Austrian forces nearest to him in Piedmont, and then the rest in succession. All at once, he altered his plans; the Army of Reserve was made to march on Milan. Acting in concert with Moncey and Béthencourt, the army was to clear the Milanese provinces of the enemy, capture his magazines, besiege his fortresses, and then attend on the Po till Melas came to recover his communications. (*Mémoires de Napoleon*—Correspondence de Napoleon, cxxx.)

When at Saint Helena, the fallen emperor, who knew well how his strategy in the Marengo campaign had been criticized, pleaded hard in favour of his march to Milan. It is interesting to examine these arguments.

★★★★★★

Melas did not dream of a French march on Milan. Writing to Lord Keith on the 23rd of May, he states: "The enemy has surrounded the fort of Bard, and has advanced as far as Ivrea. It is pretty clear that his aim is to deliver Massena."

★★★★★★

The headquarters of the Austrian Army were at Turin. But half of the enemy's forces were in front of Genova, and the other half was supposed to be, and was, indeed, on the march, coming by way of the Col di Tenda to reinforce such as were at Turin. Under this circumstance, what action will the First Consul take? Will he march on Turin to drive Melas out of it, combine with Turreau, and in this manner find safe communications with France and its arsenals of Grenoble and Briançon? Or will he construct a bridge at Chivasso, profiting by the boats which fortune has thrown into his hands, and make direct for Genova to raise the blockade of that important place? Or else, leaving Melas in his rear, will he cross the Sesia and the Ticino, go to Milan, and on the Adda make his junction with Moncey's corps, amounting to 15,000 men, which was then coming from the Army of the Rhine and had descended from the Saint Gothard? Of these three alternatives, the first was contrary to the real principles of war, because Melas had with him very considerable forces. Consequently, the French Army ran the risk of giving battle, having no safe retreat, inasmuch as the fort of Bard had not yet been captured. Besides, supposing that Melas had abandoned Turin and fallen back on Alessandria, the campaign had failed; either army would have found itself in a natural position, the French Army resting on Mont Blanc and the Dauphiné, whilst that of Melas would have had its left at Genova and in her rear the important places of Mantua, Piacenza, and Milan.

The second alternative did not appear practicable. How venture in the midst of an army as powerful as the Austrian was, between the Po and Genova, without having any line of operation, any safe line of retreat?

The third alternative, on the contrary, offered every advantage. The French Army, mistress of Milan, could lay hands on all the magazines, on all the depots, on all the hospitals of the hostile army; it formed a junction with the left, which was commanded by General Moncey; there was a safe line of retreat by the Simplon and the Saint Gothard.

******

Bonaparte always counted on the supplies accumulated by his adversary. He acted in accordance with his answer given as a boy at an examination, when he was proposed the following question: "What measures would you adopt, in case you were besieged in a fortified place and destitute of provisions?"—"As long," he replied, "as there were any in the enemy's camp, I should never be at a loss for a supply."

******

The Simplon led through the Valais and on to Sion, where all the depots of supplies for the army had been directed. The Saint

Gothard led to Switzerland, of which we had been in possession for the last two years, and which covered the Army of the Rhine, at that moment on the Iller. In such a position the French general could act according to his will. Were Melas with his united army to march from Turin on the Sesia and on the Ticino, the French Army could deliver battle with the immense advantage that, should it come off victorious, Melas, without retreat, would he pursued and thrown back on Savoy, and, in the case of the French Army being beaten, it would retire by the Simplon and the Saint Gothard.

Should Melas, as it was natural to suppose, move in the direction of Alessandria to combine there with the army coming from Genova, it was to be expected, in advancing to meet him, and in crossing the Po, to anticipate him and to deliver battle, the French Army having its rear safe on the river and Milan, the Simplon and the Saint Gothard; whilst the Austrian Army, having its retreat cut off and having no communication with Mantua and Austria, would be exposed to be hurled back on the mountains of the Riviera di Ponente, and to be totally destroyed or captured at the foot of the Alps, at the Col di Tenda or in the neighbourhood of Nice.

Lastly, by adopting the third alternative, if, once master of Milan, it suited the French general to let Melas go by, and to remain between the Po, the Adda, and the Ticino, he had in this way, without fighting a battle, reconquered Lombardy and Piedmont, the Maritime Alps, the Riviera di Genova, and caused the blockade of this latter city to be raised: these were very important results.

An ordinary general would most probably have taken the first alternative. Bonaparte selected the third, and in this he was greatly favoured by the slowness of his adversary.

The Duc de Valmy, in his *Histoire de la Campagne de 1800*, offers the following observations: Arrived on Italian soil, and at two or three marches at most from the enemy, the First Consul began to entertain doubts; he was tormented by anxieties. Where was the Army of Italy? What were Massena and Suchet about? Where was Melas? What plans was he likely to adopt? Nothing was absolutely certain; the only thing that appeared most probable was that the Austrian commander-in-chief would manoeuvre so as to escape from the Army of Reserve, and evade fighting a general engagement which would restore Italy to Bonaparte.

In this state of uncertainty, Bonaparte determined to guard at the same time all the passages of which Melas might avail himself in order to regain the line of the Mincio and Mantua, and to observe the left of the Po, towards which Melas must work back. He adopted the plan of capturing Milan, of watching the main road from Genova by which the Austrian Army was bound to come, placing himself at Stradella in the centre of the communications which he intended to close.

Some writers have admired these dispositions of General Bonaparte, others have blamed this unusual dispersion of his forces when the moment was fast approaching when he would need all the troops at his disposal. If it was certain that Melas sought to avoid a battle, no objection perhaps could be raised to Bonaparte's plan. But this dispersal was very risky in the opposite alternative; if the Austrian general, intending to offer battle, gathered all his forces around him.

The possession of Milan could not fail to produce a great morale impression both on the Italians and the Imperialists, and to renew and add fresh lustre to the halo of glory which encircled the brow of the First Consul. (Rose calls the march on Milan a dramatic stroke.) The junction with Moncey would raise the French forces to full 50,000 men on one hand, and on the other open a safe retreat over the Saint Gothard and the Simplon in case of disaster. The magazines and reserve parks established by the Austrians lay exposed to immediate capture in the unprotected cities of Lombardy.

It is all very well to applaud Bonaparte's manoeuvres, and to approve of his having closed every line of communication the Austrians had before he delivered battle. We should not lose sight, however, of the fact that the occupation of Milan was only a minor operation; that the bulk of the Austrian forces were in Piedmont, and still remained to be beaten; that by his march eastward Bonaparte gave Melas time to concentrate his forces, whereas he should have taken advantage of their state of dispersion to beat them in detail. The march on Milan was time lost, and in effecting that move he was not true to his principles, which were to seek for the main body of the enemy and to beat it in a general action.

A campaign can only be rapidly brought to a conclusion by the complete destruction of the organised forces of the enemy, and, where the circumstances are particularly favourable, it is a grave professional error to undertake unnecessary operations. The question naturally arises: Would a battle fought in the end of May with superior forces have had better ulterior results than the one Bonaparte fought on the 14th of June?

A commentator holds, with good reason, that, had the First Consul waited for Moncey so as to operate with one compact body of 50,000 men, the plan he followed might have seemed the most preferable. But if he had afterwards to cross the Po with only 29,000 men, as he did on the 7th of June, he could have done that just as well in May, whilst Elsnitz and Ott, being busy in Liguria, were not to be feared. There was nothing then to prevent his crossing the Po with 35,000 men about Cambio, and directing Moncey to come down by forced marches by Varese to Milan and Pavia, to cover the communications by the bridges and to support the army, had such a measure been necessary. In fact, Moncey had nothing to fear from Vukassevich and Laudon, who were both inferior to his two divisions. (See vol. xiii., Jomini, *Histoire des Guerres de la Révolution*.)

If there is possibly a sound principle in the art of war, it is in the concentration of superior forces at the decisive point. This principle Bonaparte neglected, and it nearly cost him dear.

In 1805, he wrote to Murat:—

On ne doit rien risquer, et la première de toutes les règles est d'avoir la supériorité numérique.

The Army of Reserve being very badly off with regard to resources, the prospect of appropriating the resources of the enemy was very tempting. The price, however, paid for this —that is to say, the delay in attacking, a delay which Melas could turn to profitable account by concentrating his forces—was very great.

Bonaparte's march on Milan may be described, as some writers have described it, as a stroke of genius, which would not have been conceived by an ordinary general. Still, no ordinary general would have ever come in for any blame had he followed a different course, and sought the enemy's army after the occupation of Ivrea, to beat it before its concentration had been completed.

Gachot makes the new plan of operations by Milan to have been settled at a conference held in the Royal College of Ivrea, on the evening of the 26th of May, at which Bonaparte, Berthier, and Murat were present.

******

Il tient, au collége royal, avec Berthier et Murat, une longue conférence. À

> *onze heures, une nouvelle marche de l'armée de réserve est copiée par Bourrienne, et Murat s'eloigne dans la nuit.*—Gachot, La Deuxième Campagne d'Italie.

******

Campana makes Bonaparte take that resolution on the 24th of May, and this is borne out by the following paragraph of a letter which Bonaparte wrote to Moncey from Aosta on the 24th of May, 1800:—

> Attack the 7th or the 8th; go on to Belinzona, to Locarno and Lugano. It is very possible that we shall be on the Ticino by the 9th.

The idea of undertaking a march on Milan can be traced further back, even before the route to be followed had been settled. The intention of doing so is contained in some indications issued to the nominal commander-in-chief of the Army of Reserve. Bonaparte writes from Paris, under date of the 27th of April:—

> Besides, it is possible that it may be no longer Milan where it will be necessary to go, but we may be compelled to go with all possible speed to Tortona, so as to free Massena, who, in case he should be beaten, will be shut up in Genova, where he has provisions for thirty days. It is consequently by the Saint Bernard that I desire that they shall pass.

The march on Milan was in contemplation when Bonaparte predicted to Bourrienne, before the commencement of the campaign, where he would beat Melas.

As we have already seen, the First Consul made a great point of drawing a body of troops from Moreau's army with which to complete his own. It was only natural, therefore, that he should wish to effect a junction with this force. This he could only do by going before it, and meeting it as it descended into Lombardy.

In a letter of instructions issued by Berthier to General Dupont, his chief of the staff, dated the 14th of May, Berthier says:—

> You will instruct the general officer commanding at the Simplon that the army now at Ivrea will probably march by its left on the Ticino, when he must impose on the enemy with regard to the number of his forces, and harass him by attacking his posts, though all this should be done without imprudence. Moncey will likewise have to be informed that the army will go direct from Ivrea to Milan by the shortest route.

All this and more appears to show that the movement on Milan was part of a settled purpose, and had been decided before the troops actually began to climb the slopes of the Alps.

Bonaparte's march on Milan has been very severely criticized by some writers. Bülow, on the other hand, calls it one of the most able manoeuvres which have ever been made.

Jomini writes:—

Leaving an observing screen before Chivasso and Trino, Bonaparte determined to cross the Ticino, to inundate Lombardy like a torrent, to drive back up to the guns of Mantua the corps which held it, so as to facilitate a junction with Moncey, who, on the 27th of May, was already descending from the Saint Gothard. This daring plan, calculated with rare precision of the time needed for its execution, met with a complete success, notwithstanding the divergent marches which it led to afterwards.

Rocquancourt holds that a march through Piedmont, with the avowed object of proceeding to the relief of Massena, overcoming all the troops Bonaparte might come across on the way, could only lead to moderate results, by no means commensurate with the greatness of the enterprise and the difficulties already overcome. It was for this reason that the First Consul, in place of manoeuvring by his right, and approaching Turin, accorded the preference to an advance on Milan and Piacenza, which would place him on the most direct communications of his adversary, whilst at the same time it was calculated to hasten his much-desired junction with Moncey. By following this course, he would acquire a large base and all sorts of resources and means. (J. Rocquancourt, *Cours Complet d'Art et Histoire Militaires, tome* ii.)

Thiers believes that the march on Milan was conceived with the principal object of concentrating the French forces before blocking Melas's communications. (Thiers, *Consulat et Empire*, vol. ii.)

Hamley views the flank march on Milan in this guise. Bonaparte's intention was to drive back that portion of the Austrian Army which lay north of the Po, and to effect a junction with Moncey's corps. He hoped to be able to keep his design from the enemy till he had thrown a force across the Po at Piacenza. Then the Austrians would be cut off entirely from the Mincio, and any concentration of their forces, which must ensue for the recovery of their communications, would go towards relieving Genova, and at the same time would enable Suchet to form a junction with Massena. Genova, however, was known to be *in extremis*; it might have fallen any day, thus rendering the last part of the plan of no avail.

Humanity and gratitude, if nothing else, should have made Bonaparte, one would think, overcome every difficulty, and get to Genova. But he turned to his left, and thus put off for eight or ten days the relief of that city.

A man like Bonaparte, who was endowed with such extraordinary insight, whose calculations were so far-reaching, whose intentions were so distinct, and whose intellect was so clear, cannot be judged on the same lines as ordinary men. The object he had in view was to interpose between Melas and Vienna, and to cut him from his base on the Mincio. This was the real scope of his move to Milan.

If he exaggerated anything it was Massena's power of resistance. He would not, otherwise, have sent repeated instructions to him as well as to Suchet, urging them to pursue the Austrians vigorously on the first indication of a backward movement.

The recall of the Austrian troops from Genova as part of the general concentration of the Austrian Army was what Bonaparte calculated upon for the relief of Massena. What more natural than for him to believe that the Austrians would have been withdrawn from Genova as soon as they found that their rear was dangerously threatened? This withdrawal did come, but it came too late.

In war, what has to be looked for is an adequate result. Bonaparte's aim was not to relieve the troops of the Army of Italy blockaded in Genova, it was a much higher one: to recover as quickly as possible all the possessions in Italy secured to France by the Treaty of Campo Formio.

It was just the difference between genius and mediocrity. Genius will often overlook small results when it beholds greater ones further ahead. The relief of the Army of Italy, desirable as it was, was for him an object of only secondary consideration. If we look at the campaign carried out in 1800 in this light, we are bound to admit that the march to Milan was in conformity with the dictates of war. It aimed not only at cutting Melas from his base of operations, but in placing him in a dire position between the Army of Italy and the Army of Reserve.

The magnitude of the enterprise justified, we think, Bonaparte's neglect of his gallant comrade struggling against all kinds of difficulties at Genova, and the non-fulfilment of the promise which he had made to him. There can be no doubt that he trusted too much to the news of his arrival in Italy alone sufficing to liberate Massena, in consequence of the scare produced by the sudden apparition of the derided Army of Reserve. And this it would have done, if Melas had not delayed too long the concentration of his army.

Bonaparte never for a moment realised the pitiable state to which famine and the horrors of the siege had reduced Massena's troops. Were such troops capable of undertaking fresh efforts? Granted that their courage was still unimpaired when they proudly marched out of the city they had so gallantly held, they were nevertheless in a state of destitution. Where could the commissariat officers obtain the necessary provisions and forage for a forward movement in a country which had been denuded of everything?

As for Suchet, what effort could he make, considering the exhausted state of the country through which he had to move?—a narrow belt of land, with the mountains on one side and the sea on the other. This is fully exposed by the statement made by Massena to the First Consul in the early part of February—

> The army is absolutely bare and shoeless.... We have not a grain of forage, nor provisions of any description, no means of transport whatever.... Liguria has no provisions of any kind, everything has gone (*est eperissé*). I have placed the troops on half rations; I myself have set the example. (De Cugnac, vol. i.)

Saint Cyr, addressing the mutinous soldiers at the gates of Genova, in the previous December, told them, "Have you forgotten that you have made a desert between your present position and France?"—a fact which of itself alone brought them back to a sense of duty.

If Bonaparte was very keen to keep his communications secure, why should not Suchet have been equally careful? For all that, he has been reproached for having undertaken the siege of Savona. But could he well leave 1,000 Austrians there, masters of his communications with France? After all, were Gazan's men, the starved garrison of Genova, troops fit for any great exertion?

The presence of Suchet's advanced guard at Acqui, as will be shown hereafter, had a very important effect on the issue of the Battle of Marengo; an effect which must be justly estimated, for to the reduction of the Austrian cavalry on the 14th of June Melas could with good reason attribute part of his defeat.

Bonaparte remained insensible to Massena's earnest appeal. The general had written on the 23rd of April:—

> I implore you, Citizen Consul, come to our assistance! The

handful of brave men that I command here, by its constancy and its devotedness, well deserves all your solicitude. (De Cugnac, *Campagne de l'Armée de Réserve en 1800*, vol. i.)

Henri Martin writes on this point:—

He had imposed untold sacrifices on the Army of Liguria, which had been accepted with an admirable abnegation. But these sacrifices and this devotedness imposed on him in turn an absolute obligation— the obligation of saving the defenders of Genova. He was pretty sure of being able to trample over Melas, and afterwards to overpower the general who directed the siege of Genova. He had already done something even more difficult. Bonaparte, however, did nothing of the kind. He abandoned Massena and his soldiers. He immolated them to the success of a more grandiose and hazardous plan which he had conceived. He desired no longer only to beat the Austrian Army, but to annihilate it at a single blow by cutting off every possible retreat. (Henri Martin, *Histoire de France depuis 1789 jusqu'à nos jours*, tome iii.)

Who can say but that the idea contained in the following words, uttered by Bonaparte, may not have been a reason for marching on Milan:—

But it is necessary to be in force before going to provoke (*d'aller provoquer*) M. de Melas?

The scarcity of artillery and ammunition may have been another of the principal causes which decided him to march into Lombardy. We find, in fact, on the 24th of May, Berthier demanding instructions, and soliciting to be informed whether it was to be a march to the right to join Turreau, or by the left to join Moncey, so as to get reinforced in guns from the Saint Gothard or from Susa.

On the same day it was decided to march on Milan. In conjunction with Moncey's and Béthencourt's troops, which constituted the left of the French forces, Bonaparte's army was to sweep the enemy out of Milanese territory, capture his magazines, besiege his fortresses, and wait on the Po till Melas should come with his army to recover his lost communications.

There certainly appears some inconsistency between the march on Milan and the line of route over the Alps chosen for the Army of Reserve. What decided Bonaparte to select the Great Saint Bernard was that, had the choice of the route been allowed to fall on the Simplon or on the Saint Gothard, it would have entailed a longer march and taken more time to go to Massena's aid. Having purposely adopted the shorter route, the object held in view when the selection was made seems, after the Alps had been surmounted, to have been thought no longer of any material consequence.

Bonaparte, at the head of 33,000 men, could have destroyed the force Melas had about Turin, which just came up to one-third of the Army of Reserve—about 11,000 men—and have afterwards dealt with the corps coming up in succession from Nice, 12,000; from Savona, 6,000; from Genova, 25,000. By his move eastwards on Milan, he allowed Melas time to concentrate a force round Alessandria numerically superior to his own; owing to which he very nearly suffered a defeat.

Nor was there any reasonable excuse for coming to Moncey's aid. For the information which he had received from Lombardy, as can be seen from a letter written to Bernadotte from Aosta on the 24th of May, proved that the enemy had there only 10,000 men. These Moncey and Béthencourt could easily have disposed of, whilst Bonaparte was free with his centre and right to devote his entire attention to Melas.

By his march on Milan Bonaparte lost the advantage of his first situation; for to accomplish what he intended it became necessary to spread his troops, whilst Melas gained time for concentrating his. The argument is that by an advance from Ivrea he would have very easily beaten the Austrians, at that time in a thorough state of dispersion, though possibly some small corps might have been fortunate enough to escape. But from the very beginning we have stated how Bonaparte craved to do something very brilliant, extraordinarily uncommon; he wished most anxiously, and with good reason, as the events proved, for a battle, a brilliant battle, with which to end the campaign with one stroke.

A series of small defeats inflicted on the Austrians by marching through Piedmont would have dimmed the brilliancy of his great strategic march over the Alps. It would have been a very tame conclusion of a grand operation. The astounding effect of that exploit needed a corresponding *finale*—a pitched, a decisive battle against the entire Austrian Army; something that would show to the French nation the full extent of his genius. This is what he so ardently desired, and risked much to obtain. Nevertheless, it was worth risking. He was mindful of the proverb, "Nothing venture, nothing have."

Bonaparte had calculated that he would beat the Austrians on the plain of Marengo, and so he had foretold; but they were not there when he emerged from the valley of Aosta. They had plunged into the Ligurian littoral. Was he, then, not to make an attempt to bar all the roads open to them for regaining the Lombard provinces? was he to keep his army united, when he was so very uncertain of what course Melas was likely to pursue?

Bonaparte deemed it a grander plan to draw round the Austrians a net formed by all his divisions, and so close the way that not one of their detachments should escape him. Had he marched on Turin, the Austrians from Nice, Savona, and Genova might have found the roads leading from Genova free. Had he moved in the direction of Genova, in that case the Austrians occupying Turin, Pinerolo, and Susa would have been free to move. In either case a portion of the Austrian Army would have been able to escape. He consequently deemed it absolutely necessary to extend the Army of Reserve on one side from Pavia to Piacenza (because this part of the Po, which runs obliquely from west to east, closes the road to Milan), on the other side from Pavia to the Ticino. Thus, advancing with clever manoeuvres, he would spread out his army in a semicircle, through which the Austrians had to break.

The move to Milan was so unexpected that all were taken by surprise when Bonaparte discontinued his advance on Genova.

If Massena was sacrificed by this manoeuvre, as Lanfry and Michelet hold, none the less was Bonaparte surprised in finding Melas so obstinate as to leave 25,000 men idle before the walls of Genova. This was one of the calculations which miscarried.

It may be questioned if the Army of Reserve did arrive in Italy too late to save Genova. We now know General Ott's hesitation to comply with Melas's orders; had he complied with them at once Massena would have been saved the disgrace of marching his troops out of Genova. In reality, it resolved itself in the end into a question of a few hours.

The drawback of Bonaparte's plan lay in the extension of the network. The wide dispersion of his forces, so as to guard many points at the same time, made his net dangerously weak. No one, however, knew better than Bonaparte how to make troops march; no commander could have appeared more speedily at any threatened point.

By the move on Milan, the rear of the French Army became the advanced guard.

On the 26th of May, Murat advanced on the road to Vercelli, at the head of 1,500 cavalry, commanded by Duvignan and Champeaux, and of the 70th regiment, commanded by Monnier. On the 27th, he occupied Vercelli, where he found that the Austrians had burnt the bridge over the Sesia. On the following day, in company with General Duhesme, Murat reconnoitred the fords of the Sesia, and made his dispositions for crossing the river.

During the night of the 28th, two batteries were constructed on the right bank of the Sesia, opposite to the position held by the Austrians. This was done to rivet their attention to that point, whilst Murat attempted to cross the river at a point two leagues further down. Early on the morning of the 29th, at about three o'clock, the Austrians, having discovered that a battery was in course of construction, and that some boats had already been collected under its protection, opened fire from four guns. Detecting a body of infantry concealed in a dike, and believing that these measures indicated an intended crossing, the Austrians opened a heavy fire of musketry, which lasted three hours.

Murat had decided to ford the river close to Palestro, and to turn the Austrian left; whilst Boudet would effect a crossing on the left of Vercelli, with the object of marching on Borgo Vercelli. The current of the Sesia was strong, and Murat experienced some difficulty in crossing, losing a few men, who were drowned. Boudet experienced the same difficulty, and likewise lost some men.

General Festenberg, with between 2,000 and 3,000 men, was guarding the Sesia; and as soon as it was reported to him by his cavalry patrols that Murat had crossed the river on his left, and Boudet on his right, he ordered a retreat. It was then about 8 a.m. This retreat was molested by Duhesme, who had sent across, in boats, a couple of companies of grenadiers. Festenberg managed to reach the Ticino before the enemy. He was vigorously pursued up to Novara.

Immediately after General Festenberg's retreat, Murat had the bridge re-established, and advanced the same day to Novara. Boudet was directed to take post the following day behind the Agogna, and to extend on the right, whilst Loison's division took post between Palestro and Bobbio. These measures were necessary, considering the fact that the Austrians, who occupied all the right bank of the Po, might suddenly cross to the left bank and harass the French right. Loison was consequently enjoined to guard himself well on the side of Mortara, and at the same time to keep a careful watch on Casale.

Santhia, Crescentino, Biella, Trino, and Masserano, were all occupied by the French, and orders were issued for the rearmost section of the Army of Reserve to close on Vercelli on the 30th.

The bulletin issued on the 29th of May relates that two special couriers had been intercepted during these operations. From them it was ascertained that Melas still remained at Turin, where he had arrived from Nice, travelling by post; that he reproached the generals who had supplied him from Turin with news of the valley of Aosta, and who had insisted that there were not more than 6,000 Frenchmen there. The largest portion of his army, which had been operating near Nice, was approaching the Po by forced marches.

On the 30th of May, Murat and Duhesme occupied the right bank of the Ticino. The rest of the army was at that moment crossing the Sesia. Lannes retained his position facing the Austrians at Chivasso. On the same day, Murat wrote a letter to Moncey, informing him that he was striving to throw a bridge over the Ticino at Novara, so as to turn the enemy and facilitate Moncey's junction with the rest of the army. He also informed him that the Austrians appeared to be in full retreat at all points.

Whilst the above movements were in progress, Brigadier-General Lechi, who commanded the Cisalpine Legion, had been directed to cover the left of the army, which had wended its way down the valley of Aosta, coming from the Great Saint Bernard. Quitting Aosta on the 24th of May, the legion marched to Châtillon, where it passed the night. On the 26th it crossed Mount Ranzola and took post at Gressoney. On the 27th it passed the Valdobbia and reached Riva, where it crossed the Sesia. On the 28th it was at Varallo. There, where the Val-Sesia commences to be practicable for vehicles, Prince Victor de Rohan stopped the way. He was in position with his legion and a gun. Lechi attacked him; the Italians boldly stormed his intrenchments, captured the gun, and made 350 prisoners. After this, Lechi, who was near Romagnano, was ordered to move on the Ticino towards Sesto Calende, at the southern end of the Lago Maggiore, and to lay hands on all available boats.

In the early part of May, Moreau drafted the men who were intended to compose Moncey's corps. By the middle of the month, these were brought together in the valley of the Reuss and in the valley of Unseren, between Lucerne and the northern slopes of the Saint Gothard. At that time, the corps was composed of two divisions, one commanded by Lapoype, the other by Lorge, with a reserve of cavalry. It amounted to 11,510 men. Moncey, writing on the 24th of May on the subject of the strength of his corps, says: "*Dont l'effectif n'est encore que de 11,510 hommes;*" by which it may be inferred that it was not complete at that date. It was very weak in artillery, which consisted of two 4-prs., 2 howitzers, and five small guns of lesser calibre than 4-prs.

According to a return furnished by Dupont, Moncey brought from the Rhine 12,092 infantry and 1,851 cavalry, a total of 13,943 men. (De Cugnac, *Campagne de l'Armée de Réserve en 1800,* vol. ii.)

The Saint Gothard route had been surveyed quite recently by Dessoles, chief of Moreau's staff, and by Boutin, a captain in the corps of engineers. The troops commenced to cross the Saint Gothard on the 28th of May, Chabert's brigade of Lapoype's division leading. Chabert occupied Airolo on the morning of the 28th. He met with no difficulty on the march beyond what arose from the bad condition of the roads.

The corps which Melas had left to guard the issues from Switzerland, and two divisions of cavalry and artillery which he had not taken with him to Liguria, were gathered together to defend the passage of the Ticino. On the 31st of May, Murat forced the passage of that river and chased the Austrians out of Turbigo. In the mean while Duhesme had commenced to cross the river at Porto di Buffalora. The Ticino was very broad, deep, and rapid, with steep banks. Bonaparte's words were, "*Il est extrêmement large et rapide.*"

On that day part of Boudet's troops took post opposite the bridge over the Ticino in front of Ponte Buffalora, whilst the other portion followed Murat's advance-guard, which had moved from Novara on to Galliate to effect the passage of the river. General Schilt was to march northwards to draw the enemy's attention to his right flank, as if the French contemplated crossing at Oleggio.

At Galliate the river was defended by intrenchments armed with several pieces of artillery. But the Austrians were principally strong in cavalry. The passage of the river at that point was effected slowly, for the enemy had destroyed the bridge, and there were few boats to be procured on the spot. The French had only two 4-prs. for overcoming the fire of the Austrian battery. These guns, supported later in the day by two pieces of Boudet's division, an 8-pr. and a howitzer, succeeded in silencing the enemy's guns.

Vukassevich had received orders to defend the Ticino as far as lay in his power. The cavalry brigades of Festenberg and Doller were assigned to him. If not able to withstand superior forces, he was instructed to fall back on Pavia, and to cross the Po there. Of Vukassevich's force, a brigade under Dedovich was at Bellinzona striving to hinder Moncey's foremost troops. Laudon, retiring before Béthencourt, had

Turbigo 1800

crossed the Lago Maggiore and landed at Angera. This brigade had orders to march on Buffalora. Festenberg's cavalry was nearly all that there was to oppose Murat on the Ticino. The Austrian line of defence from Sesto Calende to Pavia was a very lengthy one, and there were only 5,600 men to hold the ground and restrain 30,000 French.

The enemy had withdrawn to the left bank all the boats but a few which the inhabitants of Galliate had hidden in the smaller branch of the Ticino. These four or five boats were offered to the French, and were carried on the shoulder by the infantry to the main branch of the river under fire of the enemy's guns. (The Austrian account makes Murat carry on carts all the boats he had been able to find on the Agogna and the Sesia.) The French general's reports are silent on this point. By this means some companies of grenadiers were ferried over to a wooded island, whence they could bring an effective fire to bear on the enemy. Murat caused his artillery to move forward so as to take the enemy's in flank.

Under the protection of this fire, and availing himself of two boats, he crossed the river by main strength and compelled the enemy to withdraw his guns. Several small boats found on the left bank provided the means for ferrying a battalion across. Under cover of the bush this body, led by Adjutant-General Girard, who had crossed in the first boat, charged the enemy's cavalry and protected the crossing of the remainder of the corps.

As the French gradually grew stronger on the left bank, they drove the Austrians before them. The latter were weak in infantry; and, as the banks of the Ticino were covered with scrub and brushwood, it was not difficult for the French to gain a firm footing on that side of the river. Festenberg's guns were moved to several positions, from which they strove in vain to hinder the crossing; and were ultimately withdrawn to the village of Turbigo. This village was protected by the Naviglio, of which Festenberg determined to contest the crossing. This canal goes from Oleggio to Milan, and through it flows a great portion of the water of the river.

At Turbigo the Austrians received a considerable reinforcement brought up by General Loudon. Loudon marched to the sound of the guns, and hastened from Gallarate on Castano. With the main body of his troops, he entered the village of Turbigo, and at once charged Girard's foremost troops. Girard, taking advantage of all the accidents of ground, defended the Ponte di Naviglio, and thus gained time for Monnier to come to his assistance. The French crossed the Ticino slowly.

The official bulletin stated that in six hours not more than 1,500 men and two guns had crossed. Girard had carried the bridge over the Naviglio Grande, where he intrenched himself and cannonaded Turbigo with a 4-pr. gun. Murat saw all the importance of driving the enemy from his position, and night was fast approaching. Monnier at last, having gathered a portion of his troops, crossed the bridge at 8 o'clock, plunged into Turbigo, and attacked it at the point of the bayonet. The village was occupied by a large force, and was obstinately defended, for Loudon had sworn that he would compel the French to recross the Ticino. Monnier, however, carried the position by storm. General Schilt arrived at that moment, turned the village, and surrounded it. By ten that night Turbigo was in the hands of the French.

On the side of Buffalora little could be effected, for the bridges over the two branches of the river had been removed. Duhesme contrived to secure a small boat, by means of which a few companies of Boudet's division were pushed across.

The crossing of the Ticino was an important operation, and a difficult one to boot. The attack on Turbigo was carried out with considerable vigour, as the possession of that point was necessary to facilitate the passage at Buffalora on the main road. On the left bank of the river were some materials; these were quickly seized by the engineers, and a bridge was constructed. The bridge was re-established on the 1st of June, and the Army of Reserve was at once pushed across the river with its artillery and baggage. The whole of it was on the left bank of the Ticino by the 2nd.

On the last days of May, a junction was made in the north with Lechi and Béthencourt. The former with the Italian legion was at Romagnano, as we have seen, on the 30th, and had on the following day resumed his march on Sesto Calende. Béthencourt had occupied Domodossola on the 29th. These moves opened a fresh line of communication for the Army of Reserve by the way of the Simplon, for at that date the garrison of Fort Bard was still holding out.

The Army of Reserve had now crossed the Ticino, and was on the march for Milan, the capital of Lombardy. At this point it seems desirable to make a few observations on some deficiencies which the march over the Alps and the advance into Lombardy had shown to exist.

Notwithstanding all the pains taken to complete the organisation of the Army of Reserve, and in spite of Bonaparte's exceptional mastery of details, the organisation of his forces in some important matters was far from thorough. The most essential article, ammunition, was lacking. There was a constant demand for cartridges, of which the soldiers, before coming in contact with the enemy, were reported to be wanting.

Berthier writes to the First Consul on the 20th of May:—

> What perplexes me most is the question of cartridges; should we have one or two engagements by Ivrea, we should have no way to replace them.

On the following day Lannes writes:—

> I am waiting for cartridges and cavalry.

General Watrin asks for some on the 20th, and again on the 25th of May; Lannes does so again on the 27th at Romano. Paulet does so urgently after the first skirmishes which his general, Duhesme, had about Cremona.

Transport for the ammunition seems to have been scarce; for we learn that the troops marching on Ivrea were made to carry ninety rounds apiece, half of which number each soldier was to hand over at Ivrea with the object of forming a small magazine at that place. On the 27th of May, the chief of the staff is ordered by Berthier to see that the 3rd battalion of the 28th takes eighty rounds per man, with the object of handing over a portion of these cartridges to the advanced guard.

The medical arrangements left much to be desired. De Paulet de la Bastide, adjutant-general on the staff of General Duhesme, writes to the chief of the staff on the 29th of May, that the divisions of Boudet and Loison needed everything that was necessary for the dressing of wounds; that the surgeons were too few in number; that there was a dearth of medicines and of lint for bandages; that the attendants were too few, and that in consequence it was difficult to prevent many soldiers from quitting the ranks under pretence of assisting their wounded comrades.

Later still, on the 11th of June, Caesar Berthier, adjutant-general of Murat's cavalry, reported to the chief of the staff that the cavalry had no hospital.

In this campaign, as in the campaign of 1796, the French were inferior to the Austrians in guns. The artillery for Loison's division was made up of guns captured at Ivrea. This was not the only case in which the retard at Fort Bard made itself felt. Throughout the campaign a dearth of artillery was experienced. Seeing that Bonaparte himself was an artillery officer, this inferiority in guns appears strange.

A regular body of engineers does not seem to have been allotted to each division of infantry, for we find De Paulet asking the chief of the staff, in the name of his general, for one or two officers of engineers and a few sappers to be attached to General Duhesme's division, as none were forthcoming when required.

In an anonymous pamphlet attributed to Kellermann (*Réfutation de M. le due de Rovigo, ou La vérité sur la bataille de Marengo*), it is stated that Bonaparte harassed Melas with an incomplete fighting equipment.

Notwithstanding that the French Army had reached the fertile provinces of Piedmont, still on the 28th of May General Berthier complains to the chief of the staff that Loison's division had been without provisions for three days.

What was at the bottom of all these wants, was neglect and poverty. The Directory, ignorant of all that was needed for the due maintenance of an army in the field, had systematically neglected to look after the wants of their armies in a continuous manner. To do this requires care, forethought, and, above all, money; and of money there was none. Bonaparte had taken the field too soon after having assumed the reins of government for some of his measures of organisation to have reached their necessary development.

The difficulty of crossing the Alps with a large animal transport, of itself compelled the French to descend into the plains of Italy accompanied by a modest train; and their supply difficulties would have been very great had not the Austrians been careless in the location of their magazines. The French, excepting those established in Switzerland, had none. They easily obtained possession of those of the enemy, which had been located in open towns instead of being formed in the many fortresses the Austrians held in Lombardy and Piedmont. In all this the Austrians showed the grossest carelessness, for invaluable stores were allowed to fall intact into the enemy's hands, and no steps were taken to set fire to them or otherwise to destroy them.

The very incomplete state of the Army of Reserve is revealed by a letter despatched by the First Consul on the 29th of May to Carnot, minister of war. In this communication, Bonaparte complains that many of the infantry regiments were incomplete, and had at that moment detachments and even battalions in France; some formed part of, and did duty with, the fleet at Brest. Several regiments of cavalry were hardly represented in the army, and the cavalry was much below strength. He adds that the army was most in need of horses for the artillery. Bridge equipment it had none, and trusted to capturing it from the enemy. The total number of artillery artificers required was 200, but there were only thirty of these present with the army. There were no pontoniers, and a battalion of sappers was much needed.

Murat won much honour in leading the bold and swift march on Milan, passing through a country intersected by many rivers, and defended by an enemy brave and well supplied, whereas his own troops were often without bread and ammunition, armed with guns of small calibre, and badly served. He had not as yet given a proof of what he would do a few years hence, of the daring enterprise and relentless pursuit of the enemy which so distinguished him in the campaigns of 1805, 1806, and 1812, nor of the impetuosity which saved the fortune of the emperor on the bloodstained field of Eylau.

Murat, with the advanced guard, had pushed on to Corbetta, three leagues only from Milan. At four o'clock on the evening of the 2nd of June, whilst thunder was rolling in the distance, he entered Milan by the Vercelli gate at the head of six cavalry regiments. Berthier, with Monnier's division, followed the cavalry. Steps were at once taken to blockade the citadel. (This was held by General Nicoletti with 2,800 men.)

Gachot, writing on the subject of Bonaparte's entry into Milan, declares that he was disappointed with the reception he met on entering that city. When he expected to be received with open arms, and to be welcomed with great enthusiasm, he was received in profound silence; the people remained dumb before the future conqueror of Europe. A dense crowd filled the streets, but it was not demonstrative. Bonaparte was furious. However, the people were afraid lest the Austrians should return speedily into power, as had occurred before, and might inflict on them cruel reprisals; for the Austrians had certainly given proof of little conciliating spirit. (Edouard Gachot, *La Deuxième Campagne d'Italie*, chap. xvii.)

Nevertheless, it is strange that most of the writers of those events should state quite the reverse. Gachot says that the First Consul caused Bourrienne to write to his colleagues—men who, after all, had a right to know the truth:—

Milan has given him a spontaneous and touching reception.

Some of his immediate suite are said to have organised the ovation made to Bonaparte at the Scala Theatre, so as to make him forget the cold reception accorded to him on the 2nd of June, for they well knew how eager the general was for acclamation.

Trolard, who bases his narrative on ocular evidence contained in the local papers of the period, states that there were no cheers. The population, astonished at the sudden change of scenery, abstained from clapping their hands and shouting "*Viva!*" Many of the Milanese simply doffed their hats. The crowd at the Scala on the night of the reception was less than usual. (Trolard Eugene, *De Rivoli à Marengo et à Solferino*, vol. ii.) Again, in another place, he states that, notwithstanding the message Bonaparte had sent to the Consuls that he had been received by a population stirred by the greatest enthusiasm, there was on the part of the inhabitants a good deal of deference, but nothing more.

The bulletin issued on the 3rd of June runs as follows:—

> General Murat entered Milan on the 13th (2nd of June). He caused the citadel to be surrounded at once. Three hours later, the First Consul and all his staff made their entry, passing through a multitude of people animated by the greatest enthusiasm. (*Correspondence de Napoleon*, No. 4854.)

Brossier writes in the diary of the campaign of the Army of Reserve:—

> 13th *Prairial* (2nd of June).—Triumphant entry of the French into Milan. By all these measures the occupation of Milan had been rendered safe, the army headquarters went there the same day in the midst of proofs of general joy. The inhabitants, of all ages, of both sexes, bowed before him who for the second time brought them liberty and happiness.

Alison records that:—

> Bonaparte made his triumphant entry into Milan on the 2nd of June, when he was received with transports of joy by the democratic party, and by the inconstant populace with the same applause which they had lavished the year before on Suwarroff. (Alison, *History of Europe*, chap. xxxi.)

Guizot writes in the same sense:—

> The Lombard populace received the First Consul with transport, happy to see themselves delivered from the Austrian yoke, and beguiled in anticipation with the hope of liberty. (Guizot, vol. vii.)

We read in the *Campagne de Bonaparte en Italie en l'an VIII. de la Ré-*

publique (Alexandre Foudras), an account published the same year:—

> The First Consul and all his staff made their entry into the city in the midst of an immense crowd, animated by the greatest enthusiasm.

The same is recorded by the Duc de Valmy:—

> The First Consul was received with unanimous and sincere enthusiasm. (*Ibid.*)

Dampierre, writing the same day to Mathieu Dumas, states:—

> The First Consul has been everywhere received with enthusiasm by the people, but with coldness by the upper class. (Duc de Valmy, *Histoire de la Campagne de 1800.*)

Bonaparte's entry into Milan took place in the midst of an immense crowd, which shouted from every side in its semi-Oriental style, "*Ecco il sole, il liberatore della nostra Italia. Viva! viva!*" ("Behold the sun, the liberator of our Italy. Hail! hail!")—(*La Revue de Paris*, June 15, 1900, No. 12.)

Joseph Petit, the Horse Grenadier of the Consular Guard, could certainly have had no special object in giving too vivid a colouring to Bonaparte's entry into the capital of Lombardy. His words are:—

> But the finest *coup-d'oeil*, the instant most flattering to us as spectators, was when we had reached the Place du Dome, and the hero who had led us enjoyed the supreme gratification which the gratitude of a numerous people exhibited. The vast space was made to ring with reiterated shouts of '*Vive General Bonaparte! Vive l'armée Française!*' (Joseph Petit, *Marengo ou Campagne d'Italie par l'Armée de Reserve.*)

A warm reception went to the hearts of the French, for at that period they were more covetous of glory than of pleasure.

Botta, the Italian historian, writes:—

> I am not able to describe the rejoicings that took place.

He says nothing to show that the First Consul met with an enthusiastic reception; but subsequently he declares that:—

> The French were received with pleasure in the districts of Lodi, Cremona, Bergamo, and Crema, in which districts they were welcomed with considerable joy. (Botta, *Storia d'Italia,*" *tom.* iv.)

Bonaparte had hastened his march and entered Milan when the inhabitants had barely heard that he had left Dijon. Nothing could exceed their wonderment, for none were aware that he had so recently crossed the Alps.

The astonishment of the Milanese was nothing more than natural, for Europe had endeavoured to make it believed that Bonaparte was either dead or held in captivity. Just a little more than a year before, the *Foglio Lombardo*, in its issue of the 22nd of June, 1799, published the following item of news:—

General Bonaparte, with the whole of his staff, was compelled to surrender to Admiral Smith. He has been interned for a long time. (*Il Generale Bonaparte fu forzato a consegnarsi con tutto il suo stato maggiore nelle mani dell Ammiraglio Smith. Egli é stato internato per lungo tempo.*)

Milan still echoed with the success of Melas on the Var, and the capture of Nice, when behold, like a clap of thunder, Bonaparte appears and rides at the head of his troops into Milan. Jomini writes:—

The entry of the First Consul into Milan, which was for the Lombards a real *coup de théâtre*, excited amongst them an enthusiasm difficult to express. (Jomini, *Histoire des Guerres de la Révolution,* liv. xvi. chap. cii.)

We read in Marelli's *Giornale Storico:*—

The population, surprised at this sudden change of scene, did not clap hands, nor shout 'Hurrah!' Many doffed their hats in sign of respect, and he graciously responded. (*Il popolo, attonito per tale improviso mutamento di scena, non batteva le mani né gridava evviva. Multi rispottosamente levavansi il cappello, ed egli graziosamente rispondeva.*")

The Lombards were more interested in Bonaparte's success than the French themselves, for the behaviour of the Austrians on their return into Lombardy had been immeasurably arbitrary and harsh. A large number of individuals and of families had become compromised, and such as had not thought it prudent to emigrate had been deported to Austria, or were subject to a very vexatious police supervision. Others were even languishing in prison. The Austrians, in short, had occasioned so many vexations in Lombardy that their expulsion from the country came to be regarded as another benefit conferred on the people by the French. Of a host of Lombards, who had been compelled by the rigorous system introduced by the Austrians to cross the frontier and seek a refuge in France, many returned, bearing arms under the First Consul.

The previous year, the news of the arrival of the Austro-Russian Army had created great enthusiasm amongst the population of Northern Italy. On their entry into Milan, on the 29th of April, the newcomers were hailed as liberators, for the French and the democrats had disgusted a large section of the population. The illusion, however, soon vanished. The departure of the French did anything but make matters more pleasant; and the so-styled liberators, the harbingers of Providence, were found to be much worse than the former occupiers of Lombardy.

The Italians had soon come to understand all the meaning of the Austrian rule, and, in comparing it with the French, they were not slow in detecting the very marked difference which existed between the two. The contempt with which they had welcomed the cessation of the Republican rule thereupon vanished; and the Gallophobe attacks and libels, of which their Press in the preceding months had been so prolific, from that moment ceased to appear.

The unfortunate country was desolated by all kinds of vexations and of most arbitrary proceedings. The allies came to be dreaded. At the cry, "Behold! here are the Russians!" everyone fled for dear life, all the doors were made fast, and all the animals were securely shut up in their stables. The boldest of the men would take up arms and gather together in some building, determined to defend themselves, and did not venture out till after dark. Speaking of the valley of Aosta, the Abbé Fenoil declares that the heavy domination of the Austrians has left a more painful record than that of the soldiers of the Terror.

Lombardy had been made to provide for the allies, as it had previously been made to maintain the French. It was not Bonaparte alone who followed the principle of feeding and maintaining his armies on foreign ground. In eight months alone, the Austrians consumed 30,000,000 of *lire* worth of victuals and fodder, most of which remained unpaid. The consequence was that wheat rose to 86 *lire* the sack, and Indian corn to 45. The French had irritated the Lombards by imposing a capitation tax of 7 *lire*.

But during the thirteen months which the Austrians had held the country, since the expulsion of the French, this tax had risen from 7 to 30 *lire*. From the month of May to the end of 1799, 30,187,280 *lire* of fundable property were appropriated, besides 13,346,460 for military expenses. Under such circumstances it is not surprising if very great dissatisfaction existed. Nor could the Austrians plead ignorance of the cause of all this discontent. Thugut acknowledges it in a letter to Count Colloredo. He writes:—

> There is not a shadow of doubt that our army, and the men connected with it, have borne themselves in Italy in such a way that there is not a single Italian who would not prefer the French regime or that of the Cisalpine Republic to the vaunted Austrian despotism."

Bonaparte feared lest the Republican party in Italy would resort to reprisals, would break out into acts of revenge, after having been kept down, as it had been, by the Austrians with such a strong hand. He had, therefore, to take measures to provide for the general security. He invited the Milanese to re-establish the National Guard, which should be employed in the defence of their city against attack from small bodies of the enemy.

He declared that as soon as the Italian soil was free from the Austrians, he would reconstitute the republic on the firm basis of religion, liberty, equality, and order. Knowing that the clergy were the class most opposed to the French rule and ideas, he strove to dissipate every shadow of suspicion that the religious worship and other practices of the people would be interfered with. He convened an assembly of parish priests, and boldly disowned all the events which had occurred in 1796, he said:—

> All the changes which occurred then, above all in the discipline, were against my way of thinking. I, a humble representative of a government which had no care whatever for the Catholic religion, was not able to prevent in those days the disorders which had been incited purposely with the object of overthrowing it. Today, furnished with far greater powers, I am firmly resolved to use all the means necessary to guarantee it.

After the enthusiastic reception reported in the bulletin and referred to by many writers of those events, the following letter, written by Monsieur Petiet—who had been intrusted with the new organisation of the Lombard territory—to the municipality of Milan reads strangely:—

> *Plusieurs officiers français se plaignent, Citoyens, du peu d'égards*

qu'ils éprouvent de la part des habitants chez lesquels ils sont logés. L'intention du Premier Consul n'est point sans doute d'autoriser des demandes indiscrètes ou exaggérées, mais il ne pent pas tolérer que les officiers de son armée soient reçus des Cisalpine avec indifférence et souvent avec mépris. Je vous engage, Citoyens, á faire sentir aux habitants de Milan combien leur conduite vis-à-vis des Français pourrait devenir dangereuse pour eux, et que leur intérèt comme leur devoir est de traiter avec plus d'amitié et d'égards les officiers et autres militaires de l'armée auxquels ils donnent l'hospitalité.

Petiet.

Master of Lombardy, Bonaparte had secured his communications with Switzerland by the Saint Gothard, from which Moncey, with about 14,000 men taken from the Army of the Rhine, was descending. At the same time, he had interposed between Melas's army and its base of operations on the Mincio and Adige.

On entering Milan, he instantly dismissed the Austrian authorities, and one of his very first acts was to seize all letters found lying at the post-office. Amongst the mass of letters thus captured he found information of some value. But the situation of Bonaparte, reading at Milan the intercepted despatches that had been written by the Austrian Government to the general commanding their army, and the reports made by this general to his government, was a singular one.

From the letters that came from Vienna for the Austrian commander, and those from the army directed to Vienna, the First Consul gathered a quantity of useful details. He became aware of the amount of the reinforcements which were *en route* for the Austrian Army, of the actual situation of the army which was blockading Genova, with the positions it occupied, and of the situation of the parks and of the hospitals. The Austrian minister of war could hardly have furnished a more complete report than that which Bonaparte found at his disposal from the intercepted documents.

In a few hours he had learnt all that he required to know on the moral and material condition of the Austrian forces in Italy.

A letter coming from Genova revealed to him other items. From it he learnt that the city still held out, but that it was at its last gasp, that Massena was still resisting, but that in all probability he would soon be compelled to capitulate.

A courier on his way from Vienna was captured. He was the bearer of orders for the various depots, parks of artillery and equipments in the Austrian rear. This information was turned to good account, and on the knowledge thus acquired orders were issued to lay hands on all the war materials stored in the neighbourhood.

As Bonaparte gained possession of the Milanese, his first care was to lay hands on all objects useful to his army which his rapid advance had compelled the Austrians to abandon. Orders went forth that everything serviceable which the Austrians had left in their magazines or in their manufacturing establishments should be seized.

Beyond the great moral impression caused by the occupation of the capital of Lombardy, the march to Milan secured no positive advantages, for it did not lead to a concentration of the French forces. On the contrary, it was followed by a dangerous dispersion, for to carry out Bonaparte's plan a large number of troops were required. How otherwise could a line of at least thirty leagues in extent be effectively closed to the enemy?

Melas did not penetrate Bonaparte's design, and strongly believed that the relief of Genova was the principal object of his enterprise. Only when he heard that the French had entered Milan, he began to realise how critical was his position.

The Austrian generals had been warned that a large army was concentrating at Dijon. They at first scorned to believe this, and all other rumours that had reached them. When at last these were referred to the Aulic Council, all the answer they received was that the subject was not worthy of consideration.

Melas persisted in disbelieving. On the 28th of May, he had issued orders to his subordinates to rejoin him. Nevertheless, he persisted in refusing to accord credence to what he heard of the doings of the Army of Deserve.

The Austrians might very easily have stopped the French in the valley of Aosta, in the position of Bard, which had already been marked out, and where there existed intrenchments and *barracons* in a good state. The staff, however, were confident, and the cry was, "Let them come down into the plains, and we shall beat them."

When at last the French columns appeared, having crossed the Alps and traversed the district of Aosta, the Austrians abandoned Ivrea and the Canavesan. As the French marched along the left bank of the Po, the Austrians endeavoured to assemble around Turin all the forces at that time scattered throughout Piedmont. But when they had gathered a goodly number, and offered battle in the direction of Volpian on the left of the Po, the French were too alert to fall into this snare, and followed the course of the Po on the left bank of the river. Zack, when questioned on the situation, is said to have replied, "I have them in a sack." Chevalier Cavour states that from that moment the Austrians lost their head and committed many errors, one greater than the other.

At a council of war, it was decided to defend the right bank of the river. This unfortunate decision allowed the enemy complete freedom on the left bank, and plenty of time to be joined by reinforcements. In the end the plan brought about the loss of Italy to the Austrians. There were, nevertheless, at this council of war officers who objected, and who held that it was derogatory for a numerous army to observe a strictly defensive attitude in the face of an army which could not number more than 20,000 combatants, and had to defend the crossing of a river for a very considerable extent—from Turin to Piacenza—which could not have been less than forty leagues.

These officers argued that it was preferable to place the heavy artillery in safety in the fortified places, to abandon the heavy baggage, and to follow the enemy on the left bank of the Po, always offering battle, which, by reason of his inferiority as much in point of numbers as in cavalry and artillery, the French commander-in-chief would be precluded from accepting. Once on a level with Vercelli, the army should abandon this manner of proceeding, move on Novara, cross the Ticino at Turbigo, and, leaving Milan on the right, march so as to effect a junction with Vukassevich and the reinforcements coming from Austria. Then it would be time for them to retrace their steps.

The conception was good. The distance from Turin to Vercelli could have been got over in three moderate marches, one march more would have taken the army to Novara, and a longer one have brought it level with Milan. In two or three other marches it could have been within Gallarate and Varese, where Vukassevich's corps was at that time. Possibly Lannes with the advanced guard of the Army of Reserve would have harassed the left flank of the Austrian columns marching towards Vukassevich, still the Austrians had superiority of numbers on their side, and if well-handled could have swept Lannes away.

The Austrians did their scouting very badly not to get an idea of the weakness of Lannes's force at Chivasso—this in a country where the feeling was much in their favour. Chabran bears witness, for, writing from Sartirana on the 16th of June, he remarks:—

L'habitant n'est pas pour nous. (The people are not in our favour).

The reason given, and very possibly the true one, for Melas having abstained from threatening his adversary's communications by a move on Vercelli, is the sudden news he received of all the disasters on the valley of the Danube. How Kray had suffered several defeats and had taken refuge in the intrenched camp at Ulm; how Moncey had arrived at Bellinzona, and Vukassevich had retreated towards the Adda. All these circumstances demanded, he thought, more cautious measures, such as a concentration of his army under the cannon of Alessandria.

Melas had the choice of three roads by which to regain the Mincio. One leading from Alessandria to Piacenza; a second by Casale, Mortara, and Milan; the third, and most difficult, of Alessandria, Colie della Scoffera, Bobbio, and Piacenza. His dilatoriness and his state of uncertainty allowed Bonaparte to close all three against him.

At the end of May, Melas found himself exposed to be attacked by Bonaparte, and to be beaten in detail while his army was in a thorough state of dispersion. What else could he expect? Nevertheless, there was still time to do something. To concentrate his army, he was bound to bow to necessity, to make great sacrifices, to withdraw at once from Genova, to draw back from the Var; in fact, to give up a great part of Piedmont. Melas, however, for a second time fell a victim to Bonaparte's craftiness. He failed to penetrate his adversary's intentions; he believed that with some 30,000 men he could easily dispute the passage of the Po, and prevent a junction with Turreau. He was imposed upon by Lannes's bold attitude, and believed that the necessity had not yet arisen for a complete withdrawal of his troops from Genova and the Var.

When he became actually convinced of the appearance of a formidable army in Italy, he despatched couriers in all directions bearing orders for the concentration of his army. The date given by Campana for the orders sent to Ott and to Elsnitz to march on Alessandria was the 28th of May. Jomini says that the orders sent to Ott were despatched on the 31st of May, and reached him on the 1st of June. Hamley, possibly, is still more correct, for he states that Melas issued his orders for the concentration on the 31st of May, and that Ott probably received them on the 2nd of June. This appears to accord with the date given by General Melas in his letter to Count de Tige. (See De Cugnac, *Campagne de l'Armée de Reserve en 1800*, vol. ii.)

It is hard to believe that all the Austrians were badly informed. Amongst the correspondence seized by Murat at Piacenza was a letter signed "Marqui," evidently written by a superior officer of the

Austrian Army, and dated Coni, 3rd of June. This letter contained the following passages:—

> My suspicions, with regard to the Army of Reserve, were not without good grounds, notwithstanding that no one would pay attention to them. Berthier has come from the valley of Aosta, and by the valley of the Rhone into that of Domodossola, and from thence to Lago Maggiore.
> General Flavigny, who was in front of me at Barcelonnette, has descended on the side of Susa. He has not more than 3,000 men, and cannot undertake anything of serious importance.
> But at this moment I am told that Lecourbe, with a corps coming from Germany, is descending by the Saint Gothard on Bellinzona, so that if Genova does not surrender, it is impossible to foresee how things will turn out. (See De Cugnac, *Campagne de l'Armée de Reserve en 1800*, vol. ii.)

Chapter 2

Passage of the Po and Battle of Montebello

Whilst the First Consul was leading his army across the Ticino, and making Vukassevich clear for him the way into Milan, the advanced guard of the Army of Reserve was to undertake a bold march to its left. Lannes had gained his object, and his attitude had, to a certain extent, deceived Melas with regard to Bonaparte's intentions. His preparations at Chivasso, and the bridge he had thrown over the Po, could only be interpreted in one sense, *viz.* an early advance of the French Army on Turin, there to form a junction with Turreau.

To hide the First Consul's vast designs on Lombardy, and to cover the march of the army on the Ticino effectively, Lannes, at the head of 3,000 infantry and 400 horsemen, descended from Foglizzo on the 28th of May, attacked the Austrians, and drove them beyond the Oreo. The Austrian dragoons, after having withdrawn beyond that stream, burnt the bridge. Now the progress of the French Army towards Milan was sufficiently advanced for the original advance-guard to be employed in a more useful manner.

On the night of the 30-31st of May, having left General Gency with the 6th Light and a squadron of the 12th Hussars to guard the bridge over the Dora Baltea at Rondissone, Lannes quitted Chivasso and marched to his left on Crescentino and Trino, in front of Casale, driving away such small parties of Austrians as had ventured across the Po. These he compelled to withdraw to the right bank of that river. He then marched to Vercelli and by Mortara on Pavia, where he forestalled the Austrians, who were on the march to occupy it.

******

The marches were Chivasso by Rondissone to Crescentino, $14^{3/8}$ miles; Crescentino to Vercelli, $21^{7/8}$ miles; Vercelli to Mortara, 16³⁄₈ miles. The cavalry, Rivaud's brigade, 12th Hussars, and 21st Chasseurs, marched right through from Vercelli to Pavia, 38¹⁄₈ miles.

The city of Pesinum was founded by the Gauls. It was afterwards taken by the Romans, who in their turn were in the fifth century driven forth by the Goths. In 568, it fell into the hands of the Lombards, and it was for some time the capital of Lombardy. In 774, it came into Charlemagne's possession, and he founded its university. About 1477, the town, being little better than a mass of ruins, was rebuilt, when its name was changed to Pavia. Whilst besieging it in 1525, Francis I. was taken prisoner. Pavia was sacked by the French general Lautree in 1527, for three days, as a punishment for the peasants cutting his communications, and has never recovered its former grandeur.

※※※※※※

In this manner, in the forenoon of the 2nd, Lannes, at the head of his cavalry, entered the city, and a great accumulation of arms, ammunition, grain, forage, and stores fell into the hands of the French. They also captured some bridging equipment, of which they were sadly in want for crossing the Po.

It seems strange that the Austrians should have left such an important magazine without an adequate garrison. What they were about is not quite clear. Berthier, in his report to the First Consul, says:—

The enemy has abandoned the town, leaving it in our hands.

But Dupont expresses himself otherwise. He writes of Lannes, that he went:—

On the 13th, by way of Mortara, to Pavia, where he forestalled the enemy then marching to occupy it.

Brossier's words are:—

He forestalled the enemy that was marching to occupy it (Pavia), and enters therein as conqueror.

Dumas states that the Austrian troops detached by General Ott to occupy Pavia were anticipated by General Lannes' troops, which surprised the place after two days of forced marching. As Ott was busy before Genova, these troops, like those sent to occupy Piacenza, possibly belonged to some other command.

At Pavia Lannes, according to his report of the 2nd of June, found

300 or 400 pieces of ordnance, field and siege guns, on their carriages; shells and shot in large quantities, 1,000 barrels of gunpowder, and a goodly number of cartridges. Also, muskets, large stores of stuff for sheets, blankets, corn and flour in abundance, with many quintals of candles.

The number of guns found at Pavia is differently given. In the official bulletin of the 3rd of June, Bonaparte reports the capture of 500 bronze cannon, though he admits that the inventory from Pavia was not expected to arrive before the following day. Brossier, in his diary of the Army of Reserve, sets the guns captured at 200, of which number 30 were field-guns on their carriages. Dupont, reporting to the minister of war, says the same.

Dampierre shows that it was not a great catch, after all. In a letter he wrote to Mathieu Dumas he states: —

> Pavia has fallen into the hands of the French; they have found there, munitions and from fifty to sixty cannons, a real find for an army which has only just crossed the Alps.

Writing a few days later (on the 16th of June) he reviles the eight guns found at Ivrea, which he declares to have been in a worthless condition. Almost all those captured at Pavia were found spiked, and in the few days which elapsed between the capture of that town and the Battle of the 25th *Prairial* (14th of June) only five could be rendered serviceable!

The passage of the artillery through the streets of Bard had not proved a thorough success. The greater part only passed through on the 2nd of June, after the fort had capitulated. On the 3rd or 4th of June, the guns arrived at Ivrea, and could not pass through Vercelli, as that town had been surprised by the Austrians on the 4th.

When he occupied Pavia, Lannes, by good fortune, came into possession of two letters addressed to an Austrian general (one of which had been written on the 2nd of June by Prince de Hohenzollern, then before Genova). Lannes could not gather any valuable information from their contents, as unfortunately there was no one who could read German. Evidently the necessity for having interpreters or officers acquainted with the German language attached to the various parts of the army had been overlooked. In those days, when information of the enemy's doings was so eagerly sought, Lannes, to find out the contents of these letters, had to send them to army headquarters to be read. Murat, who seized at Piacenza some of Melas's letters, had to pursue the same course, there being no one with him proficient in reading German.

From the action taken by the various chiefs, it would appear that neither Murat nor Berthier had qualified interpreters at their side, for Murat sends the intercepted letters to Berthier without having fully mastered their contents, and Berthier sends them on to the First Consul, with a footnote in his forwarding letter stating that Murat reports having intercepted a letter written by Melas, in which there is some mention of the capitulation of Genova. The letters were retransmitted by Bourrienne (*Mémoires, tom.* iv), after having been duly translated.

Dampierre, who was at Voghera on the 11th of June with the foremost troops of Gardanne's division, earnestly asks the chief of the staff for an assistant well acquainted with the language of the country—a person able to gather all the information that could be got from the peasantry.

What an amount of useful tidings will be wasted when there are no competent interpreters! Without them, or without officers acquainted with the enemy's language, how will it be possible to question prisoners, deserters, and the inhabitants? to gather the information contained in foreign newspapers and intercepted letters? or to master the contents of despatches found on the enemy's couriers?

Lannes possessed a very loyal spirit; his eyes were always turned in the direction of Genova. Writing from Pavia to the First Consul on the 2nd of June, he urges:—

> The enemy is still before Genova, which it cannonades and bombards without intermission. If you desire to march against him, there is not a moment to lose. According to the information I have acquired the place cannot hold out very long.

Melas was still at Turin. He little expected that the French would march into Lombardy, for it was on all grounds more reasonable to believe that they would speed to Genova direct through Piedmont.

The Austrians could command the waters of the Po from their source up to Valenza. It was open to them to cross that river at Turin, Chivasso, Casale, or Valenza; but having done so, Melas's army was now liable to be stopped on the Ticino, which was already in Bonaparte's hands. There was little prospect of regaining Lombardy from that side, so the Austrian commander turned his attention to the lower course of the Po, so as to hold the road to Mantua by way of Piacenza and Cremona.

At this period Piacenza assumed a very important strategical value in the operations. For Bonaparte it was the real key to Piedmont, for by its possession alone could he hope to close effectively to the Austrian commander his communications with Lombardy and the empire. Melas also, as soon as he heard that the French had occupied Milan, became alive to all the importance of Piacenza. He fully realised how absolutely necessary its possession was for him; how, since the French were posted behind the Ticino and occupied Milan, the road from Alessandria leading through Piacenza to Mantua was the true line of retreat for the Austrian Army.

Consequently, he ordered O'Reilly not to await the concentration of the rest of the army, but to push on for Piacenza as fast as his horses would go. He was to assume command of the city, and with it of all the troops that had been directed to march thereto.

Melas's orders were just. But opposed to him was the best leader of the time, the man most renowned in the art of moving troops. Bonaparte had perceived before Melas that Piacenza was the key to Piedmont, necessary alike for anyone who desired to enter that country as for anyone who wished to issue forth from it. Bonaparte understood likewise that, if he had let Melas escape him, he would have lost all the fruit of his bold march over the Alps.

The Austrian troops ordered to repair to Piacenza were Lobkowitz's dragoons and a battalion of Ottochan; the first sent from Turin, the second from Casale, which set out on the 1st of June. From a small corps of observation, stationed between Turin and Valenza, were detached in the same direction two squadrons of hussars and three infantry battalions of the Reisky regiment. The infantry regiment of Klébeck belonging to Gottesheim's brigade quitted Genova, and took the shortest road to Piacenza by way of Bobbio. The fourth battalion of the Baunats had been previously sent from Genova to patrol the Po from its confluence with the Ticino to its confluence with the Tanaro. Mosel, the senior officer in Piacenza, had with him two companies of the Neugebau regiment, two companies of Tyrolese riflemen, and fifty horsemen of De Bussy.

Ott, with the troops drawn from the siege of Genova, was to follow O'Reilly, marching by way of Bocchetta and Tortona. The rest of the Austrian troops garrisoning strong places in Piedmont, and those under Elsnitz on the Var, amounting to about 30,000 men, were to concentrate at Alessandria, and afterwards to proceed in the direction of Mantua by way of the Stradella pass. The object was to reach the

Mincio, effect a junction with Vukassevich, and take up a strong position, with one flank resting on the lake of Garda, and the other on the fortress of Mantua.

Bonaparte was equally, if not more, eager to secure for his army the passages of the Po. From the very beginning of the war, his plan contemplated seizing the communications of the Austrian Army in Italy. As the campaign progressed, the most important part of his design was thoroughly to close against the enemy the road leading from Alessandria to Piacenza and Mantua. At the same time, he was bound to keep in view the possibility of the Austrians using as a line of retreat either the road leading across the Ticino to Milan or those on the lower Po which lead from Alessandria to Cremona. As long as the Austrians had the choice of three lines of retreat, he was compelled to dispose his forces in such a manner as to be ready at any moment to face any contingency.

The way in which he tried to solve the problem led to a reduction of his main force for battle. But this was unavoidable. What he had set himself to do was to close entirely the line of retreat against the Austrians, and to offer Melas no point of escape whatsoever. It was not merely a question of locating small detachments to watch and give warning of the enemy's approach, nor detachments which might easily be brushed aside; what was needed were bodies strong enough to contend against superior forces, and able to fight a retaining action till the arrival of reinforcements.

Whilst he himself was to cross the Po and advance on Stradella, occupying a central position with a force which he roughly calculated at 30,000 men, the other divisions were ordered to take post as follows. Chabran was directed on Vercelli, with injunctions to fall back on the Ticino should the enemy attempt to make for that river. Lapoype was posted on the Ticino River itself, near Pavia. These two divisions, which numbered in all from 9,000 to 10,000 men, were to fall back on each other, stubbornly disputing all the while the crossing of the river. Bonaparte from his central position at Stradella could in one day come to their aid.

Lorge was to take post at Lodi on the Adda; Gilly to contain the Austrian garrison shut up in the citadel of Milan; Lechi was at Brescia. Duhesme, with Loison's division, was to hold Piacenza and Cremona.

Thiers, in giving a sketch of Bonaparte's dispositions, says:—

Such was the distribution of the fifty and few more thousand soldiers of whom Bonaparte could dispose of at that moment: 32,000 were in the central post of Stradella; 9,000 to 10,000 on the Ticino; 3,000 or 4,000 more at Milan and Arona; and lastly, 10,000 to 11,000 on the lower Po and the Adda, all stationed in such a way as to support each other reciprocally with great promptitude. Indeed, on a report coming from the Ticino, General Bonaparte could in one day fly to the help of the 10,000 Frenchmen who were guarding it. On an advice coming from the lower Po, he could in the same space of time descend on Piacenza and Cremona, whilst General Loison, defending the passage of the river, gained him time to arrive. One and the other, on their side, could fall back on Stradella, and reinforce General Bonaparte in as short a time as he would take to go to their aid.

Bonaparte's orders sent to Lannes were to cross the Po at Belgiojoso, a little below the confluence of the Ticino and Po. Murat, with Boudet's division and some regiments of cavalry, was to seize the crossing at Piacenza.

On the 5th of June, Murat appeared before Piacenza. The city was garrisoned by a very small number of troops; nevertheless, the officer in command of the place, General Mosel, when danger threatened, made some hurried preparations. He caused twelve guns to be mounted on the bridgehead on the left bank of the Po. Other guns he had posted on the opposite bank of the river to sweep with their fire the flanks of that work.

This done, he awaited the arrival of supports, for, according to the Austrian account, he had for the defence of the bridgehead and citadel in all about 400 men. (It was calculated that the citadel of Piacenza alone required a garrison of 600 men.) The Austrian account describes the bridgehead as dilapidated, being much damaged by inundations, by time and by rains. Steps for putting it in a state of defence were only taken on the 3rd of June. The garrison detailed to hold this work consisted of one company of infantry and thirty riflemen. De Bussy's cavalry had been pushed forward in the direction of Casalpusterlengo to reconnoitre, and fell back before the French, who by 2 p.m. on the 5th advanced to attack the bridgehead. Mosel made a good show of resistance.

Boudet's division had left Lodi at three in the morning of that day, marching on Piacenza. The 11th Hussars, who were leading, fell in with the Austrian outposts near Fombio, and these they drove back as far as the bridgehead on the Po. Boudet states in his report that this work was defended by 12 guns and 500 or 600 infantry; an equal number of guns having been posted on the right bank of the Po, swept with their fire the flanks of the bridgehead, and every point from which troops could approach it.

The French advanced in three columns; one on either side of the work, whilst the third was intended to make a frontal attack, but only when the action was well engaged. The French, who had imagined that they were about to attack a post which was not likely to be stubbornly defended, soon found that they were mistaken. The two flanking columns came under a heavy fire from the guns on the bridgehead and the pieces on the right bank, the fire being so heavy that they had to suspend the action. This was to be renewed at a more promising moment, at night.

Some of the French troops had rushed forward quite close to the enemy's works. Then, taking advantage of what natural cover there was, they opened a brisk musketry fire on the Austrians, so well directed that, as Boudet reports, they acknowledge to having had 330 casualties. (They appear to have set down their losses only at 120 between killed and wounded. This is more likely, as being in keeping with their numbers.)

The several Austrian columns which had been directed to proceed to Piacenza had not yet arrived, and the troops Mosel had available for the defence of the bridgehead and citadel were quite insufficient. Those which had defended the bridgehead had held that post for eight hours, and lost heavily, so the commandant, under the protection of the guns on the right bank, caused his ordnance to be removed to the opposite shore, ordered the withdrawal of his feeble force, and lastly destroyed the communication with the Lombard provinces by removing some of the boats of the bridge.

The withdrawal of the guns was effected under cover of a brisk fire from the guns in battery on the right bank. But when the guns on the bridgehead suddenly ceased firing the French became suspicious, and made some reconnaissances. One, conducted by Major Caseau, got into the works, and found some 80 Austrians, who were ultimately persuaded to surrender. The Austrians had broken the bridge too soon, preferring to sacrifice a portion of the defenders of the bridgehead to seeing the French crossing along with them. Boudet sets down the loss for his division to have amounted to 500 between killed and wounded, most of the casualties being the result of the enemy's artillery fire.

The *Austrian Military Review* states that ten pontoons were removed from the middle of the bridge, and that it was intended to ferry the garrison to the right bank in small boats. It adds that General Mosel's force, on account of the 120 men killed and wounded in the defence of the bridgehead, was reduced to 280 men.

On the 6th of June, Murat remained facing Piacenza and searching for means wherewith to cross the Po. Dalton, having succeeded in collecting a dozen or more boats, had them brought to the village of Nocetto, situated about a league below the bridgehead of Piacenza, and little by little from that point, on the 7th, Musnier's brigade was carried across to Roncarolo on the right bank.

It had come to Musnier's ears that the enemy had received a considerable reinforcement, and was expecting a still larger one. Without waiting for the entire division to cross, he moved speedily towards Piacenza, and took post two miles from the city, on the main road to Cremona. A reconnaissance sent a mile further on ascertained that a convoy of 1,500 vehicles was moving along the Parma road, protected by a weak cavalry escort. From several sources Musnier learnt also that one of Ott's regiments was approaching by the same road.

The general made up his mind to march at once on the city, detaching one battalion to his left on the Parma road to attack the convoy. As he was advancing on the San Lazzaro gate, he was threatened by two squadrons of cavalry, but he showed a bold countenance, and the enemy did not dare to attack him. He entered the city at the heels of the Austrians, for he pressed forward with such rapidity that they were not able to keep him out. Musnier had profited by a favourable moment, and by his promptness saved the lives of many men who would have fallen in assaulting the place.

Once within the walls, he sent a detachment to secure the Sant' Antonio gate at the other extremity of the city. As this detachment arrived at the gate, the Austrian regiment of Klébeck, forming part of Gottesheim's brigade, appeared before it, coming along the Stradella road. The battalion sent by Musnier to attack the convoy, despairing of being able to overtake it, and having caught sight of this Austrian battalion, retraced its steps, and skirting the walls took it in flank, whilst the detachment at the gate charged it at the same time in front. The Austrians were either taken or dispersed; a part retired on the Trebbia, to San Nicolo, and another part towards Bobbio. The Austrian account states that the Parma gate was carried by assault, lost, and retaken.

The crossing of the Po was evidently a difficult operation, and we find Murat complaining to Berthier that he had not the pontoniers, the sappers and the engineers necessary for bridging rivers. When steps were taken to re-establish the broken bridge, a rise in the waters made the operation extremely difficult. As the waters kept steadily rising, the work had to be abandoned, and Murat had to content himself with two flying bridges.

The city of Piacenza remained in the hands of the French, but the Austrians still continued to occupy the citadel. Writing to the First Consul on the 8th of June, Berthier informs him that he had ordered Murat to join him with all his forces, minus what he might deem necessary for blockading the citadel and guarding the bridge. Murat mentions that 80 of the enemy's cavalry had just time to take refuge in the citadel. The Austrian account states that the Tyrolese riflemen and two companies of Neugebau took refuge in the citadel, and that the whole did not number more than 250 men.

As Boudet's division entered Piacenza, it was employed partly in blockading the citadel, partly in observation at the San Lazzaro gate on the Parma road, by which the reinforcements expected by the enemy were said to be coming. A squadron of the 11th Hussars was placed further forward in observation, and enjoined to scout the road. At 5 p.m. the vedettes announced the advance of the enemy. A body of between 600 and 700 men had quitted Ancona, and were marching on Piacenza to garrison the citadel. It was this body which had attacked the outposts and driven back the hussars by the fire of its two guns. But, like the regiment of Klébeck, it arrived just too late.

Two companies of grenadiers of the 59th were placed in column on the road under Dalton, and a battalion of the same regiment divided into wings on the right and left of the road; the whole advanced covered by skirmishers. The grenadiers rushed at the enemy with the bayonet, and the Austrians, unable to withstand the shock, retired. They were then pursued with vigour, but, as night was fast approaching, Boudet called on the 11th Hussars and such cavalry as he was able to collect to charge, when most of the enemy laid down their arms.

The several attempts made to wrest from Murat the road leading through Piacenza ended in failure. The troops which had come with that intent from Tortona and from the Trebbia suffered severe losses, and had to beat a hasty retreat. We learn from General Boudet what were the results of the several contests which occurred between the 5th and the 7th: 2,000 prisoners, 50 killed or wounded, the capture of 13 guns, two flags, considerable magazines, and 30 large barges full of provisions which had been intended for the supply of the enemy's army.

******

The French were short of ammunition. Berthier on the 6th brings this fact to Dupont's notice, and orders the despatch of 50,000 cartridges, and others for Murat's artillery, as all he had had been expended.

******

Whilst Murat advanced on Piacenza, Lannes, who had collected in the Ticino all the boats he could lay hands on, had these floated down to the Po. General Watrin, with a large detachment (28th and 40th Regiments), crossed the river between Belgiojoso and San Cipriano on the 6th of June, and took post in rear of San Cipriano. No sooner, however, was Watrin over than he was attacked by some 2,000 Austrians, who, as we shall see later on, were marching on Piacenza to secure that important post. The danger of being driven back into the river was great, but Watrin showed a bold front, and though entirely without artillery, fought gallantly until the boats crossing backward and forward brought up sufficient reinforcements to hold his position securely. Subsequently Lannes brought across the rest of Watrin's division, and directed a battalion under the Adjutant-General Nogues to take the enemy in flank. This manoeuvre stopped the Austrians and re-established confidence in the French. In their turn they charged the enemy, and chased him as far as Stradella.

It is at times extremely difficult to reconcile the different statements made. In this operation we have Lannes and Watrin, the two principal actors on the French side, greatly at variance. Lannes states that the Austrians had from 4,000 to 5,000 infantry engaged, 1,500 cavalry, and 7 guns, and that they attacked at ten in the morning; Watrin, on the other hand, reports that he was attacked at 3 p.m. by 2,000 men backed by 4 guns and 50 troopers of De Bussy, which were coming from Voghera. Lannes sets down the Austrian losses at 600 dead, 300 wounded, and as many prisoners. Watrin states that the enemy left 200 dead on the battlefield, and lost an equal number of prisoners. Of the two statements the reader will possibly accept the one of Watrin, who directed the fight.

On the receipt of the news that Lannes had crossed the Po, the divisions of Chambarlhac, Monnier, Gardanne, and Lepoype were directed to march as speedily as possible in that direction. Bonaparte intended to concentrate at Stradella all the forces that remained to him after having secured the line of the Ticino and of the Po, from Lago Maggiore to Cremona, so as to close every avenue of escape against Melas. But the effort to bar all the roads by which the Austrians could reach their base had so attenuated his line that a more skilful enemy might have succeeded in breaking through the toils.

Just before daybreak on the 7th of June, O'Reilly had entered Piacenza at the head of 280 infantry and three squadrons of hussars, trusting that the following day he would be in a position to collect other troops for the protection of the city; for O'Reilly had outdistanced a column of five battalions and five squadrons, which Melas had hurried off to Piacenza, fearing that Gottesheim might not arrive in time to save the place. O'Reilly soon discovered that it was not possible to undertake the defence of the city with the handful of troops he had with him, and only held his ground long enough to enable the artillery park to place itself in safety. This was a large reserve of artillery (60 pieces) escorted by 150 infantry and 60 cavalry, which was *en route* from Alessandria to Borgoforte, and had come by way of Tortona and Stradella as far as Piacenza. The Austrian account admits that there was great confusion on the Piacenza-Casteggio road, the result of the reported loss of Piacenza and the danger the artillery park was in, now that Lannes had crossed at another point and was in O'Reilly's rear.

The latter's hasty retreat from Piacenza was dictated by the necessity of saving the artillery park, which, if it got clear of Murat, who had sent a detachment of cavalry in pursuit in the direction of Rivalta-Trebbia, was yet liable to fall into Lannes's hands. It was this danger which made the Austrians hold so tenaciously to San Cipriano. In fact, the Austrian cavalry had to charge and clear away the most advanced troops which Lannes had brought up from Belgiojoso. It was not without difficulty that O'Reilly managed to get clear of the French; but he eventually reached Broni, and found for the park a safe refuge in Tortona.

This convoy escaped capture in a most marvellous manner, for at seven in the evening it passed along the main road to Tortona at a distance of only three or four kilometres from Watrin's division, which was then settling down in its bivouacs near San Cipriano.

Apparently Lannes had no cavalry to explore in advance of his infantry, or it would have brought news of the heavy artillery column moving along the high-road. This we gather from his report on the affair of the 6th of June, which concludes with the following words:—

Had I been able to take across two guns and the cavalry, I would have marched to Piacenza.

On the 8th, O'Reilly took up a position at Casteggio, where he was joined by Ott's advanced guard.

On the same day, Duhesme carried Cremona with Loison's division. The city held only a detachment which had been left behind when General Vukassevich withdrew from the place.

The French in these few days had got the control of the three main passages over the Po, and were more than ever masters of the Austrian line of communications with Mantua. They had, moreover, in Piacenza and Crema captured a considerable amount of provisions.

On the night of the 7th of June, Lannes' troops bivouacked about San Cipriano. At two in the morning of the 8th Watrin was ordered to march on Stradella. He started forthwith at the head of the 28th, and came across O'Reilly's rear-guard, which had protected the retreat of the Austrian reserve park. A battalion of the 28th attacked it and pursued it beyond Broni, making 200 prisoners. The whole of Watrin's division followed, and took post with the right on the Scuropasso brook, the centre at Vescovera, the left at Cigognola.

The first orders to abandon Genova left Melas's headquarters on the 31st of May, and reached Ott on the 2nd of June. No sooner had Massena concluded the arrangements for the evacuation of Genova than Ott despatched a large portion of the investing army to Tortona and a brigade to Piacenza. Vogelsang's division started the moment the Republican forces had evacuated the city. It marched from Genova on the 5th of June, and consisted of nine battalions. It constituted the advanced guard, and marched on Tortona by way of the Bocchetta. The same night it rested at Novi. It then pushed on for Voghera, where it was joined by Ott. On that day General Gottesheim, with five battalions, marched on Piacenza by the way of Bobbio. Schellenberg's division followed Vogelsang the next day; it was sixteen battalions strong.

Ott, having crossed the Scrivia on the 8th of June, marched on Voghera. There he was joined by the troops under O'Reilly and others previously sent in the direction of Piacenza. The following day, at the head of some 13,000 infantry, 1,400 cavalry, and a numerous artillery, he took possession of Casteggio. (These are the figures given by Victor, other accounts make his force larger.)

Fertility of resource is a great gift in an officer, and an illustration of it occurred in this march. The Scrivia is a torrent of which the bed, though very broad, is for the greater part of its course almost dry, and this is principally so at the season the operations were taking place. A storm, however, could easily swell its waters and render it impassable. On approaching the river, an Austrian staff officer, finding it in a very swollen state, was very much puzzled how to get the troops across.

Whilst thus absorbed in thought, he descried a long line of carts belonging to the commissariat advancing in his direction, evidently making for Alessandria. The carts were on four wheels, with a broad platform. The officer halted them in the stream, connected the whole with the chains and ropes they carried, and in this way utilised the carts as a bridge for the passage of the infantry. The mounted troops alone forded the river. After a time, the force of the stream broke this bridge, but this occurred when it had answered its purpose and almost everyone had got over.

Ott had received instructions to take possession of the line of retreat into Lombardy leading through the city of Piacenza, which up to that moment did not appear to be compromised. Melas evidently did not dream that it was threatened, or he would not have ventured his reserve artillery park on the Piacenza road as he did. Had Ott complied with his instructions to the letter, and raised the blockade of Genova the moment he was ordered to do so by Melas, he would undoubtedly have forestalled the French at Piacenza; but he wasted three days in negotiating with Massena, and thus allowed Murat to render himself master of that important city.

At Voghera the Austrians had no news either of Bonaparte or of Melas. Bellerose, a captain in Bussy's regiment, went forward to reconnoitre. The night was dark, and he could discover neither the position nor the strength of the French. He rushed at what there was in front of him, and was killed; his lieutenant returned to report that the enemy was approaching. The next day, the French attacked the Austrian advanced posts.

Zach, who had reached Voghera, was for avoiding any serious engagement, now that the French were already across the Po. But Ott rejected his advice. "My advanced posts are attacked," he said; "I march to their assistance." In short, Ott, being more of a hussar than a general, insisted on fighting.

He had conceived an idea that the French troops which had lately shown themselves at Piacenza and at Stradella composed a small body which was intended to mask the Army of Reserve during its march on Mantua. Under this impression he imagined that he would have a small portion of the enemy to deal with.

Ott could not now prevent the crossing of the Po, for he must have well known from O'Reilly's report that the French had crossed the river at two points. A better plan open to him was to march speedily by his right for Parma by way of Bobbio. Instead, he preferred to fight, and was defeated.

He had under his command a decent force, to which were added O'Reilly's troops—the troops which Melas had intended to be employed in defending the Po. Appreciating the great consequence to his army of having a free passage over that river at Piacenza, and knowing how eager Melas was to forestall the French at that point, Ott was strongly induced to fight. Considering how small a force he believed the French could bring to meet his 26 battalions and 15 squadrons, he not unnaturally felt confident of success.

Having made his dispositions, Ott, on the 9th of June, awaited the French, who were known to be advancing by the Stradella road from Broni on Casteggio and Montebello.

From some intercepted correspondence Bonaparte had been apprised of Ott's intention. On the night of the 7-8th, Murat forwarded some intercepted letters to Berthier, then at Pavia. On the morning of the 8th Berthier passed them on to the First Consul. One of the letters was addressed to Count Tige, vice-president of the supreme Aulic Council, and dated Turin, 5th of June.

Bourrienne relates that he awoke Bonaparte at 11 p.m. on the 7th of June to inform him that Murat had intercepted Melas's couriers, and that Genova had fallen. Bonaparte appeared much agitated, for he had hoped that the Army of Italy would display marvellous valour, and in that way make the task of the Army of Reserve more easy. Bonaparte exclaimed, "It is impossible! The letter is in German; you are not able to translate German." Well could he be disturbed by such news, for now the blockading corps would be able to join forces with Melas, whilst on the other side the troops of Massena and Suchet had been so severely tried by all that they had gone through that for another couple of weeks they would not be in a state to undertake vigorous operations.

On the morning of the 8th of June, Bonaparte wrote to Berthier the following letter:—

> I have received, citizen general, during the night your several letters.

General Murat has forwarded to me at Milan the despatches captured from the enemy. I am occupied in getting them examined; they contain some very interesting details.

A letter from Melas to the Aulic Council, dated the 5th of June, from Turin, makes known to me that Massena capitulated on the 4th. His troops are not prisoners of war; they are on the march to join General Suchet. It appears, nevertheless, that Massena has embarked on a frigate so as to arrive more promptly at Nice.

General Melas owns at the same time in his letters that Baron Elsnitz has been unable to effect his retreat by the Col di Tenda, because one of his brigadier-generals has been overthrown at the Col di Braus, and on that line his march has been cut off. He has conducted his retreat on Oneglia. General Melas states that he hopes that Elsnitz will arrive at Ormea on the 18th *Prairial* (7th of June).

Elsnitz has with him 6,000 men of his division and 3,400 men of Morzin's division, total 9,400 men; of which he will have to leave 1,000 men at Coni, 1,000 men at Savona, and 300 at Ceva.

General Hohenzollern will remain at Genova.

General Ott, with 9,000 men, will return by the Bochetta and Ovada to Alessandria.

Thus, it appears that it will not be before the 12th or 13th of June that the enemy will be able to assemble his forces at Alessandria, and that then it will have only the following forces:—

Elsnitz's division .	7,000 men.
Ott's division.	9,000 "
Haddick's division, which is on the Oreo at the present moment	6,000 "
Total	22,000 "

Move forward some parties boldly, and crush all the troops you may chance to meet.

The advanced guard may push on as far as Voghera.

Let the cavalry and artillery cross in such a manner that all the divisions may be complete, having their cartridges and everything in proper order.

Though my carriage is ready and one-half of my guides have left, I will delay my departure till the return of your post.

This was only one of the letters Bonaparte despatched from Milan on the 8th day of June, for he also sent a letter with instructions for Suchet.

It is an anomaly that whilst Bonaparte was leaving in his rear several divisions of those he had near at hand, Loison, Chabran, and Lepoype, he should have counted on Suchet's co-operation. No one should have known better how precarious is the co-operation of a secondary army which does not form a junction with the principal army before the battle. And, considering the slow ways of travelling of those days, how could he count on these instructions reaching Suchet in good time?

The following is the text of the instructions sent to Suchet on the 8th of June:—

> Citizen General,
> You will find enclosed different printed papers which will acquaint you with the situation of the army.
> We have crossed the Po at Stradella and Piacenza. We are masters of Orzinovi, Crema, Brescia, Cremona. Melas is without any communications.

******

We saw in June, 1900, a bold advance to obtain possession of the enemy's capital counterbalanced suddenly by De Wet's attack on the communications of the British Army. Bonaparte tried to close every outlet to the Austrians, and De Wet began by destroying the railway which the Royal Engineers had repaired with such labour. The disturbance on Lord Roberts' communications lasted for a fortnight.

******

> His parks, his magazines, his hospitals, his couriers,—everything has been captured.
> The despatches intercepted this morning at Piacenza inform us that Genova has capitulated. The garrison are in no wise prisoners of war; consequently, they should have joined you by the time you receive this despatch.
> Elsnitz arrived yesterday, the 7th, at Ormea. I imagine that you are on his tracks.
> Only General Gorupp, whom you have thrust back at Braus, has been able to gain the Col di Tenda. He commands at Coni, of which place his corps composes the garrison.

Battle of Montbello

If the corps of General Massena has joined you, you should be strong. I am going to undertake the pursuit of the enemy, who intends to concentrate at Alessandria. It is possible that when I shall arrive, he will not consider himself able to compete with me, and may have to retire, either on the side of the Ticino or on the side of the Riviera di Genova.

It is difficult to give you positive instructions, because I am ignorant of your forces or of what has happened. But your only aim should be this: to hold in check a corps as strong as yours. When your leading party once reaches Ceva, you will have indirectly, through the people of the country, news of the army, and that will place you in a position to manoeuvre in the best way to rejoin it.

Writing to Carnot on the morning of the 9th of June, Bonaparte says:—

You will have seen, through Melas's letters, that the very day on which the order reached Ott to raise the blockade of Genova, Massena, compelled by absolute want of provisions, asked to capitulate. It seems that General Massena has 10,000 fighting men. General Suchet has 8,000. If these two corps have, as I believe, come together between Oneglia and Savona, they may speedily be in Piedmont by way of the Tanaro, and be very useful in the period when the enemy will find himself compelled to leave a certain number of troops in Genova.

One of the stipulations made by Massena, when he agreed to the evacuation of Genova, was that two of his *aides-de-camp* were to be permitted to proceed by post to the First Consul, so that he might have timely notice of the treaty which had been just concluded. To avoid a long round-about journey, Massena stipulated that these officers should travel direct through Piedmont. Marbot states in his *Mémoires* that Major Graziani, a Piedmontese or Roman in the French service, was chosen as one, as it was desirable to send on this duty an officer who spoke Italian.

But, with a view to making things doubly sure, it was arranged that he himself should travel with that officer. Graziani, not being a Frenchman, Massena feared lest he might possibly be tampered with by the Austrians, and induced to delay *en route*. The two started on the 16th *Prairial* (5th of June), and came up with Bonaparte the next evening at Milan.

Battle of Montbello

★★★★★★

Nous partîmes le 16 Prairial de Gênes, où je laissai Colindo que je comptais y venir prendre sous peu de jours, car on savait que l'armée du Premier Consul était peu éloignée. M. Graziani et moi le joignîmes le lendemain soir à Milan.

★★★★★★

This version is quite different from that given by other writers. One declares that the two staff officers were directed by the Austrians on Casale, by way of Novi and Alessandria;. that it was only on the 9th of June that they got leave to cross the Po, after which they made for Vercelli, and thence to Milan; that it was owing to the circuitous route they were made to follow, and other delays, that they did not join Bonaparte at Stradella before the evening of the 10th. Another, the Duke of Rovigo, states that an Austrian officer, under cover of a flag of truce, brought up Massena's staff officer to the outposts; that from this officer Bonaparte learnt how the Austrians were still incredulous regarding the forces which he commanded and respecting his march; that they had taken possession of Genova with great pomp and the most rigorous formalities; that General Melas knew thoroughly that the French had descended into Italy by Ivrea, but still refused to believe that they were numerous; and that he had sent only a strong detachment to watch the banks of the River Po.

Massena's staff officer, having set out from Genova after the departure of the investing troops, had overtaken them on his way, and had been able to estimate their strength, which he gave to General Bonaparte, stating also how far in the rear he had left them. He likewise informed the First Consul that the Austrian Army had not sent any considerable detachment to Parma nor to Piacenza.

Much of what the Duke of Rovigo writes on this subject we know to be untrue. What Marbot himself relates is that the two staff officers, having reported themselves to the First Consul at Milan, the latter did not tire in questioning them on all that had occurred at Genova during the siege, as also on the strength and march of the Austrian corps which they had passed on the way to Milan.

Massena wrote to the First Consul on the 7th of June in the following words:—

> I have the honour to inform you of the evacuation of Genova under the terms of the enclosed convention. I hope that you will find it worthy of the obstinate resistance of the brave gar-

rison which was enclosed in the town. Up to the present moment we have not lost an inch of ground. Everywhere we have maintained a constant superiority, and, but for the want of provisions, we could have held Genova for eternity. Today I have given to the soldiers the last three ounces of what we call bread, which was nothing more than a miserable mixture of bran, oat straw, and cacao, without wheat. We have eaten all our horses.

The mortality, brought about by hunger, had reached the utmost limit, both amongst the population and amongst the troops. Hunger and the bombardment have given rise to insurrections, always stifled at their birth. It was in the hope of seeing you arrive to effect our deliverance that I pushed to so rigorous a length such measures as might have enabled us to await you. But the machine was breaking down, and we have been driven to retire so as not to lose everything, and to maintain for the Republic the remnants of a body of troops whose constancy has not been entirely shaken by hardships, fatigues, and privations up to this moment unheard of. Physical forces had entirely failed them, and all that remained of them was walking skeletons. The officer who brings you my despatches will be able to tell you on this point all that has been done and endured to keep Genova for you.

I am proceeding with the garrison to join the centre of the army, there to act in accordance with the instructions which I beg you to send rue. It is from there that I will send you news of myself.

On account of the breaking of the bridge at Piacenza, the difficulty of ferrying the troops across the Po, and the possibility of an attack, Berthier asked if it was not deemed safer to retire on Piacenza. The news gathered in the intercepted letters, however, showed that there was little to fear from the enemy.

On the 8th of June, Berthier sent an order to Lannes, who was at Broni, to take post at Casteggio, to attack any of the enemy's troops he should find between Stradella and Casteggio, but not to advance further than the latter village.

On the morning of the following day the French troops were not yet all across the Po. A sudden rise of that river—a thing not at all unusual in streams fed from mountain sources—had broken the bridge, and had detained on the left bank a great portion of the infantry and nearly the whole of the cavalry. Some of the latter had been sent further down to cross at Piacenza. Lannes, nevertheless, complied with his orders to take post at Casteggio on the Coppo torrent, and moved thither with Watrin's division and Rivaud's cavalry brigade.

Berthier did not anticipate an engagement that day, for he calculated that the Austrians would not reach Voghera before the evening of the 9th, where Bonaparte, in fact, purposed to attack them on the 10th. However, he had issued orders for Victor to support Lannes, should the necessity arise. Monnier and Gardanne, with their divisions, were to expedite the crossing of the river.

The postal road between Stradella and Voghera runs along the lower slopes of the Apennines, where they descend towards the Po, and leads through Casteggio and Montebello. Casteggio is situated on this road, at the junction of the roads coming from Pavia and Belgiojoso, and lies about half a league northeast of the village of Montebello. The heights which flank Casteggio command the road, and are, so to say, the key of the defile, which goes on always narrowing between the Po and the Apennines up to Stradella. From this last village up to Piacenza is 21¼ miles. At that season of the year, the fields were covered with tall crops of rye and other grain, which hid the contending troops from each other until within easy reach of their bayonets.

Bonaparte and Berthier had miscalculated the strength of the enemy, for Ott had under his command 18,000 men, and not about 10,000, as was estimated by the First Consul. This made Lannes' position at Broni somewhat hazardous. His orders, as we have said, were, that should the Austrians appear between Stradella and Casteggio, they were to be immediately attacked. These instructions from headquarters had been followed with due energy and rapidity. At six o'clock that morning (the 9th), Lannes had quitted Broni, where Watrin's division had passed the night, and moved on Casteggio. That village and the adjacent heights were already occupied by the Austrians, who were stronger in number. Lannes, who had only from 6,000 to 8,000 men, was not a man to consider the odds; still, he had to weigh the possibilities which a retrograde movement might have for an army with its back to the Po. However, warned that he would be speedily supported, he pushed ahead, and the battle ensued.

At about nine o'clock, the 6th Light, which was at the head of Watrin's column, and was led by General Gency, came into contact with the Austrian outposts at the villa San Giulietta, about a league from Casteggio, and drove them back as far as Rivetta Gandolfi, on the

Zeno stream. O'Reilly was posted on the heights near Rivetta, with some battalions, but his troops did not offer a stubborn resistance, and seemingly were only intended to gain time for the rest of the troops to take up their positions. After a resistance of about half an hour, O'Reilly and Gottesheim, who had gone to his assistance, retired to the heights above Casteggio. This is a large village, containing about 2,500 inhabitants, situated on the slope of a hill, at the foot of which runs the main road from Alessandria to Piacenza.

Ott, who had come up from Genova by forced marches, quickly grasped the advantages of the Casteggio position. He had posted the best portion of his infantry on the heights to his right, so as to flank the only available road. There, on the eminences south of Casteggio, he placed Vogelsberg's division. Schellenberg, with six battalions, held the village, the men being under cover in the houses and gardens of the same. Five more battalions of Schellenberg's division were kept in reserve at Montebello. (Montebello is a smaller village than Casteggio, about 2½ miles further back in the direction of Voghera. It is situated near the postal road, and contains about 1,000 souls.)

The cavalry protected the left, and was extended into the open country. Powerful batteries placed on the hills, on the right of the Austrian position, commanded the whole field of battle.

Against these able dispositions nothing could avail until the ground overlooking Casteggio and the road was carried.

Lannes determined to carry the heights and to capture Casteggio by an attack in front and rear. With that object, Watrin was ordered to deploy two battalions of the 6th Light on the right of the main road, and to direct them to turn the enemy's guns. The third battalion and the 40th, under General Malher, were to master the hills above Casteggio so as to turn that village. To this force was added a battalion of the 22nd.

Under a perfect shower of grape-shot and musketry the French infantry advanced with great gallantry in echelon to storm the heights, but the battalion of the 22nd, meeting with superior forces, had to give way. Fortunately, at that moment the 40th came up, attacked the Austrians with vigour, and drove them back. The position was well contested on both sides. As the 28th came up, Watrin, combining it with the 22nd and 40th, forced his way into Casteggio from the rear, and chased the Austrians from both village and heights. At about the same time, Lannes entered the village by the main road.

Ott, fully alive to the importance of the position south of Casteggio, having united his centre and right, managed to recover the heights and to reoccupy Casteggio. The village and the heights which commanded it were taken and lost several times. The Austrian soldiers, trained to war by the stiff combats they had quite recently engaged in under the walls of Genova, and stirred by the triumphs of the past year, disputed the ground inch by inch with indomitable determination. The French were led by Lannes, as undaunted a general as Bonaparte's army could boast of, an intrepid leader, impetuous and brave to excess, quick to seize any favourable opportunity which offered.

To support Lannes, Victor had marched to Broni. There the sound of the cannonade was distinctly heard; so, acting up to his orders, Victor lost no time in moving in the direction of Casteggio with his divisions.

Olivier Rivaud was the first to reach the battlefield. At 2 p.m. he arrived before Casteggio, where a fierce contest had been raging for the last hour. He was enjoined by Victor to take the 43rd and attack a body of 3,000 Austrians and some artillery posted on the hills to the south of Casteggio. Four battalions, belonging to the 22nd, 28th, and 40th, were at that moment being driven back, and the Austrians were preparing a general attack on the French forces, and by a turning movement threatening to occupy the Casteggio-Broni road, thus to cut the French off from Stradella, which was Lannes' line of retreat, and hem them in about Casteggio.

Nothing could have been more opportune than Victor's arrival on the field of action. Rivaud deployed two of his battalions in skirmishing order; one on the right, and one on the left. The third, formed in column, acted as a support to the other two. In this order he marched on the left wing of the line of battle. Having rallied the four battalions that were contending on the heights, and using them as a support, he attacked the enemy, and pressed him back till eight in the evening, three miles in front of Montebello, when all resistance on that side came to an end.

Another of Rivaud's regiments, the 96th, had been ordered to advance by the main road of Voghera through Casteggio. These troops, under a perfect hail of grape, charged with great intrepidity up the main road, and drove back the enemy's artillery and cavalry. Then, spreading out in skirmishing order on both sides of the road, they drove back the enemy at all points.

Lannes met with unbending resistance, for the Austrian general made desperate efforts to reopen the road to Piacenza. The contest had lasted over eight hours. Lannes occupied Casteggio, but Ott still held firm in his second position at Montebello. All the valour displayed by Lannes, Watrin, Malher, De Gency, De Nogues, and the brigadiers Schreiber, Macon, and Legendre, appeared to be of no avail. The obstinacy of the infantry, the daring of the cavalry, could make no impression on the enemy. It was five o'clock, and the event was still doubtful, when suddenly, enveloped in clouds of dust, Chambarlhac's division of Victor's corps arrived on the battlefield.

The arrival of these fresh troops was most opportune. They forced their way to the scene of action, overcoming every obstacle, checked the progress of the enemy, and infused new spirit in Watrin's tired men. Lannes took advantage of this moment to order the troops to make a general charge. He rushed impetuously at the enemy, forced him to yield, drove him from the neighbourhood of Casteggio, and pressed him back on Montebello.

There Ott steadily maintained his ground, and the combat raged more fiercely than ever; but Victor came up with seven fresh battalions and charged the main body of the enemy. The Austrians defended the bridge with a strong force of artillery, which swept all access to it, whilst the French strove to drive them from it at the point of the bayonet. Ott found himself nearly hemmed in on every side, and retired on Voghera. The battle, which began at 9 a.m., was not over before eight in the evening.

✶✶✶✶✶✶

The reports of this battle are very brief. Watrin barely goes beyond the first capture of Casteggio; Rivaud describes the part he took in clearing the heights on the south of the village; the official bulletin is most meagre.

✶✶✶✶✶✶

Trolard states that on the 9th two battles were fought by Lannes, one at Casteggio, the other at Montebello. He gathers from the *Corriere Milanese* that the fields round Montebello were covered with corpses, and adds that the *curé* of Montebello showed him, at a little distance from the church, a place called *Via dei Morti* (Street of the Dead) where immense graves were dug for the interment of the dead of both sides. Coignet tells us that he captured his gun at the entrance of the village of Montebello; and relates how after that there was still fighting going on.

The result of a combat shows how badly it has gone against the vanquished. At Montebello the Austrians suffered heavy losses. They had 2,104 officers and men killed and wounded; 2,171 officers and men and two guns captured. This was the first serious combat of the campaign, the first shock the Army of Reserve had to sustain. For many hours, French gallantry and efforts went unrewarded; but the tide turned in the evening, and the Austrians were unable longer to withstand their impetuosity. Their defeat was complete.

The casualties on the French side in killed and wounded was not much below that of the Austrians. In describing the battle, Lannes was wont to say:—

> The bones cracked in my division like glass in a hailstorm.

He had no other words to express the fury of the combatants.

The Austrians did not tarry long at Voghera; and though their loss in the battle had been great, only one portion of their troops had been engaged. The French had, lastly, the advantage in numbers. Nevertheless, the chances were, in the early part of the day, so often in favour of the Austrians, that had they better known the numbers against which they were actually contending, they might have deployed more forces and have unfailingly remained victorious.

At the conclusion of a long day's struggle, the victors are ordinarily exhausted and little prepared for reconnoitring. Baron de Crossard, in his narrative of the course of the battle, relates that he was ordered by General Vogelsang to take two companies of Colloredo's regiment, about 300 men, and with them to seize some advantageous position which would cover the Austrian right. Crossard established himself on a *mamelon* between the main road from Voghera to Tortona and the spur on which the latter fortress is built. The orders Crossard received were that he should hold this position, but when the Austrians retreated his party was entirely forgotten. The next morning, he set out to rejoin the rest of Ott's forces. By that time the French were in possession of Voghera, and, had they diligently explored to their left, the detachment would have been discovered and very possibly captured.

The field had been very hotly contested, and at one time Lannes despaired of gaining the victory. Nor would he have done so had not Victor reached the scene of action at a most opportune moment. Some years later, when the emperor conferred on Lannes the title of Duke of Montebello for his share in that gallant deed of arms, he ran to Victor and embraced him, saying, "It is to you that I owe my name."

The honours of the day remained with these companions in arms, Lannes and Victor. Some very fine charges were delivered; and the generals were compelled to fight like simple soldiers, so as to set an example to the battalions of conscripts and young troops which seconded the old half-brigades. Prodigies of valour were witnessed on all sides. The troops acquired great renown, and the success was a glorious one.

The supposition that the French had only insignificant parties on the right of the Po had made Ott decide on fighting. This being the case, it seems that the Austrians erred in not making a greater effort in the first phase of the battle. O'Reilly's force amounted to six battalions and four squadrons, but Watrin did not have much trouble in driving him out of the Villa San Giulietta. At the commencement of the battle, the superiority in numbers rested with the Austrians.

The news of the combat at Montebello spread dread and discouragement amongst the adherents of Austria. They foresaw that what was about to follow was not so much a question of the preservation of Italy as of the retreat of the Austrian Army. Nevertheless, the news of Ott's defeat did not dishearten the Court of Vienna; the foreshadow of a defeat on a larger scale did not receive adequate attention. On the very day that the news of Montebello reached Vienna, on the 20th of June, two days before the courier brought the distracting news of the defeat at Marengo, the Cabinet concluded a treaty with England. The representatives of the two Powers—Baron Thugut and Lord Minto—among other conditions, agreed that neither party should conclude a separate peace with France. The treaty was to be binding for both contracting parties up to the month of February, 1801.

The Battle of Montebello had been fought, and the Austrians could reckon it a real disaster. Not only was their army weakened by the loss of several thousand brave men and the morale of the survivors lowered as a natural effect of the defeat, but they had lost also all hope of securing their main line of retreat. The consequence of this event was that the Austrian Army was completely hemmed in and surrounded by the French forces.

At that moment, the line of the Ticino from Vercelli to Pavia was held by Chabran's and Lapoype's divisions, the two forming a corps of from 9,000 to 10,000 men. Béthencourt's division, reinforced by a portion of Moncey's troops, closed the road of the Saint Gothard. Gilly's division held Milan and blockaded the Austrian garrison in the citadel. Lorge and Loison, with about 10,000 men, held Lodi and Cremona, and kept Vukassevich at a distance. On the west side Suchet and Massena could rush on the Austrian flank, should the latter attempt to avail themselves of the line of retreat leading to Genova.

Many writers, German, French, and Italian, mindful of the old maxim that the general who can bring against his opponent a crushing superiority of force will win, have severely criticized Bonaparte's dispositions and found fault with the undue dispersion of his troops. It is, however, a common saying that to know your adversary is half the battle. And it is in these circumstances that a commander is almost justified in overstepping the bounds of prudence. Bonaparte had by his talent surrounded his enemy with an iron grip, from which there was little hope of escape. Melas could barely dream of bursting through the surrounding forces. He would not have succeeded if he had tried, for on whichever side he turned he would have been held in check by the French divisions, until Bonaparte could come to their aid with the rest.

On the 9th of June Bonaparte quitted Milan to rejoin the army. The sound of the cannonade was plainly heard during the best part of the journey. In the evening he reached Stradella. The small town was full of wounded brought from the battlefield of Montebello. The First Consul did not tarry long, but pushed on for Casteggio.

When he reached the battlefield, victory had already sided with the French. Worn with fatigue, the troops were not equal to a relentless pursuit; they were exhausted, but proud of the manner in which they had borne themselves in the contest, and satisfied with the proof they had given of their valour.

Bonaparte remained at Stradella for three days after the Battle of Montebello. The time he spent there has been interpreted as a regret for the fault he had committed in leaving some 25,000 men in the Milanese provinces. Some writers pretend to have detected in this a sign that he dreaded to advance into the plain of Marengo with such a small army; and that he infinitely preferred awaiting the enemy at Stradella, where the nature of the country, being so much in his favour, would add to his strength.

Some say that at Stradella Bonaparte began to perceive that he had spread out his forces too much. As the enemy made no move on Stradella, he became very impatient, and after three days abandoned his almost impregnable position.

At Saint Helena, Bonaparte endeavoured to argue in favour of this delay at Stradella. He advances that he employed his time in constructing two bridges on the Po which would make his retreat into Lombardy safe. He directed attention to the enemy's army as possessing a formidable cavalry and a numerous artillery, neither of which arms had suffered in the late engagement. With cavalry and artillery so much inferior, the First Consul did not deem it safe to venture into the plain.

The enemy, besides, could only regain its communications with Mantua by Stradella, and the position there seemed to have been made purposely for the French Army. The enemy's cavalry would be impotent, and the great superiority in artillery would be much reduced. The right of the French would lie on the Po and on the marshy plains which border its bank. The centre would be on the road, resting on substantial villages, having large and solid houses built of brick; and, finally, the left would be posted on commanding heights.

GENERAL DESAIX

CHAPTER 3

Desaix Joins the Army of Reserve

The columns under Béthencourt and Moncey had descended from the peaks of the Alps, and were steadily advancing to swell the numbers of the French in Lombardy. Still one more important reinforcement the French Army was to receive, and its importance did not consist in numbers, but in the personality of the man who came to take part in their battles and victories. This individual was none other than the brave Desaix.

Louis Charles Antoine Desaix de Veygoux was born at Saint Hilaire d'Ayat, close to Riom, in Auvergne, on the 17th of August, 1768. His parents were of old-standing nobility, and at that period had fallen into a state of comparative poverty. The military burdens, added to the necessity for upholding their position, had been for a long time a great source of impoverishment for many families in France. Desaix's mother, with her strained resources, experienced great difficulty in educating and maintaining her four sons.

Chevalier de Veygoux, as Desaix was styled up to the time of the Revolution, made his studies at the military school at Effiat. His chroniclers have not much to say in his praise during his early days. He was very far from being a diligent scholar; was idle and insubordinate, and showed more taste for botany than for any of the other sciences. At the completion of his studies in 1783, at the age of fifteen, he was appointed sub-lieutenant in the infantry regiment of Bretagne.

Once he had got into the army a sudden change came over him. He became a very studious, grave, and austere officer. The unpromising pupil of Effiat was no longer to be recognised. His companions soon came to call him *le sage* Desaix (the wise Desaix).

Though belonging to a noble family, imbued with all the prerogatives and spirit of the old feudal society, Desaix adopted frankly the reforming ideas of the French Revolution. The urgent supplications of his parents and of his friends could not shake him in this, and when two of his brothers emigrated, he stoutly refused to follow their example.

Desaix's very short life was passed in the midst of camps. From the commencement of the wars of the Revolution, he was constantly employed in the field, mostly in the higher grades. A man must get his chance, and in the piping times of peace many a brilliant soldier has passed away without having done anything worthy of being recorded in the pages of history. At the close of the eighteenth century, there were plenty of occasions for any soldier who wished to seize them.

Desaix loved war as an art. He warmed up as he held forth on any of the actions in which he had taken part, and his eyes then would sparkle with the fire of genius. All who were familiar with him were, however, agreeably surprised at hearing him all of a sudden turn the conversation from the stirring accounts of a battle to some question of natural history.

Desaix never mixed himself up with those intrigues which brought such a lasting disgrace on the Revolution. He fought, but only for the glory of the French name, with the object of doing his duty. He ignored the denominations of those numerous epochs of which every party was wont to boast so much. He smiled pitifully at the pretensions of those sects, every one of which made the safety of the Republic dependent on its temporary triumph. On the other hand, he was acquainted with all the battlefields, with all the brilliant manoeuvres, all the acts of heroism which had made the first years of the Republic so illustrious.

After the 10th of August, 1792, and the fall of the monarchy, Prince de Broglie and many officers protested against the Legislative Assembly. Desaix, who was the prince's *aide-de-camp*, protested like the rest, and was destituted by Carnot. On his way to join the prince, when passing through a village in the Vosges, he was arrested by the municipality, and on examining his baggage De Broglie's letters were found. He was then imprisoned at Epinal for two months, and when he was released, because declared innocent, Carnot appointed him to the staff of the Army of the Rhine.

In August, 1793, at the Battle of Lauterbourg, Desaix, noticing that the soldiers were hanging back, rushed forward to encourage them, and a bullet perforated both his cheeks. Covered with blood, and unable to speak, he made a signal to his men to resume the combat, refusing until after some hours of desperate fighting to have any dressing applied to his wounds. For his conspicuous gallantry at Lauterbourg, he was promoted to the rank of General of Brigade. He was then barely twenty-five years of age.

Desaix next served under the ill-fated Custine. But at that time to be fighting and shedding one's blood for France was not sufficient to silence all calumnies. Like Bonaparte and Moreau, he was denounced to the Committee of Public Safety. Some low politicians of Riom, having constituted themselves into a committee under the presidency of the infamous Georges Couthon, the representative of the people in that department, denounced him, and held that, as he possessed so few of the good things of this world, he was liable to be seduced by the gold of Pitt and Coburg. It is worthy of notice that at that very time Desaix was contracting debts to provide for the maintenance of his mother and sister, who were in prison. (They were very soon released, owing to the reports of Desaix's gallantry in the field.) He certainly was poor, he fed just like his soldiers on the ordinary rations, and refused his share of the spoils.

Pichegru objected strongly to his arrest, and when the commissioners of the Convention came purposely with the object of seizing him, the troops revolted. The soldiers said to the commissioners:—

"It is no use to make war if you will not leave us the general who has always led us to victory."

The matter was allowed to drop, but principally because the soldiers threatened, should Desaix surrender, to shoot him, not alone, but in company with the representatives of the people. (Marceau, another of the heroic soldiers the Revolution produced, narrowly escaped the guillotine at Tours and again at Mans.)

Strange enough that the same representatives of the people who had wished to arrest him a few weeks before should have named him general of division in November, 1793, for the distinguished part he played in the fighting in Alsace, especially in the engagement at Haguenau. Desaix's promotion was unusually rapid.

No one appreciated so much the importance of the intelligence service. He always kept himself well informed of all that passed in the other armies in the field; and no one was better posted up in all that had taken place.

True soldier as he was, Desaix, writing to his sister, tells her how he longs for this terrible and fearful war, which devastates and consumes, and keeps friends apart, to come to an end; how happy he would be with the restoration of peace, when he would be simply ignored, tranquil in mind, but content in having contributed to it, and in having helped to drive back the cruel enemies, the barbarous strangers, whose sole ambition it was to impose laws on the French.

Desaix belonged to the heroic age; he was a practical officer, shrewdly observant, chivalrous, perfectly brave and modest. He was not only without fear, but without reproach. He served under Pichegru, then under Hoche and Kléber. In France he was looked upon as one of the best officers in the army. He was a model general. He lived amongst his men familiarly, partook of the same fare, and shared evenly in their work. He talked in a simple way with them, offering them advice, instructing them in a thousand details of camp life.

In the present self-interested and pushing age, some words of Desaix might sound strange, and possibly might be disbelieved, but they are recorded by trustworthy evidence. In an assembly of superior officers, a question had arisen of distributing certain rewards for the campaign just concluded. The representatives of the people solicited Desaix's views. Desaix replied:—

We ask for nothing. We have done our duty, nothing beyond our duty. This intimate conviction is the sweetest and the most glorious recompense. My comrades and I desire no other.

Fine actions always appear quite commonplace to those who perform them.

※※※※※※

We may well question if all the lavishness in C.B.'s, D.S.O.'s, honourable mention in despatches, have been a move in the right direction. Certainly, Napoleon's officers and soldiers who fought and bled in many brilliant battles, returned to their homes without ever receiving distinction of any sort. To have been able to speak of having belonged to the Army of Italy, to the Army of Egypt, to the Grande Armée, was generally considered a sufficient reward. The cross of the Legion of Honour was very highly prized, and justly so, for it was distributed sparingly. How many of our officers who have their breast covered with orders and medals like a messenger-boy, have been present at a battle worthy of the name? This is not written in a spirit of criticism, but simply to call attention to the fact that rewards distributed broadcast lose very much of their value, and are, in fact, no longer a distinction. To the eagerness of our officers and men to have their behaviour noticed and reported home, to the undue craving for rewards, we believe we owe the loss of many a gallant fellow in the Boer War.

★★★★★★

Desaix, nevertheless, knew thoroughly that bestowing unstinted praise for gallant deeds was the readiest way to conciliate the friendship and devotion of his subalterns. By his talents and high qualities he had succeeded in gaining the esteem and love of both officers and soldiers.

In the terrible winter of 1794-1795, his troops alone, though dying of starvation and without clothing or blankets, maintained their discipline. Then followed Pichegru's treason; and with all the talents of Jourdan and Desaix, the war became disastrous.

In 1796-1797, Desaix was serving under Moreau's orders with the Army of the Rhine, deeply moved by the news which came from time to time of the successes of the Army of Italy. In this campaign, Desaix crossed the Rhine on the 23rd of June with 2,000 men, followed up by 2,000 more. He then carried with the bayonet the Cimetière and the Trous-de-loups redoubts at Kehl, and defeated the Austrian general Starray, who commanded on the right bank. The passage of the Rhine at Kehl was an exploit of the most glorious character.

In consequence of a false manoeuvre, the troops commanded by Moreau and by Jourdan could not combine. Jourdan had been routed, and Moreau could not continue his advance. Operating in a country a prey to open insurrection, the people exasperated by most enormous exactions, and being without secure communications with France, there remained nothing else for Moreau to do but to retire.

Desaix was besieged in Kehl, and made a glorious defence; but for want of means further resistance soon became impossible, and he was forced to capitulate. He did so on the 9th of January, 1797, was allowed the honours of war, and conducted his troops to Strasbourg.

In the month of April of the same year, during the absence of Moreau in Paris, he made all preparations for crossing the Rhine. This operation was carried out on the 20th, during which his example contributed in a special manner to its success. His former chief, Hoche, was at the same time crossing the river with the Army of the Sambre et Meuse. These movements, however, were made too late, for Bonaparte had been able to dictate peace to Austria without needing the co-operation of the French forces in Germany.

During the armistice of Leoben, Desaix left Moreau's camp to visit the headquarters of the Army of Italy. He was very warmly received by Bonaparte, and from that moment was seized with a warm admiration for him. Bonaparte, on the other hand, formed a high opinion of Desaix's talents and powers, and soon learnt to appreciate the wisdom of his views. An intimacy sprang up between the two generals; Desaix loved and emulated Bonaparte, but without desiring in any way to become his rival. At Passeriano, Bonaparte was surrounded by a brilliant court, and there Desaix enjoyed the society of Massena, Augereau, Bernadotte, Lannes, Murat, Marmont, Clarke, Monge, Larrey, and others.

When Bonaparte sailed for Egypt, Desaix joined him with a division which set out from Civita Vecehia. This division formed the advanced guard of the French on their march to Cairo, and had the first encounter with the Mamelukes at Ramanieh. Three weeks after the French Army had landed at Alexandria, the victory of the Pyramids sealed the fate of Egypt. The beaten Mamelukes retired split in two parties: one, under Ibrahim Bey, withdrew in the direction of the Isthmus of Suez; but the main portion, with Mourad Bey at their head, made for Upper Egypt. Desaix was charged by Bonaparte with the subjugation of Middle and Upper Egypt, and this he accomplished very creditably at the cost of eight months of difficult marching and tough contests. Desaix's campaign in Upper Egypt was one of the most brilliant achievements of the French Army.

In the latter part of August, 1798, Desaix left Cairo to attack Mourad Bey. This operation was brought to an end on the 7th of October, when the Mameluke chief was defeated at Sediman—a glorious battle, in which 3,000 French defeated an enemy three times that number.

The results of the Battle of Sediman were incomplete through want of cavalry, without which it was impossible to follow the Mamelukes in Upper Egypt. However, some 1,000 cavalry reinforced Desaix in the middle of December, and this enabled him to undertake a second campaign. During five months he had to fight the Mamelukes, the Arabs, the mutinous *fellahs*, and the fanatic hordes from Mecca which had landed at Kosseir. (The Arabs of Yambo and Mecca, incited by a firman of the Grand Seignior, crossed the Red Sea and landed at Kosseir to help Mourad Bey on the Nile.)

By the end of May, 1799, his task was completed, the pacification of the country had been accomplished.

In a letter to General Dumas, Desaix wrote:—

I am not in the least surprised that you have not all that you need to understand the laborious campaign of Upper Egypt. The operations in the Delta and in Syria were of an ordinary character; in the other sphere they bore resemblance to nothing which is known. It was not a war, it was an arduous chase, consisting in overcoming, with infantry alone, a bold cavalry which fought entirely according to its own liking, seldom liable to be taken unawares, still always forced to fight. Recruited at any moment from its numerous partisans and by some Arab tribes who were guided by greed of plunder and the facility with which they could withdraw from danger; hidden in an immense desert where a few springs and some grazing allowed them to subsist out of sight of the enemy; to obtain decisive success was well-nigh impossible.

It was only by dint of continual marches and a great display of activity; it was only by organising dromedary companies, that we have succeeded in destroying an enemy always remarkable for his persistence. Often surprised, beaten, and driven out of Egyptian territory, terrible hunger soon brought him back to some spot thirty or forty leagues below the place where he might have been expected. Never has his pursuit been less than 500 leagues; and of them we have made more than one. A hundred times we have surprised Mourad Bey at night, and have taken from him arms, horses, and transport; having lost everything, he has succeeded, in the immensity of the desert, in pulling himself together. There remained to him at last but a hundred horsemen out of the 4,000 Mamelukes which composed his special bodyguard at the Battle of Samhoud. The narrative of our campaign will only be that of our excessive patience, of our sufferings, but never of our combinations.

When Bonaparte suddenly resolved to leave for France, Desaix was in Upper Egypt, by the ruins of Thebes, and there, instructions to follow his general to France reached him.

In Bonaparte's despatch to Kléber—Alexandria, 22nd of August, 1799—he wrote:—

It is the present intention of the Government that General Desaix should set out for Europe in November next, unless something should arise here to detain him. (*Copies of Original Letters from the French Army in Egypt.*)

In announcing the resolution, he had taken and the political reasons which had induced him to abandon the army and return to France, Bonaparte declared to Desaix that only the hope of soon seeing him where his intelligence and devotion were certain to be needed had made him hand over the command of the Army of Egypt to General Kléber. It is well known that Desaix highly approved of Bonaparte's step, convinced as he was that he would not delay in avenging the humiliations which had been cast on his country, and that he would succeed in establishing a stable government in France.

Desaix had not unbounded ambition, and would never have contended with anyone for the first place. It was this trait that Bonaparte so admired. From his headquarters in Cairo he wrote him on the 27th Thermidor, an VII., the following letter:—

> Citizen General,
> I am sending you a sword of rare workmanship, on the blade of which I have had engraved *Conquest of Upper Egypt*—an event which may be put down to your wise dispositions and to your Constance in hardships. Accept it, I beseech you, as a proof of my regard and of the sincere friendship which I have devoted to you.

Independently of this gift, Bonaparte had already notified his satisfaction to General Desaix by presenting him with a rich dagger of rare workmanship and encrusted with diamonds. On the blade of the dagger was engraved, "*Capture of Malta, Battle of Chebr-Kheis, Battle of the Pyramids.*"

Kléber wrote a long letter to the Directory, giving a full account of the state of affairs in Egypt, and bringing serious charges against Bonaparte. Citizen Barras, cousin to Barras, one of the Directory, sailed from Alexandria on the *Marianne*, bearing this letter. The *Marianne* was chased by the English sloop *El Vincejo* and captured off the coast of France. James writes:—

> The despatches, as is customary on such occasions, were thrown overboard, but not with the customary carefulness. They were wrapped up in an old silk handkerchief, through which the cannon-shot intended to sink them immediately pierced, and one of the British sailors picked them up as they were floating by the side of the vessel. The captain of the sloop of war carried the important papers to the commander-in-chief: and Vice-Admiral Lord Keith, who had returned to Gibraltar from Eng-

land on the 6th of December, after making himself acquainted with their contents, transmitted the despatches to his government. (James, *Naval History*, vol. ii.)

The British Ministers, after reading them, sent the packet to Bonaparte, who by that time had become First Consul.

Kléber, no doubt, exaggerated the difficulties by which he was surrounded. His accusations, however, were long a source of annoyance to Bonaparte. It was his interest to keep the contents of Kléber's letter a profound secret, and in this he succeeded; for neither his colleagues nor the public heard aught of it.

In his letter from Alexandria, of the 22nd of August, 1799, Bonaparte authorised Kléber to make terms with the Ottoman Government should he receive no reinforcements from France by the month of May, 1800, or should the plague break out and carry off 1,500 Frenchmen.

Kléber, dissatisfied with his position in Egypt and eager to quit the country, had commenced treating with Sir Sidney Smith for the evacuation of Egypt. Desaix, having advanced the subjugation of Upper Egypt, and left to some flying column the pursuit of Mourad Bey—to whom he had held out proposals of peace on condition of his becoming a vassal of France—returned to Cairo. Kléber desired much to gain his influential support in the negotiations in which he was on the point of engaging; but Desaix held contrary views.

Kléber never regarded the Egyptian expedition with a favourable eye. He thought it too costly and utterly useless to France. He was eager to take part in the expedition, but once in Egypt equally eager to return. Under the conditions then existing, he considered that the withdrawal of the French Army from Egypt was the best thing that could be done. Menou, Davout, and Desaix contended that it was still possible to resist, independently of the question whether this resistance in the long run would eventually be of any use or not.

Desaix had just brought to a satisfactory conclusion a very difficult campaign in Upper Egypt against a most determined enemy. He had subdued the Mamelukes, so brave, so well-armed, so powerful, so active, and as hardy as their steeds. It was natural, therefore, for him to believe that it was feasible to hold on longer in Lower Egypt, where resistance could never be anything like as great. He therefore opposed the idea of treating for an evacuation, and made every effort to reanimate his comrades. If he eventually undertook to carry on the negotiations, he did so simply with a view of gaining time. The absurd conditions demanded by Kléber made this quite possible.

As early as the 17th of August, 1799, Bonaparte, in a letter written to the *grand vizier*, had made some proposals for an accommodation with Turkey. He had come to believe that the cause of France without reinforcements was hopeless, and as long as the British fleet remained in command of the Mediterranean it was certain that no reinforcements could arrive. In this opinion Bonaparte and Kléber agreed; for Kléber was not slow to recognise that to hold Egypt the French needed a navy, and that without one, retaining the country was an enterprise no longer capable of attainment.

As far as the new commander-in-chief was concerned, the situation had grown even worse than it was under his predecessor. Kléber was threatened by a powerful Turkish Army, whilst his own troops were in a very despondent condition. On the subject of the last Battle of Aboukir, Kléber wrote:—

> As a proof of what I say, this victory has not retarded for a single instant either the preparations or the march of the *grand vizier*.

Without waiting, therefore, for the contingencies specified in Bonaparte's letter of instructions, Kléber took up the negotiations which had been started some months before. The *grand vizier,* who had just received a check at Bogaz, was not at that moment ill-disposed to listen to his proposals.

On the 29th of December, the garrison of El-Arish capitulated. The fall of the place was hastened by the insubordination of the garrison, and showed to what extent the spirit of the troops had been shaken.

After the massacre of the garrison of El-Arish, Desaix wished to break off the negotiations, as the Turks demanded an unconditional surrender. But Sidney Smith proposed more honourable conditions; nevertheless, Desaix sent Savary to Salahieh to inform Kléber that he would not sign the convention unless he received a formal order to that effect.

A council of war was called, and all present but Davout expressed themselves in favour of an evacuation. Davout, though strongly opposed to the step, against which he had argued warmly, had the weakness to add his signature with the rest, and Desaix, rather than disobey, signed the Convention of El-Arish.

Davout sent a message by Savary to inform Desaix that if he felt inclined to break off the convention he could count on the support of the army. To this Desaix paid not the least attention; for, in his opinion, by signing the proceedings of the council of war Davout had given a clear proof that he did not dare to uphold the advice he was offering. This very unsatisfactory state of things made Desaix more than ever eager to quit Egypt. Kléber, however, would not consent to his departure, and, unwilling though he was, made him conclude the Convention of El-Arish.

The convention was signed on board Sir Sidney Smith's ship on the 24th of January, 1800. It was stipulated that the French in Egypt should be permitted to return to France unmolested, free to take the field at once against the enemies of their country. Lord Elgin, who had been appointed British Ambassador at Constantinople in the autumn of 1799, shared with Smith the belief that considerable sacrifices should be made to rid Egypt of the French forces. Nelson wrote to His Lordship on the 21st of December, disapproving his views in very strong terms, and expressing a very uncharitable hope that every Frenchman might perish in Egypt.

Admiral Lord Keith, who had relieved Nelson of the chief command in the Mediterranean, though personally in favour of this measure, had arrived bearing instructions from his government not to allow anything of the kind. Keith felt himself bound to make this known to Kléber, and wrote to him on the 8th of January, and therefore a full fortnight before the convention was signed:—

> I have positive orders not to consent to any capitulation with the French troops, at least unless they lay down their arms, surrender themselves prisoners of war, and deliver up all the ships and stores in the port of Alexandria to the allied powers.

Consequently, Kléber was informed that any person attempting to return would be made a prisoner of war.

Had the convention been carried out, it would have restored to France, at a very critical moment, some 20,000 hardened soldiers. Bonaparte's object in authorising Kléber to enter into a convention with the Turks was, of course, to save the army from capitulating.

Before Keith's return, Nelson, *ad interim* commander-in-chief, had given to Sidney Smith, who was commanding in the Levant, strict injunctions not to give any French ship or man leave to quit Egypt, and further, to oppose any such permission being given by any foreigner.

Desaix, availing himself of Bonaparte's hint for his return to France, and anxious to take no part in this dishonourable evacuation, arranged for leaving Egypt with Davout.

Davout could no longer remain with Kléber; and, though the latter offered to promote him general of division, refused to stay, alleging that it was very disagreeable to him for his advancement to date from such a deplorable event. Just at that moment Mons. de Latour-Maubourg arrived in the *Osiris*, bearing despatches from the First Consul, announcing the revolution of the 18th *Brumaire*, and the elevation of Bonaparte to the supreme power.

The news from France produced a great effect on the mind of Desaix and his suite. Such thorough trust had all in Bonaparte's genius, that they one and all foresaw, that marvellous events were sure to follow from his elevation to the Consulate. Desaix became more impatient than ever to be off, and sent Savary, his *aide-de-camp*, on board the *Theseus* to interview Sidney Smith and to remind him of the promise he had made him of a passport.

Desaix left Alexandria on the 3rd of March in a ship from Ragusa, *Madone de grâce de Saint Antoine de Padoue*. He was provided with a passport furnished him by the *grand vizier*, and with a pass signed by the English commander then blockading Alexandria. For greater security, Sidney Smith had detailed a British naval officer to sail on the same ship.

On board, the captain of the ship and others were not free from alarm, as it was well known from the latest despatches that Admiral Keith was not favourably disposed towards the clauses of the pending treaty of El-Arish. In what light, then, would he look upon the passport given by Sir Sidney Smith? Besides, the King of the Two Sicilies had declared war against France. There was a good prospect of their all being captured as prisoners of war.

On its way, driven by a tempestuous sea, the brig had to anchor at Sciacca in Sicily, but the anchor had no sooner dropped than a rumour went about that a French general was on board the ship. Immediately a multitude of savage men and women, armed with hatchets and other implements, and shouting defiant cries, rushed to the harbour. Many stones were hurled, and a few shots were fired. The ship had barely time to make sail and get away. The tempestuous sea was less inhospitable than the savage inhabitants of Sicily had shown themselves to be.

Always haunted by the fear of capture, the crew and passengers had nearly reached the islands of Hyeres, and just as every heart was in a delirium of excitement, looking forward to stepping ashore, a deep fog settled about the ship. Out of this rose the outlines of a man-of-war. It was the *Dorothy*, a British warship, which had been cruising about the coast of Provence. Neither the passport nor the presence of the British officer proved of any avail. The captain's orders were to capture any ship sailing for France, so the brig had to be conveyed to Leghorn, where Lord Keith had his headquarters at that time.

Lord Keith refused to take any notice of the passport, and was deaf to the reclamations of the British officer who had sailed with Desaix. He ordered the general and his companions to be taken to the Lazaretto and confined in a kind of a prison. He is said to have insulted the general by granting him an allowance of twenty *sous* per day for his maintenance, the same sum as was allowed to the rank-and-file, alleging that evidently with the rules about equality proclaimed in France no difference should be made between officers and soldiers. Later on Desaix was deprived of books and newspapers.

If all this is true, Keith's treatment of Desaix was undignified. It was akin to the humiliating story of Napoleon's captivity, and showed a mean, vindictive spirit, unbecoming an officer of Lord Keith's social standing.

★★★★★★

Count Balmain, in his *Mémoires*, makes some excuse for Napoleon's custodians. He writes: "Though it was impossible to satisfy his (Napoleon's) whims, and there was no sort of annoyance that the prisoner has not inflicted on the governor." Balmain's own instructions were framed in a more generous spirit. He states that they contained the following words underlined by the Emperor Alexander himself "while not forgetting the consideration due to him (Napoleon) personally."

★★★★★★

How much more dignified, how much more noble, it would have been to have treated an enemy with proper decorum, with the respect due to a gallant soldier! It is always befitting a great nation to be generous and magnanimous.

Much fuss has been made by French writers with reference to the disregard paid to the passport granted to Desaix. Still, all the evidence bears out the fact that both Nelson and Keith had given full injunctions to Sidney Smith not to furnish any person whatsoever with a passport, and a warning that it would be held valueless. Keith wrote:—

Any persons attempting to return pursuant to an arrangement

with one of the allies exclusive of the others, as the El-Arish Convention was, would be made prisoners of war.

Could anything be plainer? Nor could the French headquarters plead ignorance of the views of the British Government, since a letter written at Minorca by Lord Keith to Kléber on the 8th of January on this very subject, and containing the above words, was received in Egypt in February, consequently before Desaix's departure.

For some time, the French and Turks maintained a kind of armed neutrality. The *grand vizier* released a soldier of the 25th demi-brigade, who had been made a prisoner in the neighbourhood of El-Arish. He ordered that he should be taken round his camp, after which he enjoined him to acquaint his comrades with all that he had seen, and bid their commander to tremble.

Kléber evidently played fast and loose with the convention. Desaix was permitted to sail on the 3rd of March under the provisions of that treaty, at a time when it was known that it had been disavowed by the British naval commander-in-chief in the Mediterranean. Only a little more than a fortnight after his departure Kléber attacked the Turks and defeated them on the 20th, at the Battle of Heliopolis. Two months had barely elapsed since the signing of the convention. In the following May he consented to a renewal of the negotiations.

The injunctions sent by Nelson to Smith (and nothing could have been more explicit) were, in fact, distinctly disregarded by Sidney Smith, who plainly disobeyed his chief in letting Desaix depart, and in detailing a naval officer to go with him. On the other hand, there can he no doubt that, being on the spot, Sidney Smith considered himself as being a better judge of the actual condition of affairs at the time being, and that he could do what was needed with a sounder judgment than an officer who was at a distance, and only partially acquainted with the events.

In detaining Desaix, Lord Keith was apparently doing nothing beyond complying with the orders he had received. But when Pitt came to learn how a British officer had pledged his faith to a French general, he had orders sent out to the Mediterranean to execute the provisions of the treaty, and it was possibly under these instructions that Desaix was allowed to sail from Leghorn.

Desaix quitted Leghorn on board a Spanish ship, and sailed for Toulon, where he arrived on the 4th of May. But his troubles were not at an end, for he was compelled to undergo quarantine. When this was over, he crossed the Little Saint Bernard on his way to Bonaparte's headquarters. His bad luck followed him. On the morning of the 9th of June, he was attacked by a party of bandits at San Germano, between Ivrea and Vercelli. The ruffians killed one man and wounded three more of his retinue, and made off with his baggage. The general's party comprised several officers, three of whom, Rapp, Savary, and Auguste Colbert, were his *aides-de-camp*. With them was a servant and two negro boys, who had been sent as a gift to Bonaparte by the King of Darfoor.

Desaix was one of the most distinguished officers of his time. In military talents he equalled Moreau, Massena, Kléber, and Lannes; but he surpassed them all by the perfection of his character. He was one of those generals who knew best how, by his talents and virtues, to gain the esteem of his officers and men. But his power did not stop there, for he was able to win the respect of the Arabs of Upper Egypt, who called him *the just sultan*. (Bonaparte was called by the Egyptians *Sultan Keber*—Father of the Fire).

To a bravery which nothing could subdue, Desaix joined a rigid probity and complete disinterestedness. His character, as a writer tersely puts it, partook of the antique. De Brossier writes:—

> His campaigns on the Rhine and in Egypt render all praise superfluous. But his death robs the Republic of a rare support, deprives the soldiers of a father, and social virtues of a model.

Burning with indignation at the unwarrantable treatment he had recently received from England, on joining the Army of Reserve Desaix demanded nothing better than to be allowed to take his revenge.

Whilst Bonaparte was at Martigny, he received a letter from Suchet, in which, amongst other matters, he reported the arrival of Desaix at Toulon. In reply, the First Consul issued orders for Desaix to come and join the headquarters of the Army of Reserve as quickly as possible. From Lausanne he had written to him on the 14th of May:—

> At last you have arrived—a good piece of news for the entire Republic, but above all for me who have consecrated to you all the esteem due to a man of your talent, combined with a friendship which my heart, today sufficiently old, and having a very profound knowledge of men, has for no other person.

Bonaparte was jealous of some generals, the rivalry of whose ambition he feared. He nourished no such feeling towards Desaix, who had

The death of Desaix

an unassuming disposition. He never loved, esteemed, or regretted any man so much. An exception might be made for Duroc, who, as *aide-de-camp*, served in the Marengo campaign. Napoleon said of him:—

> He was a pure and virtuous man, totally disinterested and very generous. Throughout my career, he was the only person who possessed my unreserved confidence, and to whom I could unburthen my mind. His talents were not brilliant; but he had an excellent judgment, and his services were of the most useful kind.

Desaix arrived at Bonaparte's headquarters near Montebello on the 11th of June. The two generals had much to say to each other, and the night was spent in a long conversation regarding all which had occurred in Egypt since the departure of the First Consul.

The two divisions of Boudet and Monnier were formed into a corps, and their command was assigned to Desaix.

How greatly Bonaparte appreciated the talent and military virtues of his lieutenant will be readily understood by an episode which occurred fifteen years later. After the irreparable defeat at Waterloo, one of his generals remarked to the emperor, "What we needed was a Desaix;" to which, with a deep sigh, the dejected monarch replied, "There are no more Desaixs in our days."

CHAPTER 4

The Battlefield of Marengo

After the Battle of Montebello, Bonaparte remained at Stradella the 10th, 11th, and 12th of June up to noon. He was eager to obtain some reliable news of the Austrians, but in this he was singularly unsuccessful. His cavalry had only gathered vague information, for it had not been pushed far enough ahead.

With all the uncertainty of the Austrian plans, which so puzzled the First Consul, it is surprising to find that he did not make the best use of his cavalry to clear the situation. He was certainly weak in that arm; nevertheless, he had 3,600 sabres, a sufficient number, one would think, to conduct a thorough exploration of the country lying between the Scrivia and the Bormida, a tract of country which from east to west does not measure much more than from thirteen to sixteen miles.

The bulk of the French cavalry remained with the infantry, and when the army moved forward on the 12th, it took post on the left of Desaix's divisions at Viguzzolo, between Ponte Curone and Tortona. It was not pushed forward far in advance of the rest of the army to explore and to gather the exact information which the commander-in-chief so much needed for arranging his measures. It may possibly have been that the established superiority of the Austrian cavalry, both in numbers and in tactical excellence, may have counselled Bonaparte not to risk the little he had and might very shortly greatly need.

Up to the day of Marengo, the Austrian cavalry was held to be the best in Europe in every respect. Nothing, however, could have equalled the bravery and enterprise of the French cavalry on the field of Marengo. Its capacities were a sudden revelation, and there it acquired a prestige which was afterwards admitted by all the armies of Europe. The French cavalry was very eager to be employed, and, if sent forward to explore in front of the army, it would have brought back as early as the night of the 12th the news of Ott's withdrawal into Alessandria, and the occupation of Marengo by his rear-guard.

The Battle of Montebello was fought on the 9th of June, and, as we have said, up to noon of the 12th Bonaparte made no move. After Montebello there had been no pursuit, possibly for no other reason than because the victorious troops were thoroughly exhausted. Ott was not molested in his retreat. The contact with his troops had been lost on the 9th, and nothing had been done to regain it.

Bonaparte had begun to fear either that Melas might make for the Ticino, working round by Valenza, or that he would place his army behind the Apennines, and take advantage of Genova and the help of the British fleet.

The supposition that Melas would retire on Genova first shows itself in a letter Bonaparte wrote to Suchet on the 8th of June. In this letter, he declares that the Austrians had formed the intention of concentrating at Alessandria. But he adds:—

> It is possible that when I arrive Melas will not deem himself competent to fight, and that he will retire either on the side of Turin or on the side of the Riviera di Genova.

Bonaparte was much worried by the dread of seeing the enemy escape him after all the trouble he had taken.

As some vague rumours indicated that the Austrians were concentrating round Alessandria, Bonaparte, in order to obtain some idea of the situation and to penetrate their intentions, ordered on the 12th a move of the main body up to the Scrivia. On the march to that river, as it was expected that the enemy might be found inclined to deliver battle, orders were issued for all the disposable forces to be near at hand.

Lapoype's division was directed to advance by the left of the Po, keeping abreast of the main body; nevertheless, he had orders to retire should the Austrians have succeeded in crossing that river. In such an eventuality, he was to hold the line of the Ticino till the rest of the forces could come to his assistance.

On the night of the 12-13th, the French Army was disposed on the right bank of the Scrivia in the following manner: *Right wing*, Lannes, with Watrin's division, at Castelnuovo; *Centre*, Desaix, with the divisions of Monnier and Boudet, in front of Ponte Curone, astride of the Piacenza-Tortona high-road; *Left wing*, Victor, divisions of Chambarlhac and Gardanne, in the neighbourhood of Tortona, ready to cross the Scrivia. On Desaix's left, close to Viguzzolo, was posted Murat's

Oesterreich-Ungarn.

K. K. Infanterie-Regiment Hoch- und Deutschmeister.

cavalry division. An advanced guard composed of two regiments of hussars and one of dragoons, commanded by Kellermann, was pushed forward in the direction of Tortona. The headquarters of the army were at Voghera.

So much for the dispositions of the French Army. On the Austrian side on the same day Melas, having been informed that the French forces were about to march from Stradella towards Tortona, ordered General Ott to retire from Tortona and to fall back on Alessandria, to cross the Bormida, and to leave only a strong rear-guard between Marengo and Spinetta. Haddick's and Kaim's divisions, coming from Turin, from which city they had been withdrawn after the Battle of Montebello, had arrived under the walls of Alessandria by the afternoon of the 12th of June, as also had Elsnitz's troops coming from Ceva. Melas consequently had concentrated round Alessandria a large portion of his army. On the right of the Bormida, between Spinetta and Marengo, remained O'Reilly with Rousseau's brigade, a few squadrons of cavalry, and four guns.

Melas did not understand the full advantages of concentration. Why should he have thought it necessary to guard all points when by concentrating his whole army and beating the enemy in the field he could have guarded them indirectly? The evacuation of any strong places would have been only very temporary, as their subsequent fall would have been certain, as the necessary result of a decisive battle gained over the French.

It is remarkably strange that, if Melas had determined on giving battle in the plain, he should have made no effort to hold Marengo on the 13th, or that he should have permitted the French to capture it so easily. The position of Marengo derives its importance from the fact that many roads centre about the village, and there is the only good passage across the Fontanone brook. For a large army issuing from Alessandria and intending to debouch on to the plain, the possession of that position was indispensable.

It is likewise surprising that in expectation of a battle the Austrian commander-in-chief should not have kept a large portion of his army on the right bank of the river during the 13th, so as to avoid the loss of time in crossing the bridges on the following morning. Had a corps been detached on the left flank of the French between the Bormida and the Scrivia, to cooperate with a brisk frontal attack by the other corps, it would have turned the enemy and thrown him back on the Po.

Ott's withdrawal behind the Bormida strengthened Bonaparte's belief that Melas had marched, or was about to march, on Genova. On the 12th, he had not succeeded in getting news of the enemy. He examined the several courses open to the Austrian commander-in-chief. There were three principal ones. He might make for the Ticino, marching by way of Valenza. He might march against Suchet, leaving a corps in the neighbourhood of Alessandria to hold the Army of Reserve in check; and, after having destroyed Suchet, he could retrace his steps and meet Bonaparte's forces with soldiers inspirited by a recent victory. Lastly, he might march across the Apennines and enter Genova, where he would find Hohenzollern, and would have the support of the British fleet.

Now let us look at the vast plain of Marengo on which the eventful battle between the Austrians and French was to be fought—a battle which had immense consequences over the future of Europe.

In the centre of the vast plain of the Po lies the city of Alessandria. It was founded in 1168 to offer a refuge to the inhabitants of Milan whom Frederick II. had expelled from the latter city as the place fell into his hands.

At that period Pope Alexander III. was the recognised leader of the Lombard League, and in his honour the new city received the name of Alessandria. It was at first known as Alessandria della Paglia, by reason of the roofs of the houses, which were of thatch.

Alessandria is so situated as to guard the road which leads from Piacenza to Turin. The city stands not far from the point where the waters of the Tanaro and Bormida Rivers mingle. A little to the south-east of the walls the main road branches off due east, leading by Tortona into Lombardy; another road continues in a south-easterly direction, crosses the Apennines, and goes to Genova.

The plain of Marengo—so called after the famous battle which has acquired a well-merited place in history—commences at the bridge over the Bormida in front of Alessandria. It lies between the Scrivia and the Bormida, and in length measures from Salé to Novi approximately fourteen miles, and ten from the Scrivia to the Bormida (22 kilometres by 16). It is crossed by three main roads, the roads of Pavia, Piacenza, and Genova. These roads converge, then unite near the Bormida, and lead on to Alessandria.

The plain on the north is bounded by the Po, on the west by the Bormida and Tanaro, and is enclosed on the east and south by the Scrivia and by a circular chain of hills, which are the lower spurs of the Apennine mountains.

To the east of Alessandria, and, at the period of the battle half a mile from the gate of the city, meandered placidly the Bormida. (The river has changed its bed since 1800. It now flows much; further from the city walls, and is not so tortuous.) That river has its source far away in the mountains, above Carcare and Millesimo. It swells by degrees, turns from east to north, and describes a semicircle around the country it waters to the south of the city of Alessandria. In its winding course the Bormida makes two bends in the direction of the village of Marengo.

At one end of the plain, on the side of Alessandria, lie three villages—Castel Ceriolo, Marengo, and Spinetta, where the principal events of that memorable day in June, 1800, occurred. In the middle of the plain, two leagues beyond Marengo on the Tortona road, and about a league from that town, lies the village of San Giuliano Vecchio. At its eastern extremity, on the same road, not far from the road from Salé to Novi, stands the village of Torre di Garofoli. On the road from Castel Ceriolo to Salé we come first to San Giuliano Nuovo and next to the property La Ghilina. At Spinetta two roads branch off, that on the left leads to San Giuliano Vecchio and Tortona, and that on the right to Novi and Genova. Two other roads lead to the latter place from Spinetta, one by way of Frugarolo and Basaluzzo, the other by Pozzolo Formigaro.

It would have been difficult to find at that time a more magnificent manoeuvring-ground for cavalry. In the narrative by General Danican of the Battle of Alessandria and Marengo it is stated that Desaix's division briskly repulsed the Austrian cavalry, which found it almost impossible to act in such a broken country.

★★★★★★

Danican served in the French Navy and Army in many capacities. He was a Royalist at heart, and betrayed the Republican troops when he served with them as an officer. He was suspended several times, and fought against Bonaparte on the 13th *Vendémiaire* in command of the Royalist sections. Hoche despised him as a bad character.

★★★★★★

This statement is flatly contradicted by Chevalier Cavour, a gentleman who found himself in Alessandria at the time of the battle. He states that he cannot conceive how anyone who had been over the ground could assert that the plain between Alessandria and Tortona could be reckoned as broken ground, inasmuch as from Spinetta to the Scrivia there are no ditches, no hedges, and only a small number of barns. The country is level and clear of impediments. This is corroborated by General Duvignan's report. In this he writes:—

> At three o'clock we found ourselves on the fine plains of San Giuliano, the only ones which we had met in the whole of Italy in which cavalry could be employed with advantage.

Jomini (*Histoire des Guerres de la Révolution, livre xvi.* chap. cii), writes:—

> The plain of Marengo is almost the only one in Italy where masses of cavalry can charge at full speed.

Count Cavour admits that the country from the Bormida as far as Spinetta alone is much cut up and strewn with vineyards, cottages, and farm buildings. This is also mentioned by General Duvignan, who alludes to the difficult nature of the ground between the Bormida and Marengo, where there were broad ditches full of water, which followed each other in rapid succession. The plate forming the frontispiece of Holmes's *Précis of Modern Tactics*—taken, no doubt, from a print struck about the time of the battle—evidently conveys the impression that it was a fair battlefield. It shows the ground where Desaix advanced with Boudet's division as being good for manoeuvring, quite open, and clear of obstacles.

The student should abstain from forming an opinion on the nature of the ground from what it is in our days. From the belfry of San Giuliano Vecchio, looking in the direction of Alessandria, the plain of Marengo now appears as if covered with dense scrub. This effect is produced by the rows of mulberry trees which have been planted in continuous parallel lines. In every direction houses and small villages have sprung up, so that it is impossible to form an approximate idea of how the ground lay in 1800. Now, a retiring army would certainly find any number of points of support. The ground is cultivated with wheat and Indian corn, long rows of mulberry trees dividing the fields, but there are no vines festooned on the trees as in other parts of Piedmont.

Cavalry could now manoeuvre parallel to the trees, which generally run north and south, and in June the Indian corn must have been low. Near San Giuliano there are more vines. The ground being very flat, it would have been difficult to get a fair view of how the action was going on. The plain at the 18th kilometre slopes towards Alessandria; but there is nothing more than a gentle dip towards the city. As there had been much fighting in Piedmont quite recently, and as two other battles of Marengo had been fought in the previous year, one on the 16th of May, the other on the 20th of June, it is more than likely that the cultivation was of poor order.

The principal efforts on the 14th of June, 1800, were made round the small hamlet of Marengo. Marengo owes its name and origin to the Marici, a warlike tribe of the ancient Ligurians, which pitched its camp between the Orba and the Scrivia. In former times it had been a place of note, for the Longobard kings had made of it a summer residence, and Berengario, Guido, and Lamberto used to indulge there in the pleasures of the chase. With time, however, all the ancient glories of Marengo had faded away.

The village at that time had fallen into decay, and was of very little importance. The tower which commands the small cluster of remaining houses is the tower of Theodoric, King of the Goths. Tradition has it that the king made of Marengo a place of delight, and that he constructed there a magnificent palace, surrounded by woods and gardens. The tower is now old and dismantled; it overlooks the plain for some distance on all sides. This is all that now remains of the magnificence of the Lombard and Gothic kings.

Marengo, which in 1800 did not number more than half a dozen houses, the principal building being a modest inn, stands on the banks of the deep and sluggish Fontanone brook, and commands the bridge over it. Close by the garden of the inn is a wide brook, in the bed of which flows a fresh and limpid stream, scarcely four and a half feet deep. Verdant trees and aquatic rushes rise from the bottom of the water, which is supplied from several sources that gush forth without interruption, and rise to the surface of the brook bubbling unceasingly. It was round this humble brook, known at that period as *Il Fontanone or il Cevo di Fontanone*, and now called *Bolla Regia Ressia*, that the fiercest fighting took place on the day of Marengo.

Some writers have much exaggerated the importance of this brook, have made of it a natural obstacle of the greatest consequence in a tactical point of view, and have depicted it as filled with the corpses of the combatants on both sides. Berthier and some other French generals in their reports make mention of a stream, which was undoubtedly the Fontanone; nevertheless, none of them represent it as an obstacle of great magnitude. Whatever may have been its importance, there is no doubt that on that bright day of June, 1800, the destinies of France and of its future ruler were decided on the banks of the Fontanone.

Some writers describe it as a brook, others only call it a deep ditch. At first it flows in a direction almost parallel to the Bormida; it deviates from that river, then again approaches it, and, lastly, finishes by resuming its original direction before falling into the marshes on the verge of the Tanaro. The Fontanone comes close to the village of Marengo, as it makes its great bend to the west in drawing away from the Bormida.

It must be admitted that the deep and muddy stream which covered the position of Marengo on the west helped the French greatly on the 14th. One is consequently struck by the neglect of the Austrians, who, looking forward to a deployment of their whole army on the plain, did not provide means for crossing it at various points. As will be seen further on, it was only at about noon that the staff thought of spanning the Fontanone with a light bridge in front of Marengo.

Bonaparte, burning with impatience to learn his adversary's movements, ventured into a plain studded with strong places and watered by many rivers and streams. Such, nevertheless, was the power of his name and the dread which his talents inspired, that he alone was sufficient to paralyze the movements of an enemy superior to him in numbers, and above all, in cavalry and artillery.

It has been stated, and many historians believed it, that Bonaparte was deceived by a spy who was in the pay of both sides, and that he was by this spy's statement strengthened in the belief that Melas had really decided to fall back on Genova. The story of this spy seems to come principally from Austrian sources. (See *Œstreichische Militärische Zeitschrift, tom. xxix.*)

Whether true or not, Bonaparte should have learnt by that time to mistrust spies, for in Egypt the Arabian spies had proved far more serviceable to his enemies than to him.

Taking no notice of the Austrian garrison in Tortona, at daybreak on the morning of the 13th Bonaparte carried his army across the Scrivia. His advanced guard reached San Giuliano Vecchio without finding the least trace of the enemy. All the information he could gather was that the Austrians had retired on Marengo.

Dupont, Berthier's chief of the staff, writing on the 13th, says:—

The enemy is concentrating round Alessandria. It is uncertain if he will accept battle. But we are going to force him to declare himself.

On the afternoon of that day, Bonaparte ordered two reconnaissances to be made: one by Victor and Kellermann's cavalry brigade astride of the Marengo-San Giuliano road; the other, which comprised all the cavalry under Murat, in the direction of Castel Nuovo, by Salé and Piovera on Castel Ceriolo.

The result of the exploration of the enemy's position revealed very little indeed. On every side the information was the same. The villagers, the prisoners, the deserters, all alike reported that the Austrians were only to be seen about Marengo. The reconnaissances had one result, and divulged that the village of Marengo was occupied by the enemy, the general opinion being that apparently the Austrians had no more than 3,000 or 4,000 men there.

Petit states:—

We were joined by several deserters, and by some prisoners who had strayed and been taken; amongst others, an officer of De Bussy's legion, who wore the cross of St. Louis. The general questioned them with considerable earnestness. All the prisoners were astonished when they found that the person, they had just been speaking to was Bonaparte.

******

The name of Bonaparte, and later on of Napoleon, filled the imagination, and had a magical effect. During the Battle of Essling, as Lannes, covered with blood and fainting, was carried past Napoleon, the emperor addressed him: "Lannes, my friend, do you know me? It is the emperor; it is Bonaparte, your friend." Only the utterance of that name revived Lannes's spirits and made him attempt to speak.

******

The hypothesis Bonaparte had formed was strengthened by the cavalry exploration and the movements of the army, which had made it certain that the Austrian Army was not in the plain between the Scrivia and the Bormida. More and more convinced that the enemy had escaped to Genova, the First Consul sent Desaix with Boudet's division to his left to reconnoitre the road which, starting from Alessandria, goes to Novi. Desaix was to march from Ponte Curone towards Novi, giving a wide berth to Tortona, and taking the road over the Tortonese hills. His instructions were to cut off the retreat of the

Austrian Army on Genova, and to endeavour to effect a junction with Suchet, who was expected to be advancing from the direction of Acqui.

We can well imagine Bonaparte's astonishment in not finding the plain of Marengo occupied, and how he recognised that were the enemy retiring on Genova there was not a moment to lose if he wished to overtake them.

On the little information gained, Victor was ordered to attack the village of Marengo, to drive the enemy out of it, force him back, and strive to cross the Bormida at his heels.

Gardanne, who commanded the advanced guard of Victor's division, was instructed to do this. He divided his force into two columns, and with the larger one marched by the old Alessandria-Tortona road, bent on attacking the village in front, whilst Colonel Dampierre, his adjutant-general, and to whom he had confided the command of the lesser column, was enjoined to advance by the new road, and to work round the village of Marengo from the side of Spinetta. Victor's second division (Chambarlhac's) followed the other along the plain. Duvignan was ordered to cover the left of Victor's troops with his cavalry brigade.

Amongst the troops Moncey had brought from Germany were the 44th and 101st. These, numbering 3,697 men, were formed into a division under the command of Gardanne, an officer who had served at Genova under Marbot.

In the returns Gardanne's division is shown as having a strength of 3,697 men. But Dampierre, in a letter to General Mathieu Dumas, written on the 16th of June, 1800, states that this division, of which he was adjutant-general, was more correctly speaking a strong brigade. (*"La division Gardanne où l'on m'envoya adjutant général, ne forme pas, àt bien dire, une bonne brigade; elle ne compte gu'environ deux mille hommes."*)

It numbered about 2,000 men. (Gardanne, in his report to Dupont, says the advanced guard, about 2,000 strong, received the order to attack Marengo at 6 p.m., and that the fight lasted one hour.) Rivaud calls it *la petite division de Gardanne*. One battalion of the 44th half-brigade, the 2nd, had not more than 120 men with the colours. Dampierre says that his command amounted to 300 or 400 men, and that his column carried the village of Marengo before the frontal attack had commenced.

Towards five in the evening—Melas calls it *"vers la fin de l'après midi"*—the French, with Gardanne, marching astride of the old Tortona road, came into contact with the Austrians, who were deployed in front of Marengo. The latter numbered a little over 3,000 men, with four guns. A sharp artillery and musketry fire was opened, and just as the left column of the French was beginning to appear from the direction of Spinetta the main column advanced to the charge, and drove the Austrians out of Marengo. (The *Revue Militaire Autrichienne* sets down 5 p.m. as the hour when the cannonade commenced on the 13th.)

The French attacked Marengo with such vigour that O'Reilly, not wishing himself to be drawn into a serious combat, displayed no great resistance. The combat was at one moment interrupted by a heavy fall of rain. When the action was resumed, the Austrians were completely driven back, and sought refuge behind the ramparts of the bridgehead on the right bank of the Bormida. In this engagement the Austrians left in the hands of the French two guns, some weapons, and about one hundred prisoners.

Gardanne's troops followed up their success at the village of Marengo, and pursued the Austrian rear-guard. They were brought to a standstill by the fire of fourteen guns which the enemy had mounted on the works of the bridgehead, and by the more brisk fire of three field-batteries which General Zach had placed in position on the left bank of the river. (Zach also sent the infantry regiment of Spleny beyond the bridgehead to execute a sortie; but Gardanne had already withdrawn from the attack.)

Danican describes the attack on the 13th as being insignificant enough. He mentions that the French craftily attacked under cover of a storm; whereas the real fact is that a severe storm interrupted the contest for a time. He asserts that at about seven in the evening disorder pervaded the whole of the right wing of the Austrian Army, which retired on Alessandria, and owed its safety only to the very great superiority of its artillery, which had been posted on the left bank of the Bormida, and kept up a brisk fire until ten o'clock at night.

The Austrians made no exertion whatever to hold the village of Marengo, and soon lost that important position. It has always seemed incredible that when Melas had fully made up his mind to deliver battle on the plain on the following day, he should not have made an effort to hold Marengo in the evening of the 13th. Victor writes:—

> The position of Marengo was of the utmost importance, because, as it formed an acute angle in the plain, it offered the adversary the advantage of overlooking us without disclosing

himself, thus enabling him to throw upon us as much of his forces as he might have deemed necessary to overcome us in any weak point.

Had the enemy, therefore, held possession of the village, it would have been an indication that they meant to deliver battle on the morrow. If, on the contrary, they abandoned it, it would have afforded some sort of a proof that they purposed to evade us without giving battle.

The fault Melas committed, of so easily letting go his hold on the village of Marengo on the evening of the 13th, had a balancing advantage for him, inasmuch as it strengthened Bonaparte in his opinion that the Austrians were bent on a retreat on Genova. It caused him to persevere in a wrong forecast. He consequently subdivided his army still more, and of 25,000 men he had brought to the field of Marengo, two divisions of infantry and the Consular Guard were sent a day's march away, leaving available for battle 15,000 men; three divisions of infantry, and two brigades of cavalry.

But had Melas even adopted the plan of retiring on Genova, the position of Marengo was important, as the most direct route to that city from Alessandria passes by the village; consequently, in either case it should have been held.

That Bonaparte was *assailli ici à l'improviste*, as Jomini puts it, may be impossible to contradict. Nevertheless, there was a reasonable excuse—if there ever can be any excuse for being surprised—and that lay in what he conceived as the most favourable plan open to Melas, and that the surrender of the position of Marengo had strengthened this supposition and made it almost a certainty. His customary success made him sometimes deaf to the promptings of prudence. Had the Austrians held Marengo on the 13th, in the next day's battle Bonaparte would have had in the field both Lapoype's and Desaix's divisions. It was the very feeble defence of that village on the evening of the 13th that threw him entirely off the scent.

It has already been said how, on seeing Melas's inexplicable inactivity, the First Consul had begun to believe thoroughly that the Austrian commander-in-chief was bent on avoiding a battle, and contemplated a retreat in the direction of Genova or of Valenza. This idea, for a few days prevalent in his mind, became strengthened by the ease with which Gardanne carried the village of Marengo. The vast plain of Marengo, so favourable for the action of a numerous cavalry, appeared made purposely for the Austrian battlefield.

It was there that Bonaparte had fully expected to encounter the Austrian Army on the 13th of June, unless it had decamped. Melas not having taken advantage of such a fair field, made the First Consul distrustful. In this uncertainty as to the measures to which the enemy, finding himself in such dire difficulties, would resort, he did as he had always done; he credited the enemy with having taken the most reasonable course, and made his own dispositions accordingly.

Every consideration enjoined that, with the intention of delivering battle on the plain on the 14th, the Austrian Army should have been on the right bank of the Bormida by the evening of the 13th, ready by daybreak on the following morning to march in the directions fixed by the Austrian staff.

The easy capture of Marengo had the most natural effect on the mind of the First Consul of confirming the idea that Melas intended to evade giving battle. Consequently, Bonaparte echeloned his forces on the plain of Marengo, and issued no special orders for the morrow.

At sunset on the evening of the 13th of June, Victor held Marengo, and Bonaparte, instead of forming line on this corps, and issuing orders for a battle which might seem probable, left the other corps in echelon. Lannes and Murat at San Giuliano Vecchio, five miles in rear of Victor; Desaix was on his way to Rivalta to keep an eye on the road to Genova. Monnier and the Consular Guard were at Torre di Garofoli, seven and a half miles in rear of Marengo. Rivaud's cavalry brigade was at Salé.

Bonaparte himself decided to retrace his steps to Voghera, and there to await news from the different corps—from Desaix, from Chabran, and from Suchet. Having seen the troops established in their bivouacs, he set out, but at Torre di Garofoli news awaited him from Rivalta and from the Po that no movement had taken place in those directions, and, as the Scrivia was reported to be rising rapidly, he established his headquarters for the night in that hamlet.

★★★★★★

In the narrative of the Battle of Marengo, compiled in 1805, the version is different. The words are, "This order given, Bonaparte starts to go to the headquarters at Voghera." The order was for the burning of the bridges of the Bormida. In the bulletin of the battle there is no allusion to the information given that the Austrians had no bridges on the Bormida.

★★★★★★

With regard to the Battle of Marengo, it has always been said that Bonaparte was lulled into a sense of security by the negligence of one of his staff officers, who reported that there existed no bridge on the Bormida. Much hinges on this question of the bridge, for had Bonaparte really believed the statement made to him that it had been destroyed, he would have been correct in his belief that he had nothing to fear from an enemy on the left bank of the Bormida. He would not have thought it possible that an attack would have come from the direction of Alessandria.

The destruction of the bridge, or bridges, over the Bormida was, no doubt, a very important matter for the French, as such an operation would have prevented their being taken in flank had Bonaparte found it necessary to follow Desaix's movement in the direction of Novi to arrest Melas's retreat on Genova.

As the whole of the evidence on this mooted point is of a most confused and contradictory nature, we consider it desirable to give it so that the reader may draw his own conclusions.

The Bormida, as we have seen, was crossed by two bridges, one of which was only laid down on the night of the 13-14th June. Marmont relates that the river made a bend, and that, contrary to all military engineering principles, the bridgehead had been placed at the salient of the bend, so that it was possible for him to take it in reverse by effecting a lodgement in the re-entering bend—*dans le rentrant*. This is but one of the many mis-statements which make this battle so puzzling. Captain Pittaluga, a living author who has paid considerable attention to the topography of the battlefield, describes the bridgehead as situated in a re-entering bend of the Bormida; the bridges stood between high banks, the approaches being covered with hasty entrenchments and abatis.

It is a most remarkable fact that none of the principal officers concerned make any allusion to their having received any command to destroy a bridge or bridges. In the official narratives of the battle prepared in 1803 and in 1805, Berthier states:—

> The advance-guard receives orders to drive the enemy's posts over to the other side of the Bormida, and, if it should be possible, to burn the bridges. (*L'avant-garde reçoit l'ordre de repousser les postes ennemis au delà de la Bormida, et, s'il est possible, d'en brûler les ponts.*)

It is much to be deplored that no reliable documents have been found in the Bureau de la Guerre with regard to the order for the destruction of the bridge. Let us now see how the above instructions were carried out.

Victor states that:—

> Gardanne (one of his division generals) marched from San Giuliano on Marengo to attack the enemy concentrated in that village ... forced them to retire in disorder as far as the bridge on the Bormida.

Gardanne in his report, written on the 15th of June, simply mentions having received an order to attack the village of Marengo. Dampierre, who attacked with Gardanne's left column, writes:—

> *Nous fûmes chargés d'attaquer le village de Marengo le Soir du 24 Prairial* (We were ordered to carry the village of Marengo on the evening of the 24th *Prairial*).

Neither of the three officers principally concerned alludes to the fact of their having received an order to destroy the bridge over the Bormida, or of having received a check whilst attempting to do so, or of having found it impossible to comply with the orders of the First Consul.

The three above-mentioned officers report in the following words what followed the attack of the village. Victor says:—

> Our battalions, advancing at the charge, broke the enemy, and forced him back in disorder up to the bridge of the Bormida, leaving in our hands two guns, their waggons, and about 100 prisoners.

Gardanne reports:—

> We pursued the enemy up to within firing distance of the entrenchments of the Bormida and of the bridgehead of Alessandria, where the contest ceased at ten o'clock of the evening.

Dampierre says nothing about any attempt to destroy the bridges having been made. He deplores too much dash in the pursuit, and says that the little daylight still remaining—for the attack on Marengo was only made at half-past seven in the evening—was almost fatal to them.

> We advanced, up to the foot of the intrenchments of the Bormida. The day, which was waning, did not permit the other divisions to combine an attack capable of carrying the entrench-

ments, which had more the appearance of a town than of a field work. (The Austrian account calls it a *vaste tête de pont*, in which fourteen guns were mounted.)

After having approached to within pistol-shot of the works, the advanced guard, exposed to a regular downpour of bullets and case-shot, retired to establish its bivouacs within cannon-shot distance of the intrenchments; it was ten o'clock when all firing ceased. The left rested on the Bormida. The right stretched out as far as some cottages which stood on the left of the road leading from Alessandria to Marengo. (Petit, in narrating the events of the 13th of June, states:—

> We found the enemy at the bridge on the Bormida, whence a feeble attempt was made to dislodge him.)

There was still a fourth officer present with the advanced guard, Marmont, the commander of the artillery. As the account he gives of the events was not written immediately after the occurrences, like those we have given above, it cannot be received with the same amount of confidence. This is what he writes:—

> Arrived close to the Bormida, I discovered a bridgehead constructed on the right bank, and occupied by the enemy. At this point the river made a bend, and, against all principles, the bridgehead being situated on the salient of the river, I could attack it in reverse by taking position in the re-entering bend. I imagined that we would soon be making an attack of this bridgehead, and to prepare it I took eight guns, so as to bring an oblique fire to bear on the gorge. This drew, however, the fire of an embrasured battery constructed on the left bank, which compelled me to withdraw, after having lost several men and having had several pieces dismounted. Having taken post somewhat in rear, I went in search of General Gardanne to learn what he proposed doing. I found him in a ditch, having taken no steps either for attacking the bridgehead or for preventing the enemy issuing out and going forth. Thereupon I left him, having no orders to give him, and night being near. (*Mémoires du Duc de Raguse, tom.* ii.)

Marmont's words help to establish that neither he nor Gardanne had received any orders about the destruction of the bridge. Besides, as O'Reilly's command passed the night, 13-14th of June, on the right bank of the Bormida, this of itself would have prevented the French getting anywhere near the bridge.

There were other officers who knew of the existence of the bridgehead on the night of the 13th, and consequently, one would imagine, of the existence of the bridge. Rivaud's brigade, 43rd and 96th, about 4,000 strong, marched for Marengo and Spinetta, and reached those places at about 10 p.m., and established its bivouacs. The brigadier reported as follows:—

> The enemy on the night of the 24th *Prairial* not only retained a bridgehead on the Bormida, but also had the advanced posts between the Bormida and our advanced guard very close to the Bormida.
>
> (*L'ennemi a conservé le soir du 24, non seulement une tête de pont sur la Bormida, mais a maintenue les avant-postes entre la Bormida et notre avant-garde très près de la Bormida.*)

We find Dupont, Berthier's chief of the staff, writing to Carnot:—

> The enemy has sustained there (at Marengo) a very brisk fight; but soon hemmed in from all sides, he has precipitately gained the bridge of the Bormida, in front of Alessandria.

From Marmont's testimony it would seem that there was much carelessness with respect to the bridge and bridgehead. No one appears to have been especially intrusted with the operations at this point; no general, no superior staff officer, to have been detailed to see them carried into effect.

The lateness of the hour may have rendered it difficult to initiate arrangements for dislodging the enemy. Prudence, in any case, should have counselled the egress from the bridgehead being watched with extra care, so as to guard against every possibility of being taken by surprise.

Marmont relates that on the 14th of June, after the arrival of Victor's messenger with the news of the threatening attitude of the Austrians, the First Consul, astonished at this news, said that it seemed to him impossible.

> "General Gardanne has reported to me his arrival on the Bormida, of which he has broken the bridge." (Would not Bonaparte have said anything of Lauriston's report that there was no bridge?)
> I replied:—
> "General Gardanne has made a false report. I was yesterday

evening nearer than he was to the bridgehead, and proposed to him to render ourselves masters of it. But he refused, though I had some cannon to support him; and the bridgehead not having been captured or blockaded by our troops, the enemy has been able to issue at his pleasure during the night, without being observed; therefore, you can really believe in the battle."

In all that relates to Marengo, these *Mémoires* contain some radical mistakes. It was by no means, as Marmont states, on Gardanne's false report that the First Consul arrived at the conclusion that the Austrians were in full retreat on Genova. Desaix, with Boudet's division, had been started in the direction of Novi at noon of the 13th, several hours before Gardanne attacked the Austrian rear-guard at Marengo. By the time Gardanne could have made any report of his having reached the Bormida, Desaix's advance-guard was already trying to cross the Scrivia by Rivalta.

Marmont says: "The enemy has been able to issue at his pleasure during the night, without being observed," when, by the Austrian account, owing to the action on the previous-evening, they did not cross the Bormida in the night, but waited till morning.

Napoleon writes in his *Mémoires*:—

The scouts arrived on the Bormida at the fall of night; they sent word that the enemy had no bridge, and that there was only an ordinary garrison in Alessandria; they gave no news of Melas's army.... The First Consul was much disturbed.

Who were these scouts? They could have been no other than some of Gardanne's men—men belonging to the division which chased the Austrians out of Marengo, and pursued them towards Alessandria. Now, was it possible for these scouts to reach the banks of the Bormida and reconnoitre, when O'Reilly's rearguard remained on the right bank of the river that night, guarding the approaches to the bridgehead?

The last part of Napoleon's assertion, besides, is quite contrary to Berthier's statement contained in the account of the battle drawn up in 1803. His words were (and they bear considerable importance on Bonaparte's uncertainty as to the whereabouts of the enemy):—

We knew through prisoners captured in the fight (of the 13th) that in the morning Melas had despatched a detachment towards Acqui, but that the army corps were still round Alessandria.

What adds to the embarrassment is that the emperor's and Berthier's accounts evidently do not tally on this point. Nor can we put much faith in what Berthier states about the detachment sent to Acqui, for the Austrian account gives nine o'clock in the morning of the 14th as the time when Captain Ceiwrany brought intelligence that he had been attacked at Acqui by a large column of cavalry, supported by infantry. Captain V. Pittaluga writes on this incident:—

> It was a little after 8 a.m.... At the same hour a false report was made to the Austrian commander-in-chief to the effect that a short while before a numerous corps of French cavalry had compelled the Austrian squadron stationed at Acqui to fall back on Alessandria. Melas, imagining it might he the cavalry of Suchet's reconnoitring column coming from Genova, recalled at once Nimptsch's brigade of Elsnitz's cavalry division to the left of the Bormida, and directed it on Cantalupo."

This is what some of the historians write on the subject of the destruction of the bridge. The Duke of Valmy states with regard to the events of the 13th of June:—

> He ordered General Victor, strengthened by Kellermann's cavalry, to march on that village (Marengo), to overthrow the enemy's posts, and to push up to the bridgehead which rested on the Bormida in front of Alessandria. (Duc de Valmy, *Histoire de la Campagne de 1800.*)

The same words had been used by Jomini, but up to a certain point only, for he adds, "and to try to seize the bridge, if there existed one on the Bormida."

General Comte Mathieu Dumas gives a somewhat different version; he relates:—

> Bonaparte had ordered General Gardanne to throw himself therein pell-mell with them, and, if he could, to burn the bridges on the Bormida. But, notwithstanding the disorder of the Austrian retreat, night was approaching, and the French were stopped by the reserves which held the bridgehead, and by the fire of thirty pieces of artillery.

Now, one would imagine that either Gardanne or Victor, under whose command he was, was bound to report to the commander-in-chief that a very important part of their instructions could not be carried out. There is nothing, however, to show that either Victor or Gardanne did so. What seems strange is that at the conclusion of the fight on the evening of the 13th no report should have been made to the First Consul, and that he should not have been informed of the strongly armed bridgehead, nor of the warm reception Gardanne had met as he approached it. It is said that Bonaparte remained on the field till the bivouacs were established, to judge of the amount of the Austrian forces by the extent of their fires. If so, it was easy for Victor or Berthier to enlighten him on the subject of the bridge.

Gachot relates that whilst Bonaparte was reconnoitring from the tower of Marengo, he detected a second bridge; that he sent Lauriston with a squadron of the Consular Guard and some cannon to break it up; but that on arriving at the spot, Lauriston found the enemy in the act of removing it, so he did not molest them, and retired to Torre di Garofoli to convey the news to Bonaparte. (Trucco explains that the idea seems to have been that Bonaparte dreaded a possible night attack, the Austrians crossing the Bormida by a bridge existing lower down near the confluence of the Tanaro.) This version does not tally with the Duke of Rovigo's statement or with Bourrienne's account.

Trucco says:—

The bridge constructed over the Bormida on a level with Castel Ceriolo would have been taken away from that locality and placed alongside of the existing one during the night of the 13-14th of June, to replace a bridge of boats which had already been removed.

Pittaluga considers it possible that this second bridge was not completed in sufficient time to enable the simultaneous passage of the two columns early enough on the 14th.

Hooper's words are:—

But night was fast coming on; the staff officer intrusted with the task of reconnoitring the Bormida did not do his duty; and he returned to headquarters with the report that the enemy had no bridge on the Bormida.

Nothing, possibly, marks in a more distinct manner the necessity for having all orders and instructions set down in writing, restricting verbal injunctions to the smallest possible number. *Verba volant scripta manent.* It is to avoid errors and ambiguities, to serve for future reference, to solve dubious points, and to refute wrong accusations, that writing is needed. But it is not sufficient to have orders committed to writing. The advantages of clearness and certainty afforded by written documents are lost when the injunctions are badly worded or unintelligibly written. Amongst the orders emanating from Soult at Ligny was an important one to D'Erlon, who with his corps was bringing up Ney's rear, enjoining him to attack Blücher's right flank. This order was scribbled with a lead pencil, and badly worded. The staff officer handed the order to D'Erlon, but he, not being sharp enough to interpret correctly an obscure despatch, hastily written with a pencil, directed his corps towards Fleurus—that is, on the flank of Napoleon, and not on Saint Amand or Brye, on the flank or rear of the Prussians. (William O'Connor Morris, *The Campaign of 1815*.)

It could hardly have been the main bridge which was ordered to be destroyed, for Victor, Gardanne, Dampierre, and Rivaud would not have remained silent on the impossibility of fulfilling their orders in the reports rendered by them of the action on the evening of the 13th. Bonaparte himself in his bulletin makes no mention whatever of the failure in burning the bridge. Besides, the French troops approached the Bormida so late that it would have been very difficult to carry out the order.

The Duke of Rovigo, who as one of Desaix's *aides-de-camp* had been present at the Battle of Marengo, states with regard to this subject that Bonaparte reconnoitred the banks of the Bormida on the 14th (evidently an error, for he did so on the 13th, and not on the 14th). He persuaded himself that, independently of the bridge on the river in front of Alessandria, the enemy must have had another a good deal lower down; that is to say, on the right flank of the French.

"He had ordered that all who had crossed over should be driven back to the other side of the river, and that at any price whatever a bridge which might be fatal to us should be destroyed. He declared himself ready to go should circumstances demand it. One of his *aides-de-camp*, Colonel Lauriston, was instructed to follow the operations, and not to return until it had been accomplished.

> The combat began; the two sides cannonaded each other the whole day; but the enemy held firm: it was impossible to force him to remove the bridge. Lauriston came to report on the state of affairs. The First Consul, worn out by fatigue, either did not understand him, or understood badly what the *aide-de-camp* reported; because Lauriston, whom he afterwards reproached

for the false security he had given to his army, invariably replied that, instead of having committed such a grave fault, he had hastened to inform him how it had not been possible to execute his orders. Lauriston understood too well all the importance which attached to the bridge to make a statement to him without having first made himself personally sure that it had been destroyed.

★★★★★★

James Alexander Bernard Law, Marquis de Lauriston, was born at Pondichéry on the 1st of February, 1768. He came from a family originally Scotch. His father, known as Chevalier Law, took the name of Law de Lauriston.

Lauriston entered the artillery in 1793, and soon brought himself before Bonaparte's notice. He it was who, in 1802, brought the written articles of the treaty of peace to London for ratification, and received an enthusiastic reception. He was given command of the troops embarked in the fleet which Villeneuve took to the West Indies in 1804, and was present at the Battle of Trafalgar. After that he served in many capacities both civil and military. At Wagram he commanded the battery of 100 guns which contributed so much to the victory.

After Wagram he was commissioned to conduct the Archduchess Marie Louise, the future wife of Napoleon, to Paris. He took part in the Russian campaign, and after that commanded at the Katzbach, at Wachau, and at Leipzig, in the latter of which battles he was made prisoner. Much to his honour, it is recorded that he highly disapproved of the arrest of the Duc d'Enghien, and had an angry dispute with Cauleincourt on the subject; also, that, having in 1814 gone over to the Bourbons, he refused to take an active part in the Hundred Days, and remained in retirement at his possession of Richemont.

★★★★★★

Unfortunately, the duke's statements are full of inaccuracies. Here, for example, he declares that the two sides cannonaded each other the whole day, whereas the French, by all accounts, only got engaged between 4 and 5 p.m.

Bourrienne does not throw much light on this point. His account is:—

The First Consul slept on the 13th at Torre di Garofoli. In the evening he issued an order to send a staff officer to ascertain if the Austrians had a bridge on the Bormida.

In all this there is nothing about destroying the bridge, and his having given this order would tend to show that none had been given to the officers commanding the advanced guard. Bourrienne continues:—

> I was present when, very late, someone came to make him a report to the effect that there was none. This information reassured the First Consul, and he retired to rest very contented. But when very early on the morrow the guns were heard, and he learnt that the Austrians had issued on the plain and the troops were engaged, he showed the greatest discontent on the falseness of the staff officer's report; he accused him of being a coward and of not having advanced far enough; he even spoke of having him tried. (*Mémoires de Bourrienne, tom.* iv.)

The Duke of Rovigo's vindication of Lauriston is plausible enough, nevertheless Bourrienne distinctly states that he was present at a late hour when they came to report to the First Consul that a bridge did not exist. The report, therefore, was made before a third person, and though it is very possible that Bonaparte might have misunderstood its tenor, it is not so likely that Bonaparte and Bourrienne should both have done so. They were not likely to misconstrue the words on a point to which the First Consul naturally attached much importance.

Bonaparte cannot have borne any ill will towards Lauriston, or he would not, after what had occurred in 1800, have intrusted him with most important missions, *les plus speciales*. Amongst others may be cited the command of the expedition to Batavia, the defence of Ragusa, the siege of Raab, and the massing of the famous battery of 100 guns at Wagram, which gave the Emperor Napoleon the victory.

The Duke of Rovigo's description of the battle differs from most others:—

> General Bonaparte, believing that the lower bridge over the Bormida had been cut, refrained from changing the position of his army, which passed the night of the 13-14th astride the road from Tortona to Alessandria; the right in front of Castel Ceriolo, the left on the plain of Marengo. General Desaix was in reserve at Rivalta, and the headquarters were at Garofoli.
> The 14th of June our right was assailed at daybreak by a mass of cavalry, which crossed by the bridge which should have been

cut the previous day; the irruption was so impetuous and so rapid that in an instant we experienced an immense loss in men, horses, and materials.

In no other account have we found this attack at the break of day so unfortunate for the French. All make the battle commence between 8 and 9 a.m.; and this charge, pushed home by a mass of cavalry, finds no place in any of the narratives. The first act on that part of the field, the right, was the advance of Lannes with Watrin's division, which moved forward in aid of Victor, after Haddick's and Kaim's attacks had failed.

The duke's account, which, coming from a staff officer who had been present during the battle, should have been very valuable, cannot be accepted as accurate. Another point to which the duke makes no allusion is the difficulty Desaix experienced in getting Boudet's division across the Scrivia. He speaks of Boudet's troops commencing to march on Novi, apparently without any difficulty, and says that the cannonade was heard only just as the day was breaking. This does not tally with the reports submitted by Rivaud, Lannes, Berthier, and Victor, all of whom agree in stating that the battle really began about nine o'clock.

CHAPTER 5

The Battle

Melas had been in Alessandria since the 10th of June, but sorely perplexed by the course of events. In this state of indecision, he assembled a special council of war.

✶✶✶✶✶✶

Trucco states that this extraordinary council was held at 10 p.m. on the 13th of June, in a house, No. 1 Via Faa di Bruno, where Melas had his headquarters. Jomini and Pittaluga give the 12th of June as the date; the latter stating that the council was held in the palace of Count Aulari. We are inclined to accept the latter date as correct, seeing how little time for arrangements a council called for a ten on the night of the 13th would have left. The *Revue Militaire Autrichienne* declares that all through the day of the 13th preparations were being made for the battle on the following day.

✶✶✶✶✶✶

At this council he exposed to his generals the critical situation in which his army found itself, having lost its communications with the base, being surrounded by the enemy, and having been decimated in the past encounters. After having considered the various alternatives open to him, he gave it as his opinion that the only and creditable way out of the difficulty was to lead all the forces he had gathered together out of the city, and to fight a decisive battle on the plain of Marengo. Should the result of the contest, he added, be fortunate, and victory side with them, this would open a road for his forces to Piacenza before the Army of Reserve would have time to form a junction with the Army of Italy.

Melas greatly dreaded a junction, and an imminent one, of the Army of Reserve with the Army of Italy. He argued against a retreat on Genova, where he ran the risk of falling in with Massena's army in the defiles of the Apennines, of being pursued by Bonaparte, and thus caught between two fires.

The same did not hold good with the alternative referred to in Chapter 1, a retreat in the direction of Milan by Valenza and the left bank of the Po. This retreat avoided both Bonaparte and Massena. The Austrian Army was concentrated about Alessandria by the 12th of June, and, had Melas manoeuvred briskly by the left of the Po, he might have hoped, and with good reason, to have broken through Moncey's feeble cordon and have reached Milan, whilst Bonaparte was still seeking him on the Bormida. Melas never conceived how difficult Bonaparte found it to obtain information, and how to close him every avenue of escape he had been compelled to divide and scatter his forces. He might also have thought the price to be paid for recovering his communications too dear, if he had to leave the French masters of the whole of the country south of the Po.

The Austrian commander-in-chief laid considerable stress on the superiority of his army, both in cavalry and artillery, to the Republican forces; likewise on the nature of the ground comprised between the Bormida and the Scrivia, which was so eminently adapted for the employment of those two arms.

Melas's decision to fight had been really settled some days before, as can be seen by his letter to Lord Keith, in which he mentions that he intended to deliver battle, and, if beaten, to retire on Genova. He no sooner heard of Ott's defeat at Montebello than he decided to try the chance of a general engagement.

Retreat either on Genova or on Milan held to his mind very slender prospect of safety. It was better, he expounded, to march boldly against the French coming by the Piacenza road, to deliver battle, and to fray himself a way to Mantua, and in this manner to re-establish the communications with the Austrian empire.

Montebello had been fought on the 9th, and after three days of indecision Melas adopted a heroic resolution to fight. He decided on a rough trial of arms, trusting on the valour of his troops. This spirited plan proposed by the aged commander-in-chief was unanimously accepted by all who attended the council of war, for the Austrian generals were desirous to follow the dictates of honour, to open by strength of arms a way to Piacenza and Mantua, or to die in the attempt, as it behoved gallant soldiers. (Napoleon says in his *Mémoires* that the whole of the 13th and the night of the 13-14th were spent by the Austrians in deliberating.)

Ordinarily the Bormida is fordable in most places, but, as the banks

The Battle of Marengo

rise a good many feet above its bed and are somewhat steep, one or more bridges had to be laid to facilitate the passage of numerous troops.

From the beginning of June, the Austrians had been steadily working and improving the bridgehead which existed on the right bank of the Bormida, where the road from Alessandria to Tortona crosses the river. After the Battle of Montebello, the works were armed with fourteen guns. This intrenchment covered two floating bridges, and in the dispositions for the battle the principal attacking column was to cross the river by the right bridge; the other, or General Ott's column, was to cross by the left one.

✶✶✶✶✶✶

In the first and fifth paragraphs of the bulletin of the 26th *Prairial, an* VIII., dictated by Bonaparte, he makes out that there were three bridges over the Bormida, when in point of fact there were only two. In Melas's report the words are: "On the 14th, all the army crossed by two bridges to the right bank of that river." Not only in this point, but in others as well, many expert critics have declared that this official account of the battle was not thoroughly accurate. Impatient that the news of the victory should speedily reach France, Bonaparte evidently did not wait to compile his narrative on the detailed reports of his subordinate generals.

✶✶✶✶✶✶

All sources agree in declaring that Saturday, the 14th of June, 1800, was an exceptionally fine day, and a great improvement on the stormy weather which made the months of May and June of that year so remarkable. The day was magnificent, as splendid, indeed, as could well be found, even in lovely Italy. The sun rose in all its glory, and its dazzling rays brightened up all the country around Alessandria. It was blazing as it had not done for weeks past, and there was a hum of many insects in the air.

> *Non fu mai l'aria si serena e bella.*
> *Come alt uscir del memorabil giorno.*

The Austrians, except O'Reilly's advanced guard, had passed the night on the left of the Bormida, uncheered by bivouac fires, and, though under arms before the break of day, did not commence to cross the Bormida much before 8 a.m.

✶✶✶✶✶✶

The Austrian account states that the crossing of the river Bormida had been fixed for 8 a.m., because the French had the previous night driven back the advanced posts up to the bridgehead on the Bormida. In any case, O'Reilly commenced to advance at about 8 a.m.

******

The movement, as we have said, was executed over two bridges, one of which had been brought from further downstream, and had been established alongside of the other during the past night. (In the first official account of the battle Berthier states that the Austrians crossed by the bridges and fords of the Bormida.) The advantage of having a second bridge over the Bormida was, nevertheless, rendered fruitless, inasmuch as the bridgehead beyond had only one outlet. Here was a most glaring mistake, for which the staff officers who prepared the details of the movement appear to have been directly answerable.

It may be urged that, as the second bridge had only been completed during the night, there may not have been time to open a second safe passage in the bridgehead. Whatever was at the bottom of the omission, that single outlet leading into the plain beyond delayed the deployment of the Austrian forces very considerably. General Ott, who had to march in the direction of Salé, was ordered to keep the way clear for General Kaim's column, which was one of the two principal columns, and intended to support General Haddick's attack on Marengo.

The oversight in having a single point of egress in the bridgehead had fatal consequences for the Austrians. But for this Ott would have come into line at an earlier hour, before Lannes could have had time to come up, and the French would have been driven off the field before Desaix's arrival.

At Marengo the Austrians had nearly 31,000 men in line, and the French a little over 28,000. It was a small army that held the fate of Europe in its hands. (See chart following.)

By gathering together all the troops of Elsnitz, Haddick, Ott, and Kaim, Melas could have concentrated a much larger force than he did, but this meant leaving the places in Piedmont without a garrison.

Melas in his report computes the force he had concentrated about Alessandria at 27,000 infantry and 8,000 cavalry. From the total should be deducted the garrison of Alessandria, and seventeen squadrons of cavalry sent to Cantalupo, which took no part in the battle.

The *Revue Militaire Autrichienne* states that the effective of the Austrian Army collected for the decisive contest can be set down at 30,837 men, of whom 7,543 were cavalry.

The Battle of Marengo

STATE OF THE IMPERIAL ARMY AT THE BATTLE OF MARENGO *
(1800).

Corps.	Divisions.	Brigades.	Strength.	Remarks.
Right column	O'Reilly	Rousseau	3,000	800 of whom were cavalry
	Advanced guard	Frimont	1,300	450 of whom were cavalry
		Pilatz	1,400	
	Haddick	Bellegarde	1,500	
		Saint Julien	2,200	
		De Briey	1,650	
Main column	Kaim	Knesevich	2,200	
		Lamarsaille	1,100	
	Morzin, grenadiers	Lattermann	2,100	
		Weidenfeld	2,200	
		Pionniers	400	
	Elsnitz, cavalry	Nobili	1,900 } cavalry
		Nimptsch	2,300 }	
Left column (Ott)	Advanced guard	Gottesheim	800	250 of whom were cavalry
	Schellenberg	Retz	2,000	
		Sticker	2,600	500 of whom were cavalry
	Vogelsang	Ulm	2,200	
	Total present at Marengo		30,850	7000 of whom were cavalry

DETACHMENTS AND GARRISONS.	Strength.
At Casale, 2650; at Feliciano, 1000; at Acqui, 115; at Bobbio, 1000 ...	4,765
At Alessandria, 3000; at Tortona, 1200; at Turin, 3800; at Coni, 4400	12,400
At Genova, 6000; at Savona, 1200; blockade of Gavi, 1200; Riviera di Levante, 1000 ...	9,400
At Mantua, 3500; at Peschiera, 500; Castle of Milan, 2800	6,800
Castle of Piacenza, 300; of Pizzighettone, 800; of Parma, 350	1,450
In Tuscany	3,000
In Venice, Verona, and Istria	6,350
Total	44,165

The Imperial army, showing a total of 75,000 men, had, since the opening of the campaign on the 6th of April, lost nearly 30,000 men.

* Jomini, "Histoire des Guerres de la Révolution," Livre XVI. chap. cii.

Olivier Rivaud gives to the Austrians 28,000 infantry and 7,000 cavalry, making the whole of their army 35,000 strong. Many writers think Jomini's estimate too low. Possibly Rivaud was nearer the mark. Some compute the Austrians at 30,000, the French till Boudet's arrival at 22,000, and at about 28,000 after his arrival on the battlefield.

With an army about 31,000 strong, with numerous and well-horsed artillery, with a fine and well-mounted force of cavalry, with tried and disciplined infantry, Melas was in every respect well-furnished for a combat on which hung important results. Though advanced in age, for he was seventy-one years old, the record of his services showed that he was not deficient in skill and valour; besides, he was inspirited by his recent successes.

Melas should have striven to bring together every man he could lay hands on, for the simple reason that he was not quite sure of the strength of Bonaparte's army. Whilst at Milan, according to Bourrienne, the First Consul had sent him through a double spy a misleading return showing the French Army to be double what it really was.

The Austrians must have experienced considerable difficulty in provisioning their troops, when we recall how the north of Italy had been the scene of a long conflict between the Austro-Russians and the French the previous year. The local resources must have been well-nigh exhausted, a fact which of itself would make open communications with the base ever more valuable.

It has never been explained, except under the excuse of jealousy, why the Austrians so determinedly refused to accede to the solicitations of the English to take charge of Genova. By letting the English hold that city, the garrison left there under Hohenzollern would have been free either to reinforce Melas or to arrest Suchet's progress. This would have given the Austrians a superiority of numbers on the battlefield.

There appears to have been something unexplained beyond British unreadiness with regard to the British troops at Mahon. Jomini states that, in order to replace Hohenzollern at Genova, Melas sent an officer to Lord Keith with a request that he would bring over in all haste a portion of the 12,000 British soldiers then lying inactive in Minorca; also, that Melas sent a second officer to Keith to depict the embarrassing situation he was in, and urge him to comply with the above demand. Keith is said to have replied that he had not the disposal of Abercromby's corps, and must wait till Abercromby arrived to replace Stuart. This possibly was the case, seeing how in our country the army and the navy are two quite independent services.

Moreover, Lord Keith, being a very methodical, attentive, and correct personage, and not an officer of extraordinary talents, may not have relished assuming any responsibility in the matter, not knowing what instructions Abercromby might have received; or it is possible that he may have known that the government destined the troops for important operations on the shores of Provence. With regard to this demand of General Melas, Dundas stated in Parliament that Melas's *aide-de-camp* came to make the request on the 22nd of June, the very day Abercromby reached Mahon and assumed command. Nor does the general appear to have lost any time, for with 8,000 men he arrived before Genova on the 25th of June, the day after Suchet had marched in and taken possession of the city. If Dundas's statement was correct, and Keith was only asked for troops on the 22nd, the demand was strange, as by that time the fate of Genova had been sealed on the field of Marengo.

The troops at Mahon might in any case have been brought over to Genova, where they would have relieved 5,800 Austrians who had been left to garrison the place and 1,192 more who were investing Gavi. In this manner nearly 7,000 men would have been able to join Melas on the day of battle.

Bülow shows undisguised contempt for the abilities of the British generals and for the discipline of their soldiers. (Bülow, *Histoire de la Campagne de 1800*.) Nevertheless, a few months after the victory of Marengo the very troops that were at Mahon under Sir R. Abercromby defeated Bonaparte's famous troops in Egypt, and Sir Ralph's successor entirely cleared the country of them.

The troops the Austrian general retained to garrison the strong places in Piedmont proved simply a cause of weakness. No advantage whatsoever was to be gained by them.

The following was the strength of the Army of Reserve on the 14th of June, as given by the Duke of Belluno (Victor):—

	At Marengo.	Before the forts.	On the march.	Total.
Infantry	22,938	21,339	3,468	47,745
Cavalry	3,220	2,382	1,424	7,026
Consular Guard	1,232	—	—	1,232
Artillery and engineers	618	1,400	—	2,018
	28,008	25,121	4,892	58,021

In his *Relation de la Bataille de Marengo*, Berthier gives a table of the French forces in Italy at the time. The totals are very nearly the same as Victor's:—

In line at Marengo—
Infantry   23,791
Cavalry   3,688
Artillery   690
                 ─────
Total   28,169

Guarding the communications and holding strong places—

Infantry	24,964
Cavalry	3,312
Artillery	1,400
Total	29,676

The artillery of the troops which crossed the Po made a total of 41 guns. Of these 36 were divided amongst the division and 5 formed a reserve. On the day of the battle Bonaparte had not more than 15 to 20 guns.

The returns of the battle, as given by Berthier and Victor, show that more than one-half of Bonaparte's force was absent from the field of Marengo. Wishing to close every point of passage open to the enemy, he had been induced to forget one of his soundest maxims, which was to concentrate all his forces in view of an impending battle.

Bonaparte, whose avowed object in marching to Milan had been to form a junction with Moncey's forces, after quitting Milan was always scattering his troops. To such an extent did he do this that his own subordinates became surprised at it. (Marmont, *Mémoires, tom. ii.*) Conversing amongst themselves, they remarked how thoroughly contrary such action was to his habits, that it seemed as if he were bent on capturing his enemy by mastering all his communications before having beaten him; whereas it would have seemed more prudent to insure first all possible means for subduing him, leaving his capture to a future moment.

Bonaparte could well be reproached with the large dissemination of his forces. But Melas committed the same error. He had left 25,000 men to garrison Cuneo, Turin, Genova, Acqui, Gavi, Tortona, and Alessandria. Number is a factor which counts for much in a battle, but both commanders in 1800 appear to have taken little account of it.

Goldsmith wrote of Frederick the Great that his manly acknowledgment of a lost battle made him win others. For political reasons, Bonaparte could not afford to confess that he had made serious blunders at Marengo. Nevertheless, no one understood better than he did to what dangers he had been exposed. The lesson sank deep into his mind, and he did not commit the same mistakes again.

Bonaparte's officers were young, confident, and brave; ready to uphold the glorious destinies of France. The career of arms, freely opened to personal courage and talent, had in a short period given to the army from its ranks an excellent number of generals. These leaders, though young, had been formed in battlefields. They had risen, step by step, in the hard contests the Republic had to sustain to exist, in the Italian campaign of 1796, and in Egypt. Their reputation was solidly established; it had not been cheaply acquired in Egypt fighting against an inferior enemy, nor were they in any way afraid to lose it.

Bonaparte's artillery and cavalry, however, bore no comparison with that of the enemy; his guns were few in number and poor in quality. From 14 to 15 guns were all that the French had in the battle up to five in the evening, when Boudet arrived, bringing eight more. The ranks of the infantry were full of conscripts—a marked difference to the German infantry, which was composed of men well inured to war.

On the 14th of June, a complete army fell suddenly on Bonaparte's corps and surprised them. The Austrians advanced in three columns. O'Reilly, who had remained on the right bank of the Bormida, led the way. He commanded the right column, composed of 4 battalions (2,228 men) and 6 squadrons (796 sabres). This column attacked Gardanne's outposts at Pedrabona, and afterwards inclined to the right, and moved up the Bormida towards Stortigliona and Frugarolo. The centre column was composed of the troops of Haddick, Kaim, and Elsnitz, 28 battalions (14,204 men) and 22 squadrons (3,694 sabres).

With this column, which took the road to Marengo, marched the general-in-chief. General Ott commanded the left column, which counted 16 battalions (6,862 men) and 6 squadrons (740 sabres). It marched on Castel Ceriolo, making for Salé. All the three columns marched with their artillery; the baggage and impedimenta had been collected and parked to the north of Alessandria.

Able military writers have expressed their opinion that the plan of battle, as conceived by Melas for the 14th of June, had been well thought out, that his forces had been well distributed, and that, if defeat overtook him, the fault could not be laid on the commander-in-chief. But plans, however good, when their execution is not in capable hands are apt to miscarry. General Danican, who was a spectator of the operations on the Austrian side, states, in his version of the events of that day, that the Austrian soldiers were sad and dejected, and that many of their officers were tired of war. Other writers do not confirm this statement; on the contrary, they say that everything had been done to put the troops in good cheer.

The defiling of the Austrian columns through the one opening in the bridgehead had been long and laborious. Victor, though in a manner surprised—a fact admitted by the words used in the official bulletin—*surprit notre avant-garde*—had time to make his preliminary dispositions, for Quiot, who was his *aide-de-camp* at the battle, tells us that throughout the still summer night of the 13-14th of June, Victor's men heard the unmistakable sounds of a large force standing under arms. The general, expecting to be attacked at daybreak, posted the troops himself, and established his headquarters at the presbytery of Spinetta.

Coignet, who was in Chambarlhac's division, states that his division was under arms all night. Also, that at four o'clock in the morning all the troops were made to take up their positions.

Jomini reproaches Bonaparte with having been assailed unexpectedly. But such was hardly the case. And this is pretty clearly demonstrated by Victor's evidence, he writes:—

> The night (13-14th of June) was so calm and peaceful, that an attentive ear could catch from quite a distance and distinguish the slightest sounds which happened to break the calm. Then, about one o'clock in the morning, whilst everything was hushed in silence, there arose in the plain, on the left bank of the Bormida, intense and confused sounds, as of a multitude which stirs and assembles; many sounds rang out clearly—the murmur of voices, the roll of drums, the calls of trumpets, the pawing of hoofs, a grinding noise of chariots and of cannons. It was impossible to doubt that the enemy was preparing to deliver battle, and the day was longed for with impatience.
>
> The dawn at last lighted up the horizon, and soon one of the most brilliant suns of Italy illuminated the scene. All the Austrian Army stood there revealed under arms....
>
> Mons. de Melas had the intention of marching against the Republicans at the break of day, and on the previous day he had issued orders to his generals to that effect. It is unknown what caused him to alter his mind. Some German accounts, and Melas by his own words, pretend that the loss of the village of Marengo, and the fact that the Austrian advanced guard had been driven back to the bridgehead on the Bormida, decided him to postpone the attack. But this reason does not appear quite satisfactory. Possibly he desired to await more positive news of the strength and disposition of the French Army. It may be, after all, that he hoped that Bonaparte might be impru-

dent enough to come and attack him in the strong position he occupied by Alessandria. Whatever the reason may have been, more than four hours elapsed before he gave the order to his troops to march to the attack.

Pittaluga states that it was 6 a.m. when the two columns moved towards the bridges and commenced crossing.

That the French Army was surprised, seeing that Melas adopted a course quite contrary to Bonaparte's expectations, we grant. But, in the real sense of the term, there was no surprise; for Victor had sufficient warning of an impending attack. The morning sun had revealed him the dense masses of Austrian infantry and glittering squadrons of cavalry, and from afar many sounds rung out clearly in the morning air—the murmur of voices, the pawing of hoofs, the clatter of arms.

One of the most important obligations when detecting a marked change in the situation is to hasten to call the attention of the responsible officer to it. Considering the position that Victor held in the Army of Reserve, he must have been aware of Bonaparte's idea that the enemy was striving to elude him and slip away. The noise in the very early morning, and the appearance of the Austrians under arms at daybreak, were circumstances which should have been speedily reported to Berthier and to the First Consul.

There can be little doubt that it was the thunder of the artillery that gave Bonaparte the first intimation of the battle. If he was in a manner surprised at Marengo, it was owing to one of his lieutenants, who did not hasten to dispel from his mind the idea that the Austrians were escaping from him, when, in the very early hour of the morning the Austrian Army stood revealed to his gaze—even if we ignore the fact that the tumult at an earlier hour, in the dark, could but have indicated the assembly of a large body of troops on the banks of the Bormida.

Victor, who recognised all the importance of the hamlet of Marengo and of the Fontanone brook for the defence, failed in giving to his superiors a sufficiently early warning of what might be expected. That the enemy was about to do something else than retire can be gathered from Coignet's declaration that his regiment was under arms the whole night. And his regiment did not form part of the advanced guard.

Olivier Rivaud, in his report on the battle, expresses the same opinion as Victor, namely, that Melas delayed attacking in the hope that Bonaparte would assume the initiative. This, nevertheless, does not quite accord with the bold decision arrived at at the council of war that was held in Alessandria.

The *Œsterreichische Militärische Zeitschrift*, quoted by De Cugnac, vol. ii, states that the passage of the Bormida was fixed for eight o'clock on the 14th.

General Victor, who commanded the French advanced forces, having made a rough estimate of the enemy's strength, arrived at a conclusion that the whole of the Austrian Army was in the act of crossing the Bormida, intending to attack. He thereupon despatched Captain De Blou, or Deblou, one of Murat's staff officers, to Torre di Garofoli, to warn the First Consul that the enemy was evidently bent on bringing about a decisive battle on the plain.

We should here note that when Victor acknowledges having, from the very early morning no doubt that a battle was impending, and after his having confessed to having beheld the Austrian Army in battle array, the warning sent to the commander-in-chief of what was threatening should have been sent off at an earlier hour. The sun rises at 4.36 on the 14th of June, and Victor acknowledges that with the return of light he saw the Austrian forces under arms.

Victor declares that De Blou made his report to Bonaparte at eight o'clock; if so, his message had so little effect that between nine and ten o'clock that morning we find Bonaparte despatching orders to Lapoype and to Desaix to manoeuvre in such a way as to stop any attempt the Austrians might make to reach Milan or Genova. Lapoype's division being at Ponte Curone at ten o'clock on the morning of the 14th of June, received an order to march on Valenza. The bearer of this order most likely quitted Torre di Garofoli at about 9 a.m., showing, we might well imagine, that no intimation of the coming battle had reached Bonaparte by that hour. The issue of these orders to the two divisional commanders seems strange, for Victor is quite positive that De Blou informed the First Consul precisely at eight o'clock of the enemy's preparations, and warned him that he would have a big and decisive affair during the day.

Bonaparte, who did not dream of a battle for the 14th, seems to have attached little consequence to De Blou's report. He evidently remained in that state of mind for some time, persisting in considering the hypothesis of a retreat on Genova as the most probable contingency. It is always hard to discredit one's sagacity; had he entertained the slightest suspicion of what was really about to happen, we can well imagine how he would have hastened to recall the orders he had just sent to Lapoype and Desaix.

General O'Reilly's column, which had bivouacked on the right bank of the Bormida, commenced at about 8 a.m. to advance on Cascina Pedrabona—at times called Perbona or Pietrabona. Shortly after, it attacked Gardanne's outposts.

The Marquis of Faverges, in his *Extrait de l'Histoire des Guerres Européennes*, writes:—

> We find nowhere set down at what hour the battle commenced; one is led to believe that it was about nine o'clock.

This agrees with the hour given in their reports by Victor, Gardanne, Dampierre, and Olivier Rivaud—all officers who were foremost at the commencement of the battle. Gardanne's report is very short and modest, as becomes a brave man. He states that the previous night the advanced guard bivouacked within cannon-shot distance of the intrenchment, and in that position was attacked on the 14th at nine o'clock.

Kellermann says that it was nine o'clock when his brigade arrived at Marengo, and took post in front and on the left of the village. Pittaluga and Fontana make him bivouac at San Giuliano Vecchio, from which place Murat sent him off to reinforce Victor as the first guns were heard. This would lead us to suppose that the battle began before nine, as Kellermann had to make ready and march from San Giuliano to Marengo. Possibly the order to move to the front had been given before nine, when Victor was making his preparations to meet the impending attack. If he called on Lannes to come to his aid, why should he not have also called up the cavalry?

Moreno says that, having only one issue from the bridgehead, the Austrians took three hours in coming out and forming line of battle. As they set out at about 6 a.m., the attack would not have commenced much before 9 a.m.

Various hours have been given by the generals and principal officers engaged. Lauriston and the Duke of Rovigo say it was at the break of day; Marmont at 6 a.m., Berthier at 7 a.m.; Lannes and Watrin, who were together at Giuliano, at 8 a.m.; Dupont, chief of the staff, gives no hour. The unanimous evidence of Victor and his officers may be taken as coming very near the truth. In the face of this the statement of the Duke of Rovigo is strange reading. He writes:—

> *Nous quittâmes la position de Rivalta; nous marchâmes sur Novi; mais à peine le jour commenqait à poindre que nous entendimes time cannonade redoublée s'ouvrir au loin en arriere de notre droite.* (We

quitted the position of Rivalta; we marched on Novi; but day had barely commenced to break than we heard the sound of a fierce cannonade in the distance, in rear of our right).

Little reliance can be placed on the evidence of some of the principal eye-witnesses of this important battle. Marmont, for one, states that after his conversation with Gardanne near the bridgehead on the evening of the 13th, as given in the previous chapter, he wended his way towards army headquarters; but that a storm and the bad state of the roads prevented his getting there that night. He set out for Torre di Garofoli at daybreak the following morning, and no sooner had he got there, at six o'clock, than the cannonade began to make itself heard.

Now, not only have we the evidence of several of the officers in the fighting line, who positively state that the Austrians attacked at about nine, but Melas's statement that his troops were not put in motion till several hours after daybreak. The Austrian account declares that the crossing of the Bormida was ordered for 8 a.m.; and, though O'Reilly was already across, it does not seem likely that he would have attacked before sufficient troops had had time to cross to be handy to reinforce him if necessary. This would have brought the attack up to about nine.

The words in the Austrian account are:—

Already, at nine in the morning, when the Austrian Army was busy in effecting its deployment and in driving Gardanne's division from Pedrabona and neighbourhood, Captain Ceiwrany made his report.

Marmont goes on to state that a little after his arrival at headquarters, one of General Victor's officers came up to the First Consul and reported a general attack of the enemy—*et lui rendit compte d'une attaque générale de l'ennemi*. Against all this we have the testimony that, far from expecting an attack, Bonaparte at 10 a.m. was issuing orders which would keep Lapoype's and Desaix's divisions, 8,778 men strong, still further from the scene of operations. (Lapoype's division, 3,462 and Boudet's 5,316.)

Evidently Bonaparte ignored the full extent of Melas's attack, and waited at Torre di Garofoli till he could get decisive news of Desaix's return and of Monnier's march from Castel Novo. There can be little doubt that it was Savary who first brought to Bonaparte the news of Desaix's whereabouts. As he had crossed Bruyère on the way, Bonaparte could make sure that his order would be delivered, and that there was nothing now to keep him from going to the battlefield. Before setting out, a little before 11 a.m., he received a message from Victor to the effect that the Austrians were steadily bringing up fresh forces. According to Boudet, his division, having got across the Scrivia, commenced its march on Pozzolo Formigaro at about noon. It had got a mile beyond Rivalta when the order of recall arrived. Now, from Torre di Garofoli to Rivalta is not more than eleven or twelve miles, which distance a rider going at his best pace, and, as the Duke of Rovigo relates, across country, could well cover in an hour. The *aide-de-camp* bearing the order would, under these circumstances, have quitted Bonaparte's headquarters at somewhere about 11 a.m.

In determining the hour at which the Austrians attacked there is a retarding circumstance which has not received sufficient attention. This was the counter-march of Nimptsch's cavalry brigade, the brigade detailed to proceed to Cantalupo. This brigade had already crossed over to the right bank of the Bormida, and when recalled to the left bank must have checked the progress of the troops then in the act of crossing, and thereby caused a certain loss of time in the deployment of the Austrian Army.

Up to the moment when they were attacked by O'Reilly, the French outposts had remained concealed and silent. It would appear that in this initial phase of the battle the French were to blame for having displayed a lack of enterprise, and for not having fallen on the Austrians when in the act of filing out of the bridgehead. The distance between Pedrabona and the Bormida is very short, and it may well be asked, why did Gardanne abstain from punishing the Austrians when they were in a critical position streaming out to assume an attacking formation?

Let us return to Melas. It was about nine in the morning when an unfounded report reached him. This was to the effect that his rear was threatened by a large body of French cavalry which had driven an Austrian squadron out of Acqui. Uneasy for his rear, which Melas believed might have been seriously molested whilst he was engaged with Bonaparte, and not relishing being taken between two fires, he recalled the brigade Nimptsch, which formed part of Elsnitz's cavalry division, made it recross the Bormida and move through Alessandria in the direction of Cantalupo.

By this false move the Austrian commander deprived himself of seventeen squadrons of cavalry. Thus 2,340 men of the very arm of the service on which he counted so much, looking at the level and open nature of the country in which he purposed to give battle, were withdrawn from the field. (On the previous day the hussar regiment of the Archduke Rodolph had been detached to Casale.) In his report of the battle, Melas states that Suchet, who had been advancing at the head of 12,000 men towards Savona and Voltri, had sent detachments in the direction of Acqui in the valley of the Bormida, and that Massena, at the head of 10,000 men, had advanced likewise in that direction on the 13th.

This was one of the many errors made on that memorable day. Melas did not reflect that he could very well have neglected to look after Suchet, and that it was on the field of Marengo that it behoved him to be strong. It was there where the fate of his army was about to be decided. Acqui was sufficiently far off, being twenty miles from Alessandria.

Melas was alarmed without cause, for the forces of Massena and Suchet were still on the Littoral, unable to move for want of bare necessaries.

The situation Massena was in is fully explained by his letter to the First Consul from Finale, 13th of June:—

> Had I on my arrival here found some little artillery and some ammunition, I would have at once set out marching. My position is more difficult than it has yet ever been. I am in want of everything, of absolutely everything.
> I reckon on having within seven or eight days the little artillery and ammunition which are indispensably necessary to me. Then I will march on Asti to join you as soon as possible. I shall have from ten to eleven thousand infantry.
> At this moment I occupy the heights of Savona, Montenotte, Carcare, and Dégo.

In war the commander who neglects to avail himself of the people of the country to bring him information lays himself open to miscalculations and erroneous conceptions. The Austrians, who entertained a great dread of Suchet's column, appear to have made no effort whatever to surround him with emissaries, so as to be able to be thoroughly well informed with regard to his numbers and movements. It may be observed that there was a strong party in Piedmont and Liguria opposed to the French Republic and to the innovations which followed the footsteps of the Revolution.

With a little skill and enterprise there should consequently have been very little difficulty in acquiring accurate intelligence of the movements of the French forces.

★★★★★★

After the defeats which had overtaken the French the Legitimists and enemies of Liberal ideas in Piedmont began to look up. Under the name of religion, they committed many excesses. The Bishop of Asti became a cruel persecutor of the patriots, sacked the municipal palace and the houses of the Jacobins. At Alba, too, the reactionary bands grouped themselves round their bishop, and committed many acts of cruelty. Mondovi and Ceva became the headquarters of several bands; arson and sack were frequent in Fossano, Cherasco, and Ceva.

★★★★★★

What really did occur was this: The cavalry of Suchet's advanced guard, having reached Acqui, the 13th Dragoons attacked a squadron of the Emperor's dragoons commanded by Captain Ceiwrany, which had been detached to watch Suchet, and compelled the squadron to beat a hasty retreat, leaving in their hands forty of their number. This insignificant encounter was badly reported; for Ceiwrany stated that he had been attacked by a large cavalry force followed by infantry. It was on this exaggerated report that Melas was induced to weaken his army at a most inopportune moment.

On the evening of the 13th, Berthier had established his headquarters on the high ground to the west of Cascina Buzana. From that point he had a good view of the movements of both armies.

★★★★★★

This locality is now known as *Regione Trono*, on account of a throne which was erected there for the Empress Josephine when she witnessed the sham fight held on the field of Marengo in 1805, to give her a representation of the actual battle.

★★★★★★

When the Austrian attack commenced, he had sent word to Victor to offer a stubborn resistance; at the same time he sent a report to the First Consul at Torre di Garofoli of what was likely to occur.

It is desirable to form a just idea of the formation of the Republican forces at the commencement of the action. The Austrians had a bridgehead resting on the Bormida, but their advanced posts had passed the night between the Bormida and the French advanced guard, which lay not far from the riverbank. In the early morning Gardanne, with most of the 44th and the 101st half-brigades, was in position at Pedrabona, strengthened by the few guns Victor could dispose of. His orders were to resist as long as possible, and to gain time for the other divisions to get into line.

On Gardanne's left, resting on the Bormida, was Colonel Dampierre with a portion (two or three hundred men) of the 44th half-brigade, and a platoon of riflemen. This detachment had a gun; however, it was useless, there being no ammunition for it.

Ismert, with a squadron of the 11th Hussars, was sent further still to the left, to the Orba and Lemme, to cover the French Army, to watch the enemy's movements, and to harass him.

The second division of Victor's corps, Chambarlhac's, 24th, 43rd, and 96th, had its right resting on Marengo, the centre in front of Spinetta, and the left on the Fontanone brook. Chambarlhac had instructions not to join in the battle without first receiving some definite order. In rear of him and towards the extreme left were the 8th Dragoons and Kellermann's cavalry brigade, which had been sent forward by Murat from San Giuliano Vecchio, possibly before the sound of the first guns was heard. Lannes's corps and part of Murat's cavalry division were still at San Giuliano Vecchio.

John Rivaud's cavalry brigade had marched that morning to Salé. The general had orders to watch the road going to Castel Ceriolo, and to cover the line of retreat leading to Pavia.

A little later Champeaux's cavalry brigade came up from San Giuliano to protect Victor's right flank, and deployed on the plain to the north-west of Marengo.

Gardanne, with the advanced guard, had bivouacked within cannon-shot of the Austrian intrenchment. According to his report he was attacked at nine in the morning. This is fully corroborated by Dampierre, whose words are:—

> The enemy attacked the right at about nine o'clock, and half an hour later fire was opened all along the line.

Gardanne's division, holding Pedrabona, was exposed to a heavy artillery fire. A most terrible fusillade followed, and was kept up with fury by both sides for two hours. O'Reilly, in conformity with the general plan, cleared the front for the troops that were following him, and inclined in the direction of Cascina Stortigliona, to make room for the advanced guard of the central column. This gave the French a breathing time; but it was very short, for soon Haddick's division came in view and commenced to deploy.

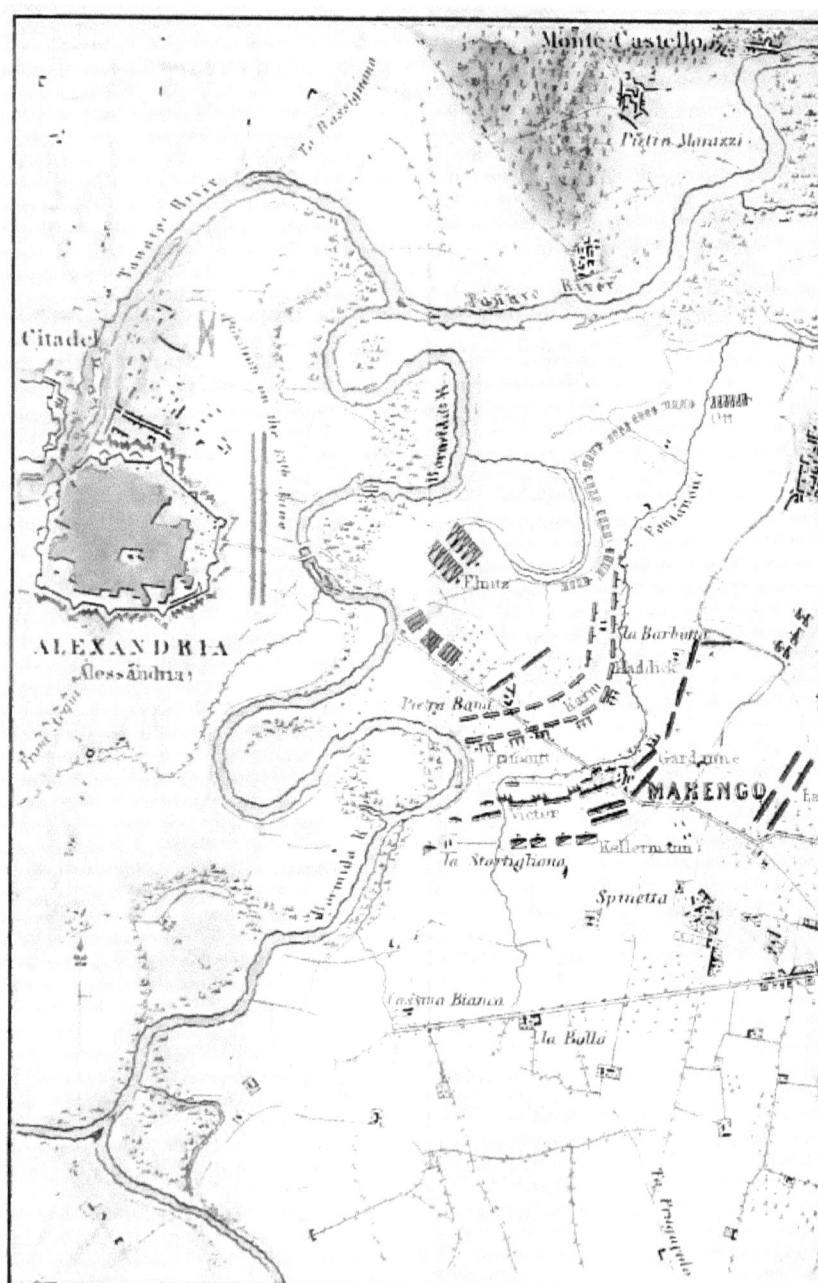

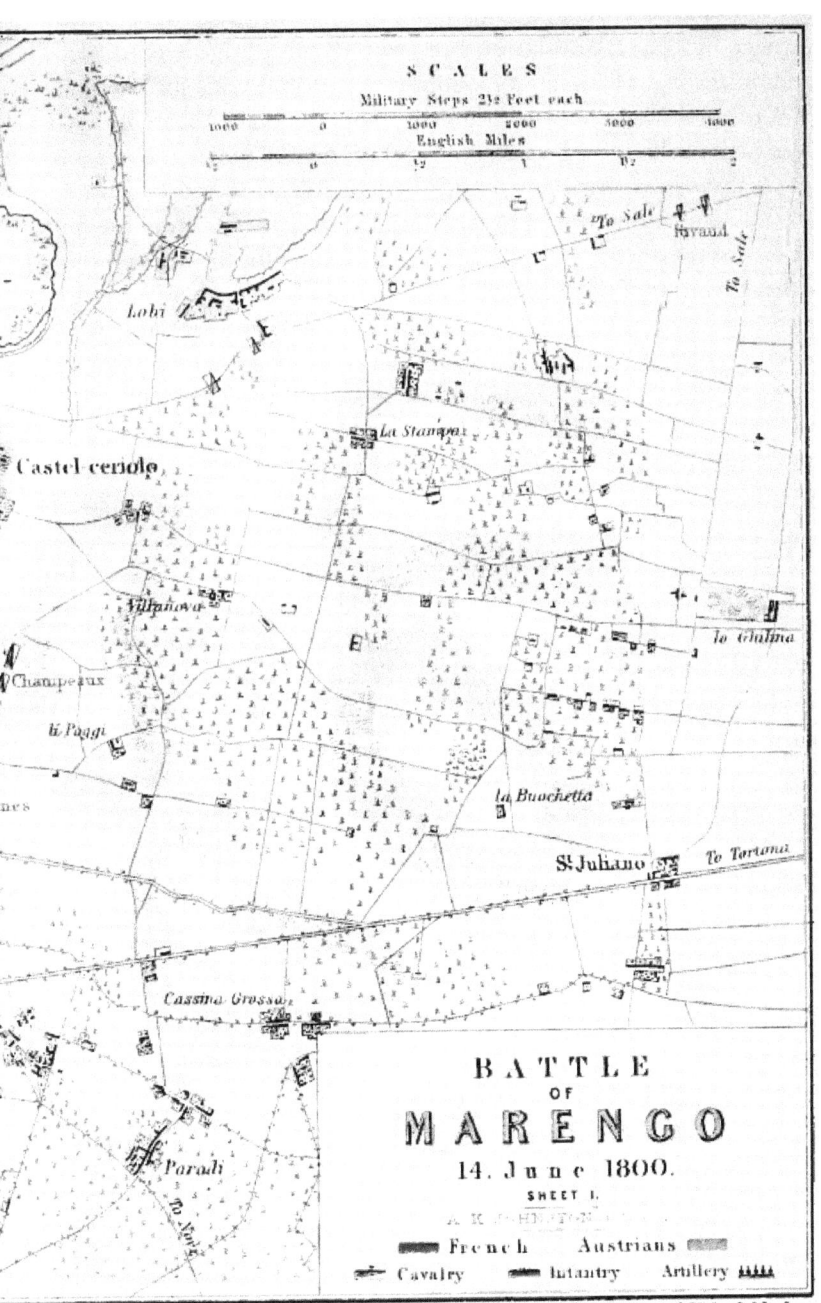

Gardanne endeavoured to obstruct this deployment, and with that object brought a very heavy musketry fire to bear on the enemy, but all to no purpose. Soon attacked in front by many Austrian battalions covered by a battery of sixteen guns, by O'Reilly's brigade on the left, and on the right flank by some squadrons of cavalry, his six battalions had to give way before such greatly superior forces. Victor ordered him to get behind the Fontanone brook, under the protection of some of Chambarlhac's battalions, which he had ordered to move forward.

The Fontanone was an obstacle in itself sufficient to arrest the first efforts of the enemy, and calculated to gain time for the arrival of the other divisions of the French Army.

On Gardanne's left was Adjutant-General Dampierre, to whose detachment had been intrusted the defence of the extreme left. Taking advantage of the configuration of the ground, Dampierre had posted one half of his men in a kind of intrenchment formed by the ditches running round a small cottage that stood on the banks of the Bormida, the remaining half being extended to the right, hidden away in some ravines which protected the soldiers up to their heads.

The Austrians tried to form within musketry range of this detachment, and suffered severely. Dampierre held his ground stoutly during the retreat of the rest of his corps, which took place at about three o'clock, and was not overpowered by the Austrians until seven o'clock in the evening. It was when bombarded by six guns firing case, and surrounded by Nauendorf's hussars and several regiments of infantry, that he found himself compelled to lay down his arms. The detachment was without ammunition or artillery, and all sound of firing in the neighbourhood had died away. The last cartridge having been expended, all further resistance in face of such overwhelming numbers was profitless.

In a letter to General Mathieu Dumas, written on the 16th of June, 1800, Dampierre states that the troops on his right had retreated in the greatest disorder, and that his men when carried away as prisoners had no sooner entered Alessandria than they perceived that fortune was again siding with the French, and that the latter had resumed the mastery.

Early that morning Melas had become alive to all the importance of the position of Marengo, which had been so heedlessly abandoned to the enemy. He recognised how great an error he had committed in not supporting O'Reilly the previous evening. He had simply given away the key of the plain of Marengo, the main issue to the country beyond. The first object, and doubtlessly the most important for the success of the day, was to recover that village, so as to make it a pivot of operations. Accordingly, to repair his mistake of the previous day, Melas issued orders to Haddick to recapture Marengo at all costs.

Notwithstanding the first success gained over Gardanne's division, the Austrians lost the opportunity of getting to the other side of the Fontanone by crossing that marshy stream at the heels of the French. Their remaining on the other side for a deployment, carried out according to all rules, was soon to cost them dear.

It took nearly two hours for Haddick to deploy, form up his division, and post his batteries, and Kaim, who was to support him, was not much smarter. In this manner much precious time was wasted.

When the slow and pedantic deployment of the central Austrian column was completed, the Austrian Army stood in the following order: In first line, on their extreme right, resting on the Bormida, came O'Reilly's brigade; then, on its left, stood Frimont's detachment, which had furnished the advanced guard of the central column; next in order came Haddick's division, which stood opposite to the village of Marengo. Kaim's division was in second line; in reserve were Morzin's grenadier division and the greater portion of Elsnitz's cavalry division. Ott was at that time crossing the Bormida.

Bonaparte had sent orders to Lannes and to Murat to proceed from San Giuliano Vecchio to the assistance of Victor, an order which had already been anticipated. Lannes was at that time marching across the plain, making for Cascina Barbotta, where the right of Victor's corps stood, which was seriously menaced.

Shortly after 10 a.m., the first line of the Austrian Army, under the protection of five batteries, advanced against Gardanne's division. Haddick was keen to make up for lost time, and attacked as soon as the deployment was completed. At the head of Bellegarde's brigade he advanced on Marengo, but he was received by the French, who were posted around the village and in rear of the Fontanone brook, with a most violent musketry fire and some rounds of case. Rivaud, who had been posted on the left of the village, in a bend of the brook, took the Austrians in reverse.

Undaunted, they continued to advance up to the Fontanone, and Haddick was on the point of crossing the brook when a small reserve came to the aid of the French. This support arrived very opportunely, for Gardanne's men were hard pressed. Haddick several times tried to get across the Fontanone, but that insignificant and muddy stream, swollen by the previous day's rain, which art itself could never have designed, continued to shelter the French position. Forming as it did a re-entering bend in front of Marengo, it enabled the French posted in the village and on either flank of it to pour a converging fire on the attacking columns. Recognising the futility of his efforts, Haddick had just given the order for his troops to withdraw when he fell mortally wounded. Deprived of their chief, the troops fell into disorder.

Kaim with his division was following close on Haddick. Having protected the retreat of the troops of the first line, which their defeat had put into confusion, he renewed the attack, but with no better result. His battalions, smitten at point-blank range, suffered severely without being able to gain ground. At about eleven o'clock Kaim found it necessary to withdraw his men.

Reinforced by Melas, he returned to the attack, his well-served artillery playing great havoc amongst the French. Chambarlhac's division, which was posted on Victor's right, was already giving way, when, at about eleven o'clock, Lannes was seen approaching with Watrin's division.

Fighting is dreadfully uphill work when there is an insufficiency of men, and it is discouraging in the extreme for the soldier to find himself overmatched and outnumbered. When Lannes came up on Victor's right rear, the battle was continued under more even conditions. Still the French had in line Victor's and Lannes's troops, at the most from 15,000 to 16,000 men, with which to keep 30,000 Austrians in check, and these had to bear the brunt of the battle until the reserves could arrive from Torre di Garofoli and Rivalta. French pluck made up for deficiency in numbers. So obstinate was the resistance, that for a long time the Austrians, notwithstanding all their efforts, could not dislodge them from Marengo.

Lannes, with Watrin's division, had bivouacked in front of San Giuliano. On the morning of the 14th, as has been said, the division marched two leagues across the plain to come and reinforce Victor's right. Watrin states that he deployed his division between Spinetta and Marengo, the right extending in the direction of Castel Ceriolo, and the left being a little to the left of the Alessandria-Tortona road. The 28th and 40th were kept in reserve on the left of Spinetta.

As to the 6th Light and the 22nd, deployed between Marengo and Castel Ceriolo, these two corps drove back impetuously a numerous body of the enemy, infantry and cavalry, which had already made rapid progress on that side. They rushed at the enemy, threw him into great disorder, and pushed him back behind the Fontanone—Lannes says as far the banks of the Bormida, where the cannon from the bridgehead compelled his troops to fall back out of range. (Lannes states that this occurred after Victor had been fighting for two hours It must, therefore, have been 11 a.m.) These two regiments, though exposed to a murderous fire, continued to hold their ground for a considerable time.

As the enemy in great strength moved on Castel Ceriolo and deployed a deep column on Watrin's right, Watrin moved up a battalion of the 22nd in that direction, so as to support the 6th Light, then on the point of being turned by the enemy, who were outflanking the French right. General Lannes had brought up the 28th Regiment with the same intent. At that time the 40th, on the main road of Marengo, was making head against several charges of cavalry.

It has been said by eye-witnesses that the Austrians attacked feebly and slowly, and that it was this that enabled Victor to hold his ground as long as he did. For the French it was, of the highest moment to defend the mean brook on their front, for on that alone depended the timely arrival of Monnier's and Boudet's divisions, and the bringing together of the scattered divisions for a combined effort. Though suffering severe losses, the Republicans made a vigorous resistance, which reflected great honour on the troops. Of the Austrians Victor says that the enemies, drunk with *eau de vie* and despairing in their position, fought like lions.

Fully to realise the nature of the contest, we should not overlook the description of the weapons with which the troops were armed a century ago. The arm of the infantry at that time was the flintlock muzzle-loading musket, an arm which was not only very poorly sighted, and of very limited range, but which from the materials of the cartridges after a certain use became difficult to load. In this very battle we have the evidence of Captain Coignet, who states that from constant firing the muskets fouled to such an extent that the cartridges could not be rammed home. He adds that the soldiers were compelled to make water in the barrels to free them of deposit from combustion.

Soldiers in the old days were enjoined to trust to the bayonet rather than to powder, and when the bayonet could be used it was strongly recommended that not a shot should be fired.

Not only were the range and accuracy of the firearms very poor in those days; but the troops were trained to move with rigid precision in close formation, and did not turn cover to profitable advantage. Troops attacking under such conditions were liable to suffer serious losses.

Disquieted by the stubbornness of the defence, Melas determined to attempt a further effort. At about noon he ordered Pilatti with his cavalry brigade to find a passage across the Fontanone between Marengo and Stortigliona, so as to attack and turn the French left. Pilatti was in this manner to draw the attention of the French to their left, whilst Bellegarde and Nairn made a fresh effort to carry Marengo. With the greatest difficulty Pilatti got some squadrons to tread their way across the marshy brook above Marengo.

Kellermann had been posted in the morning not far from Marengo village and on its left. His brigade consisted of the—

2nd Cavalry Regiment	182 sabres.
6th " "	340 "
20th " "	280 "
	802 "

With him, and to the right of his brigade, were the 8th Dragoons.

The Austrian horsemen, under cover of a small wood which partially concealed their movements, crossed the Fontanone one by one and deployed in two lines in a field. Kellermann was quick in detecting Pilatti's intention. Without losing time he sent the dragoons forward, and made ready to support them with his brigade, which was drawn up in line. The dragoons swooped down on the Austrian squadrons, which they overthrew; when in their turn they were assailed by the Austrian supports and driven back. Kellermann gave them time to clear his front and rally behind his line; he then went headlong with his brigade, charged the Austrian cavalry, and drove it back to the Fontanone, where many found their death. Others were captured, and only a very small number were able to effect their escape.

This charge took place near La Stortigliona, to the south of a small house which bears the name of Cavalla Rotta. Tradition has it that the house derives its denomination from the defeat of the Austrian cavalry—*rotta della cavalleria Austriaca*.

An Austrian account says:—

These dragoons once broken, in disarray and at a fast gallop, made for the brook, which was very deep. Men and horses fell into it pell-mell. Those who did not perish in this frightful disorder were sabred or taken prisoners. Only a very small number of men were sufficiently fortunate to be able to regain the opposite bank.

The two regiments, the Emperor's and Karaczay's dragoons, suffered heavily.

Kellermann's bold counterattack succeeded for the moment in holding the enemy in check on the French left. The position in which Pilatti placed his cavalry was extremely risky. Formed with a deep brook in rear, one which had allowed the horsemen to cross only one by one, the slightest reverse would inevitably bring about a disaster; and so, it did.

The retreat of Haddick's line, Kaim's vain efforts to carry Marengo, and the orders to Pilatti to attack the French left occurred at about the same time. It was nearly at that time that Lannes arrived on the battlefield. The defeat of Pilatti's cavalry and the arrival of Lannes inspired the French with confidence.

Melas has been credited with having thrown nearly the whole of his army upon the head of Bonaparte's echelon so as to strive to crush his divisions in detail. There is nothing, however, to support this intention of his, for on the morning of the 14th he was not a bit better informed than his adversary; the want of compactness in the French forces was totally unknown to him.

Moreno declares that the plan arranged by the Austrian staff was for the Austrians to outstrip the French right wing, to attack it with vigour, to drive it back in the direction of Stortigliona, and in that manner to render themselves masters of the Tortona road. (Gennaro Moreno, *Trattato di Storia Militare, vol.* ii.). He states that this plan had to be abandoned owing to the late arrival of Ott's corps on the battlefield; and that on that account it was changed into an attack of the French left.

There is, however, nothing to support these statements. For, had it been Melas's intention to commence by attacking the French right, he would have made Ott's force much stronger than it was; and that corps would have been sent across the Bormida and through the single egress of the bridgehead first, having the longest way to march. In fact, the course of the contest gives no evidence of this intention to attack the French right.

The thunder of the guns and the rattle of the musketry went on without intermittence, and awakened echoes all along the banks of the Fontanone. Though exposed to the murderous fire of forty guns, the French still held their position, and showed no sign of giving way.

It was now about noon, and up to that moment the French had not lost a foot of ground. The Austrians were taking steps for delivering a fresh attack, and for one hour there was a cessation of fire. At 1 p.m. their artillery reopened fire, if possible, with more energy, and Gardanne's division was attacked by O'Reilly. The French strove to stem the torrent which was about to burst through their line, but the ammunition began to fail, and the division was driven back on Marengo.

Kaim, covered by the fire of eighty guns, now directed a third attack, supported by five battalions of Lattermann's grenadiers. The troops were directed to carry the Fontanone under cover of a very heavy artillery fire. A small portion of the Archduke Joseph's regiment waded across the brook and reached the further side. Chambarlhac's division, posted on the left of Marengo, took them in flank, but the Austrians succeeded in making their footing good. Their engineers with great difficulty managed to throw over some small trestle bridges, and Lamarsaille with great promptitude posted his guns so as to command the locality and by canister fire to sweep the approaches and pave the way for the passage of the other troops.

Rivaud, who commanded Victor's last reserves, marched against the assailants, and was on the point of precipitating them into the brook, when he and many of his men were smitten by the heavy fire of the Austrian guns. The French having been checked, Lattermann's grenadiers profited by this advantage, rushed forward, and carried Marengo.

Rivaud, covered with blood, hereupon put himself at the head of the 43rd half-brigade, charged the grenadiers, and drove them clean out of the village. He could do no more; for, after leaving the shelter of the village and coming into the open, he was stopped by the enemy's artillery and musketry, and soon the grenadiers were again masters of Marengo.

Of all natural fortifications, villages are the most difficult to carry. To commence with, to deprive the enemy of their protection the assailant tries to set them on fire with a few shells, a process which very seldom meets with the desired success. Round shot do not succeed any better in driving the defenders out, for they soon find shelter behind the ruins of the houses. A fusillade can even do less damage. These kinds of attack are very deadly. It is well known that it requires the fire of artillery, much time and much blood to carry a well-defended village which has baffled all attempts to set it on fire.

In his report Rivaud makes it 2 p.m. when he led his last charge. After this the Austrians, now masters of Marengo, crossed the Fontanone in many places, and deployed to the left of the village under the protecting fire of eighty guns. Kellermann states that, at about the same time, being exposed to a murderous fire without the support of infantry, and threatened by a column of 3,000 cavalry preceded by numerous artillery, he felt himself compelled to retire.

Marengo and its few buildings, as well as the Fontanone brook, were important points on which the Austrians had concentrated their efforts, with the object of dislodging the French, and thus opening a way for the recovery of their communications. The village of Marengo had been taken and retaken several times in succession; the victors and the vanquished disputed this ensanguined post hand-to-hand. The defence was stout; the men beheld their ranks thinning without any emotion of terror; they closed in as fast as their comrades fell, and still dared the death that menaced them. The continuance and length of the attacks, however, exhausted both the means and the forces of the French soldiers.

It has been mentioned that the brook, which covered the front of the French Army, had presented a very serious obstacle to the deployment of the Austrians. Possibly, deeming it a very trifling impediment, or not expecting to fight on their side of it, they had not prepared anything to facilitate its crossing, and for a certain time found themselves massed in the ground between the brook and the Bormida. Once a temporary bridge was thrown athwart the Fontanone, the Austrian grenadiers crossed over and drove Victor back in great disorder into the plain, when they made first for Spinetta and afterwards for San Giuliano.

This would have been the moment for launching the Austrian cavalry forward, so as to turn to full account the disorder which reigned amongst the French, and by a general charge to scatter them completely over the plain. The Austrian staff, however, had not employed the cavalry economically, and at the most propitious moment it was not forthcoming.

By this time O'Reilly, having crossed the Stortigliona, had advanced by La Bolla on the Tortona road. Nevertheless, Kellermann, who was posted in that part of the field, maintained a bold front. By his attitude he imposed on the enemy, who dreaded to display too much enterprise.

The village of Marengo may well be considered as the centre of the battle-ground, for the whole of the Austrian efforts were directed, as we have already seen, to oust the French from that point. This, by facilitating the forward movement of the two wings of the Austrian

Army, contributed to dislodging the French entirely. The several attacks on the village, nevertheless, held the troops on the wings in suspense, when they might have come into play at an earlier hour. They would have been better employed in pushing forward to attack beyond Marengo the troops which were destined by the French to support those engaged in holding the village. These supports should have been attacked and destroyed by cavalry and artillery.

The remnants of Victor's corps, the divisions of Gardanne and Chambarlhac, exposed to the fire of fifty guns, could barely hold out any longer. For two hours Victor's corps had resisted single-handed the repeated and dashing onsets of the Austrians, who were continually bringing up fresh troops to the attack. His divisions had fought the longest, and he had lost twice as many men as Lannes. Rivaud's brigade alone had suffered as much as the whole of Watrin's division. Unable to resist any longer the efforts of Haddick's and Kaim's troops, supported as they were by their reserves, Victor was obliged to abandon the village after it had been several times lost and retaken. The Austrians then issuing from Marengo took a firm footing on the plain.

Victor had to go nearly to San Giuliano, for a distance of two leagues or thereabout, before he could find a point of support. The Austrians brought such a powerful artillery fire to bear on the retreating troops that one might have expected to see at every moment the retreat degenerating into a flight.

Kellermann, however, withdrew his cavalry by alternate troops, and kept the Austrian horsemen from charging Victor's disordered divisions. Retiring in this manner, Kellermann's cavalry brigade covered the retreat until threatened by a large column of 2,000 or 3,000 cavalry preceded by a numerous artillery. The brigade suffered heavily, and on reaching the extremity of the plain did not muster more than 150 troopers. To it afterwards were added a platoon of the 1st Dragoons and two squadrons of the 8th. Kellermann states:—

> My brigade formed line, extended to the right and left of the main road. Always exposed to a deadly artillery fire, covering the infantry, finding for it opportunities for rallying, it withdrew by platoons at a walk, turning about from time to time, and not suffering the enemy to capture a single prisoner in this part of the field. Under trying circumstances, it displayed a cool courage which, whilst recognising danger and death, meets them with firmness.

Victor's extreme left was protected by a squadron of the 11th Hussars, which was likewise compelled to fall back before the superior numbers of the enemy. The Austrians assailed this squadron on all sides, but were never able to break it. After a while it became incapacitated for rendering any further service to the infantry, and had to retire to San Giuliano. The 12th Chasseurs were also in this part of the field, and charged the enemy several times, to prevent their cavalry pressing and attacking the flank of Victor's retiring columns.

General Baron Quiot, who was Victor's *aide-de-camp* at Marengo, wrote:—

> The French carried out their movement of retreat with all the order which it was possible to maintain in such a critical moment, the corps which were in the centre checkerwise being supported by close columns in mass ready to form squares if needed: our feeble cavalry, likewise, on the wings, seconded by the infantry columns, drove off such corps as pressed on too close, and compelled them to follow at a slow pace. The Austrians consequently contented themselves by pounding us with their artillery.

Crossard states:—

> We continued to push the enemy before us, and we saw him evacuate Marengo as its wings were turned.

It was possibly at that time that Murat told the First Consul, "General, it is time for us to retire; there is the Austrian cavalry turning our flanks."

All agree that the defeat would have been irretrievable had the Austrian cavalry taken up the pursuit.

The French losses on their left were heavy, for the Austrians pressed the Republicans steadily back, halting from time to time to open fire with a battery of fifteen guns. After a time, the squares mowed down by this artillery fire broke up, and the plain was covered with fugitives. The French had not far to go, for they rallied at San Giuliano.

On the Austrian left, Ott, who had been sent by Melas towards Salé, arrived at Castel Ceriolo, and formed his troops between that village and Barbotta. Astonished to find no French in the direction of Castel Ceriolo, but hearing the thunder of fierce cannonade on his right, he conceived, notwithstanding the orders he had received, that it was his duty to turn in the direction of the firing. He therefore made a change of front to his right, came into contact with Lannes, and threatened to sweep his line from end to end.

Lannes made head against the attacks delivered by Ott. But, as his numbers did not permit him to extend as far as Castel Ceriolo, he wheeled back a portion on his right so as to confront the enemy. To stay the advance of the Austrians, Champeaux delivered two charges. The enemy's cavalry was driven back, but the Austrian infantry continued to press forward, menacing to outflank Lannes and take his line in reverse.

Dense smoke obscured the glitter of bayonet and lance, and the groans of the wounded were silenced by the roar of the many guns.

The French still held their ground, but all the reserves Victor and Lannes could count upon had joined the fighting line, and by this time the ammunition had begun to run short.

Counting from 8 a.m. to 1 p.m., the battle had by this time lasted some five hours. During the first two hours Gardanne's division alone, barely 3,000 strong, with Kellermann's cavalry, had borne the brunt. Afterwards, by degrees, all of Victor's and Lannes's troops had come into line, and these 13,000 men had repulsed repeated attacks made by 16,000 infantry, supported by more than 4,000 horsemen. Ott also was pressing on the French right with 7,000 infantry and some six squadrons.

On the French right their troops took and retook several positions under a heavy fire, until Lannes, finding his forces almost surrounded by the enemy's troops (which had broken the centre and compelled the left to give way entirely), felt compelled to order the retreat. The troops were to retire, keeping in line with the left of the army.

The Austrians continued to assert their superiority with a terrible artillery fire, their line being steadily strengthened by fresh batteries and battalions. Lannes acknowledges that after a five-hours' cannonade and heavy musketry fire the enemy broke the centre and thus compelled Victor to retire. Also, that at this moment, seeing himself nearly surrounded by the troops which had overcome the centre, and with the whole of the left in full retreat, he ordered his division to retire.

Uncovered on his left by Victor's retreat, there was nothing left for him to do but to fall back. Though his corps was without guns, and he had only a few squadrons of cavalry for protecting his right, Lannes manoeuvred with great deliberation under a most murderous fire. He withdrew slowly by echelon; he repelled every charge; and kept his troops from being broken. The courage and the devotion of their leaders were beyond praise. The division lost ground at the rate of a quarter of a league per hour, but this admirable retreat cost Lannes cruel losses.

Danican, though showing great animosity against Bonaparte, does not deny that the French retired methodically, disputing every inch of the ground.

Early on the forenoon of the 14th, Bonaparte, as has been already mentioned, heard from Berthier and Victor that a battle was imminent. The sound of artillery also soon bore out this intimation. Entertaining no longer any doubts about what was happening, he sent *aides-de-camp* and other officers towards Rivalta to search for Desaix, and to convey him orders for the immediate return of Boudet's division, which was to march by the shortest way to the battlefield. Bonaparte himself remained at Torre di Garofoli, anxious not to miss an early reply. Late in the forenoon one of his *aides-de-camp* returning from Rivalta brought the welcome news that Desaix had been found, but that various circumstances made it probable that Boudet's division would not reach the battlefield much before 5 p.m.

This news reassured Bonaparte. The Consular Guard and Monnier's division had already marched in the direction of San Giuliano Vecchio, and, mounting his horse, he hastened after them. (Petit states that the First Consul mounted his horse at 11 a.m.) The last news he had from Victor, sent a little before 11 a.m., stated that the enemy was continually deploying fresh forces.

In his narrative of the campaign of Marengo, trooper Petit states that the enemy's dispositions were not fully known at headquarters till towards the latter part of the morning; *aide-de-camp* after *aide-de-camp* had been apprising the Consul of the enemy's steps; that Bonaparte mounted his horse at eleven o'clock. Apparently, the Guard followed him, for he remarks:—

> Both cannon and musketry, on certain points, began by this time to be heard.... By twelve o'clock we were well convinced we had the whole of the Austrian forces against us.

★★★★★★

Petit's account is somewhat incongruous; he narrates how the Consular Guard he belonged to slept at San Giuliano on the 13th; further on he shows it was with the headquarters on the morning of the 14th. Bonaparte on the night of the 13th had rested at Torre di Garofoli and not at San Giuliano; we imagine that his Guard bivouacked where the headquarters were.

★★★★★★

Evidently it was only at about eleven o'clock that Bonaparte detected the seriousness of the attack. Monnier's departure from Torre di Garofoli shows this; for it was at about that hour that he ordered Monnier to march, and that he sent messengers to recall the detached divisions of Lapoype on the north and of Boudet on the south. Desaix was reached at about 1 p.m., but the messengers did not come up with Lapoype before 6 p.m.

Monnier's division was one of the two assigned to Desaix after Montebello; but it did not proceed to Rivalta on the 13th, for it passed the night at Torre di Garofoli. Monnier set out from his bivouac at Torre di Garofoli between 11 a.m. and noon, and had to march eight kilometres (five miles) to the spot where the French and Austrians were contending. He reached this, according to his report, at 2 p.m.

Bonaparte appeared on the battlefield at the commencement of the retreat, and consequently at the most critical moment. On arriving he found his left wing broken, and his right, though seriously menaced, still withdrawing in good order and showing a bold front to the enemy.

With his infallible intuition he judged in an instant what was the state of the battle. The point was to prevent the Austrians from overreaching the French position on the Tortona road, and fraying for themselves a passage to the Mincio. This could be secured in two ways, either by offering a stout resistance on the Tortona road itself, or by taking such a position on the right as would threaten to take any advancing Austrian troops in flank.

The First Consul judged that the first plan was hopeless, but that the second was by no means so. From the course of the contest the majority of Melas's troops had gathered in the direction of Spinetta. On the other-flank the opposition was by no means so strong, and Lannes could almost hold his own. Consequently, the right was the best side to reinforce, and the one where the greatest hope lay of doing something effective. It was not a case of abandoning the line of retreat, but of adopting an alternative one.

Bonaparte feared lest Ott, by extending on the French right, should take the whole of his line of battle in reverse, and cut off his communications with Salé, which place was only guarded by Rivaud with 600 sabres. It was on this account that Monnier was directed to proceed to Castel Ceriolo, with orders to seize the village and to hold it. The occupation of that post the First Consul believed would disengage Lannes, might oblige the enemy to halt, prevent his pressing vigorously against the retiring left, and might give rise to some favourable chance of resuming the offensive, or, at all events, might gain time for Desaix's arrival.

Monnier's division arrived on the field about the time when Bellegarde and Ott were on the point of overpowering Watrin. It advanced in the unoccupied space between Lannes's right and Castel Ceriolo. Carra Saint Cyr, at the head of 700 men of the 19th Light, formed in column of attack, moved on Castel Ceriolo, and carried that village with little opposition. Schilt, at the same time, with the 70th half-brigade, threatened to take the Austrian line in reverse. (The 72nd belonging to this division was held back in reserve.) The French pressed forward with vigour, and the Austrians, unable to withstand their onset, were driven back on to the swamps in front of the Bormida. At that time the French left was already in retreat.

Dupont describes this phase of the battle thus:—

> But on our right, finding ourselves threatened by a corps which was extending on the side of Castel Ceriolo, we abandoned Marengo and took up a position in rear of that village. . . . Monnier's division, which had been encamped at Garofoli, then reached the battlefield. The 19th Light and the 78th half-brigade, under the orders of Carra Saint Cyr and Schilt, marched on the right, and recaptured a portion of the ground which we had abandoned.

This attack reduced the pressure on Lannes's right. But Ott sent Vogelsang with five battalions of his second line to recapture the village. The two French regiments, surrounded both in the village and on the plain, after fighting lustily for an hour, being unsupported, and finding themselves the last on the battlefield, retired in good order on Torre di Garofoli. They moved across vineyards, the vines protecting them from the action of the cavalry.

According to the Austrian account, it was the regiment of Stuart which attacked Castel Ceriolo, and drove the French out of it.

Jomini questions the expediency of sending Monnier's reserve division to occupy Castel Ceriolo. On this point he is not in accordance with Mathieu Dumas, and the greatest portion of the historians. Lannes was not strong enough to occupy that important post as he deployed, and when Monnier received his orders to move on Castel Ceriolo, Victor was hard pressed. In this critical state of affairs any other officer might have reinforced the left wing, and not the right, arguing that to protect Lannes's retreat was not so important a matter as to arrest the flight of Victor's troops. The occupation of Castel Ceriolo proved indeed fortunate, whether it was the result of insight or of luck. By reinforcing his right, Bonaparte stayed the pursuit of his left wing, and, what was of far greater importance, he gained by this measure time for Desaix to arrive on the battlefield.

The battle at that time resolved itself into a purely defensive action. It was necessary to gain time and to prevent the Austrians from overlapping the French position, with the object of opening themselves a way to Piacenza. All offensive action had already become impossible by reason of the inferiority of the French and the disorder reigning in their ranks; nothing remained to be done but to draw the enemy's attention to their left flank, indirectly preventing any brisk action on their right. The course of the contest and Victor's vigorous resistance at Marengo had drawn a very large portion of the Austrian troops towards La Stortigliona. On the opposite flank, about Castel Ceriolo, they were not so numerous that Lannes could not keep them in countenance and still offer a stout resistance. Every consideration, therefore, showed that it was the Austrian left against which the reserves could act with the greatest effect.

It was at about this time (2 p.m.), when Watrin had been instructed to drive Bellegarde back, Victor to prevent Kaim from debouching from Marengo, and Monnier to carry Castel Ceriolo, that Bonaparte, in the hope of arresting Ott's advance, and of relieving the pressure on Lannes, flung forward the 800 or 900 grenadiers of the Consular Guard.

These orders only partially attained their object. The Consular Guard formed in column at deploying distance, and, preceded by a line of skirmishers, advanced along the plain between Li Poggi and Villanova. Ott made Lobkowitz's dragoons charge it, but the Guard speedily formed square, planted its guns, poured several rounds of canister on the dragoons, and made them turn about. A portion of Champeaux's brigade pursued the dragoons to clear the way for the Guard, which then continued its forward movement. Champeaux's brigade in its turn was attacked in flank by Spleny, and obliged to beat a hasty retreat. Gottesheim then advanced against the Guard, and attacked it with Spleny's Hungarian regiment and a battalion of Froelich's, supported by a formidable artillery.

The Guard had deployed and held out for forty minutes, and was only shaken and broken by Frimont, who charged it in rear at the head of a few squadrons of hussars. But though their formation was broken, and they had left 258 of their number on the ground, the Consular Guard held together, and, fighting all the time, managed to gain Poggi. Providence always watches over the brave, and all that Frimont could secure was a few unserviceable guns. The Austrian account states that this occurred at 1 p.m., but, as it relates that the advance of the Consular Guard occurred subsequently to the arrival of Monnier's division on the scene of action, which the latter general fixes at 2 p.m., there must be some error in this. The hour given in the bulletin of the 15th of June, 3 p.m., appears much more correct. According to the same narrative the Consular Guard was broken and almost destroyed. It is very unfortunate in this conflict of opinion that De Cugnac has not been able to discover any report made by the officer who commanded the Guard.

The foot grenadiers of the Consular Guard advanced against the enemy, marching with the same steadiness and precision with which they had been previously beheld on the parade-ground. Without the support of cavalry, they were left to experience the brunt of a victorious army. Charged repeatedly by cavalry, fusilladed by infantry at fifty paces' distance, they remained undaunted; formed in a hollow square, they surrounded their colours and their wounded, and after having exhausted all their ammunition fell back slowly. Many brave men had fallen, mown down by the Austrian guns and musketry, meeting death with rare stolidity in the blinding heat of that June day. Patiently they had endured all things, and failed to reach the goal.

Marmont, who should have known, writes all that has been said and written of a change of front left back, of this post of Castel Ceriolo, held during the whole of the battle, with the object of issuing therefrom on the enemy's rear at the moment of the retreat, is pure supposition and invention conceived after the events:—

> In retiring the army kept the same direction as it had followed in the advance—that of the main road, withdrawing in good order.

It was owing to the heroic conduct of the Consular Guard that Monnier's troops had time to arrive at Castel Ceriolo. With regard to the tenacity displayed by the Consular Guard on this occasion, the illustrious Italian historian Botta remarks:—

> I know not whether I ought most to laud their prowess or condemn Elsnitz's incapacity. But certain it is that the German general, although he had hemmed them in on every side, was never able to break them; for either he did not do all that he ought to have done, or the nine hundred did more than could be deemed possible.

A matter which gave rise to a good deal of discussion was the best formation to be adopted by the infantry to withstand cavalry. Two of Monnier's battalions, of the 72nd, surrounded by a large body of cavalry, received it in line; the two front ranks firing to their front, whilst the third, having faced about, fired directly to their rear. After having executed several charges, the enemy's cavalry cleared off, not having succeeded in breaking the French infantry.

To save the troops from the swarms of Mamelukes, they had been formed in squares at the Battle of the Pyramids, and other actions in Egypt, and Bonaparte had brought back from Egypt a sort of predilection for squares. This formation has two radical defects. One defect, and the principal one, is that it seriously diminishes the firing front. The other is the difficulty experienced in marching in square. At Marengo the Consular Guard was formed into a large square. The men behaved with great courage, and repelled many attacks delivered by the Austrian cavalry. The square, Jomini states, was eventually broken, and no wonder, for it was attacked by all the three arms.

The merits of the two formations for withstanding cavalry do not appear to have been settled by the events of that day. What is certain is that during the greater part of the nineteenth century the rule was for infantry to receive cavalry drawn up in square and not in line. Possibly preference was given to the square on account of the Consular Guard having changed its formation to resist the Austrian infantry. It was after they had deployed that General Frimont charged them in rear with a body of hussars, managed to get the best of them, and compelled the corps to commence its retreat on Poggi.

At Waterloo, in the last of his battles, at the close of the struggle, Napoleon formed four battalions of the Guard in four squares, and made them fall back slowly in the same formation which the Consular Guard had assumed at Marengo. Behind these four squares he hoped to rally his army; but it was then too late. When the French were rapidly breaking up, these four living redoubts of brave soldiers alone maintained a hopeless struggle, and stood at bay against two victorious armies. They were charged over and over again, but they repulsed more than one fierce attack of cavalry. Their heroic bravery was no proof against overwhelming numbers; and, hemmed in on all sides, they were at last overpowered. It was with such noble efforts that that sanguinary battle was brought to a close. Much heroism had been displayed by the French on that ill-fated 18th of June, but possibly none outshone that of the old veterans of the Guard.

Not sufficient importance has been accorded to the position assigned by Bonaparte to the Consular Guard, and to the effect resulting from the bravery displayed by that corps, to the time it gained for the arrival of reinforcements and, in short, to the share it could claim in the day's glory. The intrepidity of the Guard stopped the intended wheel of the Austrian left wing, and allowed the troops of Monnier's division to arrive from Torre di Garofoli and to cover Lannes's right, already outflanked by Kaim. Monnier's division was for a time surrounded by the enemy; but leaning on the unshaken square of the Guards, Carra Saint Cyr and Schilt approached Castel Ceriolo and took part in the battle.

This occupation of Castel Ceriolo had considerable influence on the future course of the action. As had happened with Marengo the previous night, the Austrians became alive to the importance of Castel Ceriolo only after they had lost it. Their losing it and having to recapture it was a gain of time for the French.

Melas in his report states:—

> A fresh and decisive assault by Marshal Lieutenant Ott was sufficient to recapture from the enemy the lost place. The enemy showed but little resistance, and retired in haste and disorder all along the line.

With regard to what happened there it must be confessed that the accounts given by Bonaparte, by the Austrians, and by Carra Saint Cyr, are very contradictory. Bonaparte had an object in denying the French retreat: that was to foster the belief that the retreat formed part of a settled plan with Castel Ceriolo as a pivot of manoeuvre. Carra Saint Cyr, writing to the minister of war on the 21st of October, 1800, states:—

> At the Battle of Marengo, at the head of 700 men of the 19th Light, I carried the village of Ceriolo in face of the enemy's army, at a moment when our army was effecting its retreat; I carried

out mine in good order, supported only by the 70th of the line.

The officers of Carra Saint Cyr's brigade wrote that:—

> They had started in the morning for Torre di Garofoli, where they had spent the night. On their reaching the battlefield they had been directed on Castel Ceriolo. After having captured the village and defended it for some time against the Austrian Light Infantry, seeing that the plain on their left had been entirely abandoned by the French, and finding themselves the last left on the battlefield, they quitted Castel Ceriolo, and went back to Torre di Garofoli.

Monnier's account is as follows:—

> Our attack disengaged the right, but the enemy, which had reinforced its centre, having obliged the troops who supported our left to retire, our two columns found themselves surrounded in the village and in the plain. They defended themselves with vigour, and the enemy could never overcome them. After having so resisted for an hour, not having been reinforced, they disengaged themselves, and effected their retreat in the very best order on San Giuliano, where the army was rallying.

De Brossier writes:—

> General Monnier's division succeeded in breaking through the Austrian line, and, under the protection of the brigade under General Champeaux's orders, in effecting its retreat on San Giuliano, when the entire army was joining Boudet's division, which, led by General Desaix, was arriving at that point.

Mathieu Dumas makes out that all the attacks of the Austrians were unsuccessful, that they could not recapture the village. The above evidence, however, is sufficiently convincing. It shows that Carra Saint Cyr complied with the movement of the rest of the army, and retired in the direction of San Giuliano. Jomini states that Bonaparte purposely left Carra Saint Cyr in Castel Ceriolo, but this is evidently contrary to the Austrian account.

Notwithstanding the discordant statements of the operations of Monnier's division at Marengo, the evidence goes far to prove that a part of the division (Carra Saint Cyr's brigade) resisted for a certain time the attacks delivered by Ott's light infantry against Castel Ceriolo, and that it afterwards followed the movement of retreat of the

French left and centre. The abandonment of this village appears to have taken place at about 3 p.m.

According to Monnier's report, Carra Saint Cyr reached the battlefield at 2 p.m., and retired from Castel Ceriolo after an hour's fighting, therefore at 3 p.m. According to the brigadier's statement that he found himself alone on the battlefield, which fact induced him to retire, the action of the Consular Guard must have come to an end before 3 p.m. Dampierre sets down the rout of the right at 3 p.m., which in a way agrees with Saint Cyr. Pittaluga speaks of Carra Saint Cyr's half-brigade (evidently the 19th Light) at four o'clock to the east of Castel Ceriolo, intrenched in the vineyards close to the village; this, however, does not tally with the statement made by the officers of the 19th.

A writer states that Monnier's division did not do all it could have done, especially in the evening, when Ott's corps were falling back on the bridges of the Bormida. He adds that the displeasure of the First Consul was evinced by the fact that shortly after the battle General Monnier was shelved, and that no reward whatsoever was decreed to any of the troops of his division.

******

De Castres, *maréchal de camp*, in his notes on the account of the battle, issued in 1803 and 1805, relates that, so annoyed was Napoleon with General Monnier for having remained with the 72nd, which was held in reserve, instead of keeping with the other two half-brigades of his division at Castel Ceriolo, that he would not mention his name in the narrative. He substituted the name of Carra Saint Cyr, the senior brigadier-general, who had commanded the two half-brigades in the advance and attack of the village.

******

Somewhere about this period the Austrians directed their efforts in outstripping the left flank of the French Army, with evident intention of driving it on its centre clear of the Tortona road. In this manoeuvre, however, they neutralised the efforts of their cavalry, which was mostly posted with the left wing.

CHAPTER 6

Desaix Takes Part in the Battle

Amongst the alternatives that were open to Melas was a withdrawal to Novi. By taking post there, and resting on Genova and Admiral Keith's fleet, he might have awaited the arrival of Abercromby's force, which was at that moment concentrating at Mahon. By following this course, the Austrian Army ran no chance of falling short of supplies or munitions, and would have even been in a position to receive reinforcements, inasmuch as its communications with Florence and Bologna were open, and a Neapolitan Army occupied the Tuscan provinces. Her communications by sea were also open, by which means the Austrian commander might, if he deemed it desirable, march by the Corniche on Tuscany, and attain Parma or Modena, having a considerable portion of his artillery and war materials conveyed to Lerici, in the gulf of Spezia, by sea.

Melas had accorded full consideration to this plan. On the 10th of June, a few hours after hearing the results of the Battle of Montebello, he had written to Lord Keith that it was his intention to give battle, and that, should fortune go against him, he would retire to Genova. He therefore begged the admiral to collect all the necessary provisions. Prince Hohenzollern likewise had received instructions to collect supplies at Genova as a precaution in case the Austrian Army should, owing to the unfortunate issue of the battle, find itself compelled to retire on Genova by way of Novi.

In the afternoon of the 12th of June, Bonaparte was tormented by the utter absence of information. He feared lest the Austrian Army should have retired either on Genova or on the Ticino, if it had not marched against Suchet, with the object of crushing him, and of afterwards returning to confront the Army of Reserve. It was this uncertainty that made Bonaparte quit the excellent position of Stradella, which he had carefully prepared, and where he had counted on awaiting Melas's attack.

Stradella was a strong position, formed by a lower ridge of the Apennines which juts out towards the Po, where the intersected and broken nature of the ground promised to render the numerous cavalry of the enemy ineffective. In this position Bonaparte had remained for three days, fortifying and intrenching himself more and more, and covering with bridgeheads the two bridges over the Po in his rear.

★★★★★★

Je ne vois pas encore comment M. Melas s'en tirera: ou il viendra attaquer à Stradella, et il sera battu et perdu.—From the First Consul to the Minister of War. Milan, 20 *Prairial* (9th June).

★★★★★★

But, becoming impatient under the influence of the suspense which the utter dearth of information brought about, he resolved to quit such a favourable position, and to approach the plain of Marengo.

The importance of being adequately informed in war has been admitted by all great commanders, and possibly no one devoted keener attention to this point than Napoleon; for he well knew how timely and reliable information is indispensable for success. Here we have an instance in which the absence of information induced Bonaparte to order a portion of his troops to make a false movement, and caused him to remain up to the last moment in the dark as to his adversary's projects.

The scarcity of news may truly be imputed to the cavalry, which had not been able to gather anything beyond the most vague scraps of information, and this because it had not reconnoitred far enough to the front. In justice to that arm, it must be stated that it had been studiously held back and kept with the infantry. Kellermann's brigade was the foremost one, but this brigade was employed as an advanced guard, more with the object of screening the French Army than of discovering what was passing in front of it.

Its action, as Commandant Picard puts it, "*Avait plus pour mission de couvrir quo de découvrir.*" (Commandant Picard, *La Cavalerie à Marengo*.) At that period the exploration service, so eminently necessary to enable a commander-in-chief to make his dispositions, was still in a rudimentary state. It was not then fully recognised that the role of the cavalry before the battle is more important even than its role during the battle and after it. Neither was a cavalry general accorded all the liberty of action necessary to conduct a thoroughly effective exploration.

The opposite side was not a whit better informed. Melas's cavalry was far superior in numbers to the French, and enjoyed the reputation of being the best in Europe. Nevertheless, in the way of exploration, it did nothing.

We have before us Bonaparte's feeling of uncertainty as to his adversary's plans. On the morning of the 13th, this was augmented by the statement made by a peasant who had been brought before him at eleven o'clock. This peasant informed the First Consul that Melas was actually preparing for a retreat on Genova; that Elsnitz's cavalry, in fact, was already on the march. Bonaparte was disturbed by this report, made, as it appears, by a man in the pay of the Austrian staff. This caused him to send an order to Desaix to march on Novi. (Gachot, *La Deuxième Campagne d'Italie.*)

An able general will move detachments of his troops in different directions, so as to puzzle his adversary, and drive him to weaken the point where he intends to strike. But Melas did not resort to any clever manoeuvre of this kind, and what puzzled Bonaparte so much was that the Austrian forces seemed to have quite vanished, leaving no trace of themselves anywhere.

Frederick the Great maintained the ancient adage that he who separates his forces will be beaten in detail. Napoleon laid it down as a rule that:—

> No force should be detached on the eve of battle; because circumstances may change during the night, either by the retreat of the enemy, or by his being joined by large reinforcements, which might enable him to resume the offensive, and render all premature dispositions disastrous.

It was a maxim ever on his lips to prepare for a decisive action by bringing in every available man, for no one could tell when the result might turn on the presence of a few men more or less.

Those being his convictions, how was it that, on the eve of the Battle of Marengo, we find Bonaparte acting in contradiction to them? Evidently everything originated from his fixed idea that Melas was endeavouring to escape from him. The only way still open to Melas was that of Genova. It may be presumed that Bonaparte felt thoroughly convinced that the Austrians were ready to march to Novi, if they had not already shown themselves on the road, towards the important city which was to place them in connection with the sea and the British fleet.

His surprise in not finding the Austrian Army drawn up ready to give him battle on so fair a field as the plain of Marengo must have raised in his mind a strange doubt as to their forces being still in the neighbourhood of Alessandria.

Another circumstance also tended to indicate that Melas contemplated a retreat. That was his having despatched the reserve artillery park towards Mantua. He was evidently desirous to free his army of its cumbersome impedimenta.

A commander with a deep intuition in all the intricacies of war would most naturally expect his adversary to follow what he himself believed to be the best alternative under the existing conditions. Of an officer like Melas, who had shown so very little enterprise, the last thing Bonaparte was likely to expect was that he would have attacked him on the 14th of June.

He himself proceeded to Castel Novo di Scrivia on the 13th of June, from where he enjoined Murat to cause the whole ground between the Scrivia and the Bormida to be explored in every direction by the light cavalry. The movement of that day was nothing less than a reconnaissance of the plain of Marengo, performed by nearly the whole of his army.

The information which the cavalry gathered—at a time when the true principles of cavalry exploration were insufficiently understood—being found very scanty, the First Consul himself traversed the plain in every part. Both the cavalry and the scouts failed to explore sufficiently ahead to discover the main body of the Austrians concentrated under the walls of Alessandria. Everything was against the reconnoitring party. It was difficult to obtain a fair view, for the Austrian Army was located in rear of a broad and winding river, with wooded banks, the crossing being protected by a well-armed and defended bridgehead. Certainly, had any of the French patrols shown themselves on the right bank of the Bormida, they would have been received with musketry, which, possibly, would have indicated the extent of ground occupied by the enemy's army.

When Marengo was carried on the evening of the 13th, Gardanne made about a hundred prisoners. Probably little information was extracted from them, for these troops had come from the field of Montebello, and had been halted outside Alessandria, at the village of Marengo. Besides, we know now, what was not known then, that most of the Austrian troops had crossed the Tanaro only that very day.

The enemy's retreat across the Bormida in the evening of the 13th gave good grounds for forming a fair opinion of Melas's intentions. Who would have ever believed it possible that an army of over 30,000 men would have left the important position of Marengo to the enemy, with hardly any opposition, when its chief fully intended to deliver battle on the right bank of the Bormida the next day, with the object of opening itself a passage through the French Army?

An anterior prepossession existed in Bonaparte's mind—he strongly believed that the enemy would avoid the battle, and withdraw to Genova. All that had hitherto occurred he interpreted in the same sense, and we all know how very difficult it is to shake off an idea once it has been allowed to take firm root in the mind.

There is much excuse, after all, to be made for Bonaparte, when we consider that a retreat behind the Apennines was the best move Melas could make, therefore the most likely one to be made.

Everything considered, it was prudent to take steps for preventing his escape. This appears to justify the detachment sent to Rivalta on the 13th. Special circumstances and the peculiar aspect of affairs seemed to demand it. Bonaparte, who had quite lately given the following advice to Massena, "*Gardez vous d'avoir une ligne trop étendue,*" was not likely to fall into the same error without some very good reason. The great dispersion of his forces was in a certain way imposed on him from not knowing precisely the place where the enemy's forces were going to concentrate.

If Boudet's division was to form an advanced guard for offensive operations in the direction of Novi on the 14th, so as to interfere with any movement of the Austrian Army, there is nothing to censure. If, on the other hand, Bonaparte simply desired to ascertain the truth of the reported retreat of the Austrians on Genova, it appears to us that a detachment of cavalry sent direct from the plain of Marengo on the 13th would have sufficiently answered the purpose, and would have obtained the information more speedily. The cavalry, having sent in their report, would have remained in observation.

Bonaparte's army, already weakened by many detachments left to close the way to the Austrians, was not sufficiently strong to dispense with a division to reconnoitre in the direction of Novi. His numbers did not sanction such an extension of his forces as he ordered on the 13th, and but for the timely swelling of the Scrivia, Desaix, on the 14th, would have been much further from the battlefield.

Moltke, in his *Franco-German War*, remarks:—

> In war it is for the most part with probabilities only that the strategist can reckon; and the probability, as a rule, is that the

enemy will do the right thing.

In this case the total absence of information, the abandonment of a fair battlefield, the false news purposely given by a peasant, and the scarcity of the bivouac fires, were all circumstances tending to show that the enemy was bent on doing the best thing in his power, *viz.* to withdraw in the direction of Genova.

Bonaparte always formed his plans and manoeuvres on the capacity and system of his opponent. In this instance he calculated on the little initiative and enterprise hitherto shown by the Austrian general, and was fully convinced that he would be all for effecting a retreat. He left out of account entirely that Melas might take heart at the last moment, and might resolve on cutting his way through to Piacenza, and so recover his communications. It is so true that the unexpected very often occurs in war.

The position of an army at night can be best gauged by the bivouac fires. The reflection of these fires on the sky is a very good indication of the size of an army, possibly a more accurate indication than what can be obtained by day. Before returning to his headquarters on the night of the 13th, Bonaparte had beheld so few of the enemy's fires that he was more than ever strengthened in his conviction that the Austrian commander-in-chief contemplated a retreat. In this frame of mind, he sent orders to Desaix to push on to Novi in the early morning with Boudet's division.

A very heavy storm had broken out in the afternoon of the 13th; nevertheless, the Austrians lighted no fires, lest these should betray their presence.

The Duke of Rovigo writes that the Austrian Army had lighted no fires; but he falls into error when he states that Melas had led the whole of his army across the Bormida. It was only his advanced guard that passed the night on the right bank of that river.

★★★★★★

The duke states that Bonaparte had remained on horseback by his vedettes for a good part of the night, and had beheld a very small number of the enemy's fires. This does not tally with Berthier's narrative, for his words are: "As soon as night had come on and the divisions had settled in their bivouacs, Bonaparte left in all haste to return to the headquarters at Voghera, and to receive news from all the points occupied by the army."

★★★★★★

Historians have allowed their imagination to run wild regarding Desaix—the reasons which caused him to retrace his steps on the eventful 14th of June, his pithy words to Bonaparte, and the hour of his arrival on the battlefield. The statements about the hour he reached the battlefield are, above all, very conflicting. Dupont says:—

Il était alors 5 heures du soir. (It was then five o'clock in the evening.)

And Boudet's journal shows that his division did reach San Giuliano at about that hour. The Austrian account runs:—

It might have been about five o'clock when this general arrived from Rivalta. (*Il pouvait être 5 heures environ, lors que ce général arriva de Rivalta*).

Crossard likewise states that the division from Novi reached the field at about five o'clock:—

Il pouvait être alors cinq heures du soir.

★★★★★★

Il Buonaparte poco prima di mezzo giorno viene alfine informato da uno dei suoi aiutanti, giunto dalla parte di Rivalta , che il Desaix é stato trovato, ma die la divisione Boudet non potrà essere sul luogo dell' azione prima delle 5 di sera.—Capitano V. Pittaluga, La Battaglia di Marengo.

★★★★★★

Let us go back to the previous day, and see what had happened to Desaix's command. We may reasonably do this, as the various incidents had a marked influence on the events of the 14th.

It was already noon on the 13th when Desaix gave the orders for Boudet's division to march from Ponte Curone, to proceed by way of Sarrezano to Rivalta, and thence to Serravalle. The division set out at once. As Tortona, however, was occupied by an Austrian garrison, Boudet's division kept the fortress well on its right, and marched along the right bank of the Grua rivulet as far as Sarrezano to the south-east of Tortona, and thence by the hills of the Tortonese. Under ordinary circumstances, the division should have reached Rivalta the same evening; but it had been overtaken by very heavy rain, which had rendered its march extremely arduous. The rain had also swollen the Scrivia to such an extent that its passage by a large body of troops had become an excessively difficult undertaking.

The same swelling of the Scrivia, which was to detain Bonaparte at

Torre di Garofoli on the evening of the 13th, when bent on returning to Voghera, was to keep Boudet's division from crossing over to the left bank of that stream.

At about 5 p.m., the 1st Hussars and the 9th Light Infantry, which were leading, approached the banks of the river. The few foot-soldiers who tried to get across by holding by the horses' tails were swept away by the impetus of the current, and their lives were saved with great difficulty. An attempt was made to effect a passage elsewhere, at Valvernia. This met with less success, for three of the men were drowned. The general tried next, with not much better success, at Castellar Ponzano. During the night, by the aid of a boat, a small part of the 9th Light Infantry was ferried across; the bulk of that corps bivouacked on the right bank of the Scrivia opposite Rivalta. The 30th and 59th of the line, under the command of Brigadier-General Guénand, spent the night on the hills of Sarrezano to guard the artillery. It was only by the assistance of twenty pairs of oxen that the guns could be brought to the banks of the Scrivia, and then not before nine o'clock the following morning.

Desaix, with his customary energy, made every effort, and tried every possible expedient for getting his troops across to the left bank of the swollen river. But the enterprise was full of difficulty, and the crossing took much time. Fortunately, when Desaix was about driven to despair, a priest, one Guasone, a very ardent partisan of the French, stepped forward and volunteered to aid him. The good man soon gathered all the country folks, peasants, boatmen, and fishermen; boats, carts, and materials were everywhere sought, and by all this combined aid the French were soon ferried to the left bank of the Scrivia.

★★★★★★

This is what Captain V. Pittaluga writes with regard to Boudet's division, gathered from local tradition. Nothing of what is reported to have been done by the priest is contrary to Boudet's report.

★★★★★★

We consider it best to follow General Boudet's version, which was written when the events were quite recent. As De Cugnac justly observes, Boudet's journal was written with great candour; his story, therefore, should be accepted as very trustworthy. Boudet reports:—

At the break of day (on the 14th of June) the water did not yet permit us to ford, but a boat had been secured by the help of some boatmen, whom a detachment had carried off from Tortona during the night. The troops crossed speedily, and went to take post at Rivalta. Towards ten o'clock in the morning the waters had fallen, and the artillery was able to ford the river.

This report shows in a very clear way the locality and manner in which the division got across the river:—

> Desaix had despatched to headquarters to know what dispositions were to follow the occurrences of the previous evening. He received the order (fortunately too late) to march on Pozzolo Formigaro, an intermediate position, from which he could have proceeded certainly, but with a good deal of time, to Alessandria, or to the Genova road, in case the enemy should have attempted to effect its retreat that way.
>
> My division had not got a mile beyond Rivalta, when one of the commander-in-chief's *aides-de-camp* came in hot haste to bring me the order to march to San Giuliano, and thence on Marengo, where the two hostile armies had been fighting from the break of day. (The last paragraph contains an exaggeration, inasmuch as Gardanne was only attacked at about nine o'clock—"*à 9 heures du matin.*")

Boudet makes no mention of any sound of heavy firing; neither does Dalton in his report to Dupont, chief of the staff. This last report is understood to have been sent from Rivalta at 9 a.m. on the 14th. Savary, on the contrary, writes that hardly had the day broken when a powerful cannonade was heard in the distance in rear of their right.

Marmont in his *Mémoires*, as Savary in his, states that Desaix, on hearing the clamour of the battle, had stopped his movement in the direction of Novi, and waited for orders; which probably would be sent him, as the enemy was not effecting a retreat as it had been supposed he intended to do. In the face of what Boudet writes in his *Rapport des Marches et Operations*, we can dismiss this story of halting for orders. Boudet distinctly states that the division was marching on Pozzolo Formigaro when the order of recall arrived.

According to Savary, Bonaparte never so much as dreamt that Melas would advance to attack him, though two emissaries from the enemy, who appeared at Voghera, seemed sent especially for the purpose of finding out if the French Army intended to advance against the Austrians. His fear was lest Melas should escape him to avoid a battle which held little prospect of success. Novi was the place through which he expected the enemy's troops would pass in making their way to Genova.

Desaix had been directed on the evening of the 13th of June to push a reconnaissance as far as that town. Savary was ordered to undertake the duty. He went to Novi, but could find no trace of the enemy, and returned to Rivalta; and his report was forwarded to the First Consul. Trucco states that Bonaparte was having supper with Baron di Garofoli, when at a late hour he received Savary's report giving the result of his reconnaissance at Novi, and stating that the town was not occupied.

Dalton speaks of reconnaissances pushed as far as Serravalle on the evening and night of the 13th along both banks of the Scrivia, when it was found that the enemy occupied that post. The explorations showed also that some Republican troops were occupying Novi. To what corps these troops belonged he does not say. They may possibly have been Savary's party.

Even Savary's report does not seem to have reassured Bonaparte. It was difficult to persuade him that the Austrians would not have tried to evade him by using a road which was yet sufficiently safe and not watched.

But if Melas had any intention of using this road it was high time to be moving, for shortly it could no longer have been considered safe. He must have known that Suchet was advancing on Acqui, if he was not there already, and the chances were in favour of his crossing the Bormida, leaving Alessandria well to his left, and making for Novi and Tortona.

Desaix, by what has been stated, and by the very trustworthy report of General Boudet, the next officer in seniority to him, neither marched to the sound of the guns, as some writers pretend, nor did he do the next best thing to it—halt on hearing the cannonade on his right and send for orders. He received orders to proceed to Pozzolo Formigaro. These orders were possibly despatched at about ten in the morning—when the real extent of the Austrian attack was not fully known at headquarters—and may have reached him at about noon of the 14th. The order of recall did not reach him till later, at about 1 p.m. This, alas! destroys the happy inspiration which Thiers attributes to Desaix:—

> To that Desaix who, guessing before having received them the orders of his chief, came to bring him victory and his life. "*Magna est veritas, et prevalebit.*"

✶✶✶✶✶✶

One is distressed at having to say anything that may deduct from Desaix's reputation; but in the interest of history the truth must be told. He was the soul of honour, and would have been the first to discredit all the legends. His glory, after all, is so great that it cannot in any way be lessened by exposing fictions.

✶✶✶✶✶✶

Savary, by his own account, when heavy firing was heard on the right rear, was again sent to Novi to reconnoitre. He states that he set out early in the morning, taking with him fifty horsemen, and lost no time in getting to his destination. On reaching the town, he found things there exactly as he had left them on the previous afternoon. Everything was quiet, and there was not a vestige of the enemy.

Savary returned as quickly as he had gone, and in two hours was back by the side of his general. He states that he went to make his report in person to the First Consul, and to inform him how Desaix had stopped his movement and was waiting for fresh orders. This does not coincide with the statements contained in the diary of Boudet's division, according to which orders were solicited from headquarters before the waters of the Scrivia had fallen, which did not occur before ten o'clock.

Savary states that, being quite alive to the importance of his mission, he wended his way across country, taking for his direction the sound of the fire and the smoke. As luck would have it, he crossed Bruyère, one of the First Consul's *aides-de-camp*, who was likewise galloping across country in search of Desaix, to deliver an order for his immediate march to the battlefield, where a reinforcement was greatly needed.

✶✶✶✶✶✶✶

Bruyère's name is inscribed on the Arc de Triomphe. He was a light cavalry officer, and died of his wounds at Gorlitz on the 5th of June, 1813.

Lockhart states that Desaix was already half a day's journey from headquarters when Bonaparte received intelligence which made him recall all his detachments. Berthier, in giving a recapitulation of the French forces, places Desaix's troops in the reserve, being on the march from Rivalta, from whence they had been summoned as soon as the enemy's designs had been penetrated.

✶✶✶✶✶✶

The two *aides-de-camp* by this fortunate meeting found out the whereabouts of the general officers they were respectively in quest of. Bonaparte was pleased to hear what Savary had to report about Desaix's division. He was very anxious for his arrival, and put some questions to the *aide-de-camp*, evidently imagining from the replies that he was very close at hand.

'Go,' he said, 'and tell him to form up there (pointing to the locality with his hand); to quit the high-road, to allow all those wounded to pass on, as they would only obstruct him and possibly sweep away his men.'

We have remarked on some inaccuracies and errors in Marmont's accounts, and we have the same complaint to make against another eye-witness. In the Duke of Rovigo's narrative there are several points almost impossible to explain. He says absolutely nothing about the difficulty experienced in crossing the swollen Scrivia, which was an important point. His narrative would seem to convey the idea that at daybreak on the 14th Boudet's troops were all concentrated at Rivalta, so that nothing remained but to set them in motion; whereas we have Dalton's report, in which he distinctly states that early that morning only a small portion of Boudet's division was on the left bank of the Scrivia, and that the best part of the said division, the 30th and 59th of the line, and the artillery, were still at Sarrezano. The whole, in fact, were not really concentrated on the left bank of the Scrivia much before noon on the 14th.

If Desaix, as Savary states, heard the sound of the guns as day was breaking—and the day breaks very early in the month of June—and, as Gachot puts it more definitely, at seven o'clock in the morning, and it took Savary two hours to ride to Novi and back, he would have left Rivalta at 9 a.m. to go and make his report to the First Consul. Gachot makes Desaix receive his orders of recall—"*à 8 heures et demie, il reçut la dépêche de Bonaparte;*" and this does not quite tally with Savary's account of his accidental meeting with Bruyère.

The narrative of the Duke of Rovigo is very disappointing. As he was one of Desaix's *aides-de-camp*, one might have expected him to elucidate many points regarding the Battle of Marengo of which history was deprived by the unfortunate death of his chief. However, what he writes is very brief, and his statements do not tally with those of Boudet and Dalton, who took a more conspicuous part in the battle.

The dates of certain memorable events sink into men's minds, besides which it is easy for a careful writer to look them up. But even here Savary errs, though he admits that, possibly, the exact dates may have slipped from his memory. (See note, *Mémoires du Duc de Rovigo*.) It detracts much from the interest of the duke's narrative that no statement is made of the time when he reported having left Desaix at Rivalta.

Bonaparte, taking out his watch, asked, 'At what hour did you quit him?'—'At such and such an hour,' I replied. (*'À telle heure,' lui repondis-je.*)

In war precision with regard to time is essential. To give an indefinite hour would imply that the duke attached no importance to this point. These *Mémoires* were published some years after the events, for they first appeared in 1828, and are evidently too incorrect to serve as a guide. We may note the following passage to show how unreliable the *Mémoires* are. Referring to the passage of the guns over the Alps, the duke writes:—

> The ardour was such that the First Consul found the next day at the foot of the mountain, on the Italian side, fifty guns on their carriages. They were accompanied by their waggons filled with ammunition, which had been sent over on the backs of mules. The guns and carriages were horsed and ready to march. (*Mémoires du Duc de Rovigo*, tom. i.)

The duke says that it was three o'clock on the 14th when Desaix came up with Boudet's division. But Marmont, who also took a more prominent part in the battle, writes: "It was nearly five o'clock, and Boudet's division, on which our safety and our hopes depended, had not yet arrived. At last, shortly after, it rejoined us."

Alison states that the vehemence of the cannonade convinced Bonaparte that a general battle was at hand; and that he instantly despatched orders to Desaix to retrace his steps from Novi, and to hasten to the scene of action. This idea Bonaparte apparently formed at about eleven o'clock. It was then evident to him that the Austrians had not retired along the Novi road, as he had all along imagined that they might possibly have done.

This clearing of the doubt may have been the result of Savary's report. In any case, however it came about, he became convinced that the storm was on the point of bursting in the direction of Marengo, and accordingly sent orders to hasten Desaix's return. Some writers have given the exact words of the order:—

I have always anticipated attacking the enemy. He has forestalled me. In the name of God come back, if you are able to do so.

V. Pittaluga, in his narrative of the Battle of Marengo, refutes the authenticity of this order. It is the Duke of Valmy who gives it in his *Histoire de la Campagne de 1800*. In a footnote the duke explains that the letter, *billet*, was seen in General Desaix's hands, as he received it, by a young Hungarian, attached to the general as orderly officer; that it was General de Faverges who gathered this fact from the mouth of the ocular witness. Pittaluga questions the genuineness of the message on account of the style being so unmilitary. He declares that Bonaparte was not given to make use of such despairing exclamations, or to giving ambiguous orders to his generals. He often enjoined them to do things seemingly impossible, never to *do if they could*.

This order, whether verbal or in writing, was despatched from the Torre di Garofoli, where the headquarters were. Rivalta being about twelve kilometres away, it would have been in Desaix's hands by noon or thereabouts, and allowing for the necessary dispositions and the time employed in marching, the division might have been expected at San Giuliano between four and five o'clock in the afternoon.

Boudet's division, quitting its position a mile beyond Rivalta at about 1 p.m., and marching at the rate of 2½ miles per hour, would not have reached San Giuliano much before 5 p.m. Boudet says truly that the march was accelerated, but it was carried out in the early hours of a very hot afternoon, so that 2½-miles per hour would have been considered good marching for a division. The distance and the late hour at which the order was received would account for the division not appearing on the battlefield much before five o'clock.

Let us return to the battlefield. It was now about four o'clock in the afternoon, and by all appearance victory seemed fully inclined to side with the Austrians. The French Army was in full retreat, and on the plain of Marengo no other position remained in their hands but the one of San Giuliauo. To the advance of the Austrian columns the French in certain parts of the field made hardly any show of resistance. And even the few troops of Monnier's division which hung yet about the vineyards of Castel Ceriolo, after having for some time made head against the attacks of Ott's troops, had ended, as we have said, by retiring in the direction of Torre di Garofoli.

Coignet states that at 2 p.m. the officers already looked upon the battle as lost. The state of the contest at 2.30 p.m. was, the French left routed, the centre and right in disorder. Lannes in his report says that, after a cannonade and fusillade which had lasted eight hours, Victor had to beat a retreat. This might lead one to believe that Victor only withdrew his forces at 4 p.m., when by that time his men had already gained the neighbourhood of San Giuliano. All that the French could do at that hour (4 p.m.) was to offer a passive resistance.

Whilst matters were in this distracting plight, there were some in the ranks of the French Army who studied the demeanour of their commander-in-chief. On that day and at that dreadful hour, Bonaparte remained perfectly unmoved, encouraging his men. His perfect self-possession and the sudden inspiration so thoroughly peculiar to him never deserted him. Watching every turn of the contest and grasping the importance of every movement, his assurance never gave way for an instant. He gave his orders with his accustomed coolness; he beheld the tempest increasing without fear; while the shot flew incessantly around him, some of his attendants falling every minute by his side, he remained quite oblivious to all personal danger.

His voice and his traits were not altered in the least. His generals, the officers, and even the soldiers, showed more concern. Voices were heard on all sides calling that his proper post was not in the midst of the fire. (He remained untouched. Fortune disappointed the speculations of those Frenchmen who hoped that he might have fallen in battle.) Victory, however, was not far distant, and, faithful to him, came heralded by the gallant Desaix, his friend, the model of great men.

Melas had been in the saddle from a very early hour that day. He had several times ridden over the battlefield. He had received a slight wound in the left forearm, and had had two horses killed under him. He had lost the alertness and eagerness of youth, and the heavy responsibilities of the latter weeks had preyed on his constitution. Shortly after 2 p.m., convinced that Bonaparte was drawing off the field, that the battle had been gained, and that the French were irretrievably beaten, he left the battlefield and wended his way back to Alessandria. He not only desired to take the rest of which he was much in need, but also to forward to the Austrian Court a message announcing the victory.

Crossard relates that as Melas was about to quit the battlefield, he told General Saint Julien:—

It is now an accomplished thing. They are retiring at all points.

You will not proceed beyond San Giuliano, where you will post the right of the infantry. You will see that the enemy is pursued by your cavalry and light artillery, which must kill as many of their men as possible whilst in the act of crossing the Scrivia. As for myself, I am old; I have been in the saddle since midnight, therefore I will go and lie down. (Crossard, *Mémoires Militaires et Historiquos pour servir à l'Histoire do la Guerre depuis 1792 jusqu'en 1815, tom.* iii.)

As long as a battle lasts, a commander can only look for a probability of success, and on nothing positive. So many things may occur, so many accidents come to grasp victory out of his hands. An *aide-de-camp* carrying an order is killed, injured, or taken prisoner; one of the generals misconceives his role; a column kept back by bad roads arrives too late; reinforcements may come up for the enemy. One or more of such mishaps may make the most promising battle fail.

Many generals are clever enough to win a battle, but are quite incapable of drawing any advantage from the victory. Melas was here a case in point. As soon as the aged chief was back in Alessandria, he hastened to inform his imperial master of the splendid victory he had obtained over the French. It was Colonel Radetsky who was commanded to convey the announcement, which was couched in the following words:—

> After a lengthy and bloody battle on the plains of Marengo, the troops of His Majesty the Emperor have thoroughly beaten the French Army which was led into Italy and directed in the fight by General Bonaparte. A subsequent despatch will descend into particulars, giving the results of the victory, which Zach's lieutenant-generals are now collecting on the battlefield.

★★★★★★

At the time that Radetsky was charged to execute this mission he was simply a staff officer, a young colonel thirty-four years old. More than possibly, it never entered his head that, close on half a century later, he would, as commander-in-chief of an Austrian Army, become renowned for his brilliant campaigns in Italy.

★★★★★★

There have been other battles in which the troops on both sides fought with great determination, and with fluctuating success during the day, and in which a vigorous effort towards the close of the day, after so many hours of hard struggling, accorded victory to the side that made it. So, it was at Marengo.

Melas came to a very hasty conclusion, and committed an egregious blunder. Had he reflected that the adversary he was contending against was a general of brilliant talent and endless resources, he might have deemed it possible, or even probable, that the day would not be allowed to close without his making some unexpected effort. The commander-in-chief's abandonment of the battlefield was found to have a bad effect. On one side was a leader who quitted the battlefield before the battle was actually over, on the other an alert general, who was doing his best to restore the supremacy of his troops. The change of commanders on the Austrian side led to hesitation and want of unity.

At four in the afternoon, or thereabouts, Lannes, then in position between Valmagra and La Buschetta, was skirmishing with Ott's and Frimont's advanced guards. Victor, less fortunate, taking advantage of the defile of San Giuliano and under the protection of Kellermann's and Champeaux's horsemen, had succeeded in getting some 2,000 or 3,000 men together. Carra Saint Cyr, almost cut off in Castel Ceriolo, had not been able to prevent Ott's advance on Villanova. The head of Rivaud's brigade, which was intact, had marched up from Salé; it was showing itself at Piovera and threatening Ott's left, then advancing on Villanova.

The French were in full retreat. The retreat of one corps had entailed the retreat of the others. It began on the left more in the guise of a flight than of a retreat; on the right it was conducted with more steadiness, still only two of Lannes's regiments adhered to the orders he had issued for the good result of the manoeuvre. In falling back, the right withdrew steadily and slowly, showing a bold front to the enemy from time to time. The left was completely broken; confusion, terror, and indescribable disorder prevailed on that side of the battlefield. There was no intentional change of front such as Napoleon endeavoured to make people believe in his various accounts of the battle.

De Cugnac dubs Napoleon as the inventor of a premeditated retreat pivoting on Castel Ceriolo. He shows that the battle was fought without any settled plan. He states that:—

> It was fought by a natural succession of unforeseen episodes: attack and defence of the Fontanone and of Marengo; reinforcements of troops of the first line; critical position of the French, whose artillery was much inferior in number and whose am-

munition had become expended; retreat towards the localities in which they had camped on the eve; lastly, appearance on the scene of Boudet's division, which, seeming at first only capable of staying the pursuit, attacks with such vigour, is assisted to such purpose by Kellermann's cavalry, that the enemy's advanced guard is dispersed, and the entire Austrian Army, seized by a panic, flies in disorder, quitting the battlefield.

An ocular witness, Petit of the Consular Guard, declares that at 4 p.m., in a line of five miles or more, there were not more than 6,000 men standing with the colours, 1,000 cavalry and six serviceable cannons. He shows that fully a third of the army had been rendered ineffective, and that, owing to a want of transport, more than another third was occupied in removing the wounded. He adds that fatigue and thirst had driven a large number of officers from the field, and with bad consequences. Against these discouraged troops was advancing an enormous mass of infantry protected by a most powerful artillery.

At that moment, the French were in a sad predicament, the demeanour of the troops in every part of the field alike showed most clearly that the battle was lost. The French at that hour could only offer a mild resistance. The bad plight they were in is no secret, for even the official bulletin issued on the 14th of June admits it.

The enemy was advancing all along the line, over a hundred guns were firing case-shot. The roads were crowded with fugitives, wounded, and abandoned materials. To all appearance the battle was lost.

The right wing of the Austrian Army, whilst pushing back the remnants of Victor's and Lannes's corps, was slowly advancing by the road which goes from Marengo to San Giuliano.

Zach, in whose hands Melas had left the completion of the defeat, instead of following the French in hot pursuit, satisfied himself by occupying the Marengo-Tortona road with the object of cutting the French from their proper line of retreat. To this effect he formed a deep column to be preceded by an advance-guard.

This advance-guard was composed of Saint Julien's and Lattermann's brigades, flanked on the left by Lichtenstein's regiment of dragoons. A mile or so in the rear followed Kaim, with the brigades of Bellegarde, Knesevich, and Lamarsaille. With a like interval Weidenfeld's grenadier brigade brought up the rear.

On the left of this main column rode the cavalry in two lines, a regiment of the Archduke John's dragoons, and what remained of Pilatti's brigade.

Flanking the main column on the right, and marching along the Lungafame-Cascina Grossa road were three battalions of De Briey's regiment. Frimont with some troops marched on Poggi, to keep the connection with Sticker's regiment of Ott's corps. O'Reilly, from Frugarolo, moved on Cascina Grossa, having found no trace of Suchet in the direction of Novi or on the Orba.

Zach marched with the advance-guard, at the head of which was Wallis's regiment.

The Austrians were drawn up more in order of march than in suitable attack formation. They had been under arms from the earliest morning of a very oppressive day, overcoming an obstinate resistance. Before launching this column forth in pursuit, no steps whatever had been taken to restore order or anything like a regular array. Crossard remarks on the disorder amongst the Austrian troops when they saw the French defence becoming so feeble. Elated by the prospect of victory, which seemed thoroughly within their grasp, the Austrians imagined that by this time all resistance was at an end, and advanced in a loose and disorderly style. Experience seldom fails to show that negligence of this kind is rarely allowed to pass unpunished.

In Chevalier de Cavour's notes on the *Mémoires du Général Danican sur la Bataille d'Alexandrie ou Marengo*, the writer refers to this point, and alludes to a warning which Zach received.

> In vain, did the talented Lieutenant-Colonel Iclkman remind him that the army was completely tired out, and several battalions in disorder, prostrated on the ground by weariness; that there was no longer a line, some regiments being too far forward, and others having remained too far behind; that it was expedient to give breathing-time to the troops, to reform the line, to get up some guns, and afterwards to carry the said village. (The village alluded to evidently was San Giuliano, though the Austrians never reached it; for they were met by Boudet's division before getting up to it.) He would hear no reason, and ordered the attack, which had a thorough success, but it was the last.

Something quite similar is what Baron Crossard writes in his *Mémoires*. He was a French emigrant attached to General Vogelsang, who commanded a division on the left wing of the Austrian Army. He writes that disorder pervaded the ranks; that the troops marched on the high-road, without feelers, with bands playing; that the soldiers, unchecked, quitted the ranks to strip the dead; and that the officers, much elated, were leaving their places to join in mutual congratulations. Troubled by seeing these irregularities, he brought them to the notice of his general. Vogelsang, apparently, did not receive these observations in good part. Crossard's strictures were allowed to pass unnoticed, and he was told not to make himself unpleasant. (S. Crossard, *Mémoires Militaires et Historiques pour servir à l'Histoire de la Guerre depuis 1792 jusqu'en 1815*, tom. ii.)

As Zach's formidable column was advancing, the French had received a reinforcement in that part of the field, and this was to decide the fate of the day. It has been shown how, as soon as it had been definitely made clear that the entire Austrian Army had crossed the Bormida to give battle in the plain of Marengo, the First Consul had hastened to recall the troops under Desaix's command.

At about 4 p.m., Bonaparte, having charged Berthier to superintend the retreat—which was to be directed on San Giuliano Vecchio, but as slowly as possible—repaired to the Villa Ghilina. He was extremely impatient regarding Desaix's arrival, on whom he greatly relied; and it is said that from the top of the villa, where he was with the Marquis Ghilini, he first caught sight of Boudet's approaching division.

At last, this so-much-looked-for reinforcement was at hand. It would give him a fresh body with which, if nothing else, to cover his retreat, for little hope there was of accomplishing anything more. Bold would have been the man who could have dreamt, as things were going, of anything beside it. Possibly Bonaparte might have conceived turning an incipient defeat into a victory, but it was a thing that no one else would have thought of at that supreme moment. Bourrienne writes:—

> *On ne parlait à San Giuliano que de la retraite à laquelle, disait-on, Bonaparte seul s'opposait avec fermeté.*

Quiot was alongside of General Victor when Bonaparte accosted him, he declares:—

> The latter was not moved, but had the appearance of being much ruffled, I believe, on account of the retiring movement. I cannot recall any of his words.

So anxious was the First Consul that he hastened to meet Desaix.

It was about five o'clock in the evening. The French Army, almost entirely disorganised, was retiring to the right and left of San Giuliano in the direction of Torre di Garofoli. Bonaparte, who had pinned his hopes on Boudet's division, decided that it was adequate to re-establish the balance, and to give another air to the battle. He was not likely to let the first pitched battle of the campaign go against him without one more desperate attempt to retrieve the fortunes of the day. It is often so that battles are won.

At the sight of Desaix's troops, full of enthusiasm, and eager to take part in the battle, he stopped the retreat. Victor's and Lannes's corps had suffered very severely. For all that, the soldiers were not entirely devoid of ardour, and when Boudet's division came level with San Giuliano, Bonaparte, from whose perspicacious eye nothing escaped, seized the favourable opportunity; orders flew everywhere in a moment. Lannes, Monnier, and Watrin were bidden to suspend their movement to the rear. To reform, however, a proper order of battle, with troops fatigued by heat and the toil of the contest, required a certain amount of time, and this Zach had given to the French by staying his advance to form his deep column of attack.

Jomini states that what made Bonaparte reject the idea of a retreat was the spirit of the troops, and their eagerness to attack the enemy. This fixed the resolution of the First Consul. It was after he had stayed the retreat that he addressed a few inspiriting words to his men—words which had the effect of increasing the ardour of the troops a hundredfold.

> We have gone back enough today. You know that my custom is always to sleep on the battlefield.

The army replied to this appeal by one loud shout—a fair promise of victory.

With the troops in so high a state of tension, a spark only was needed to fire their enthusiasm into action. The slightest favourable incident sufficed, and it was forthcoming. Nevertheless, the credit belongs to the man who had the power to work them up to such a pitch.

Desaix preceded Boudet's division, and reached San Giuliano. At a hundred yards from the village, he met the First Consul, and learnt from his mouth the principal events of the day. The conversation which followed is given in various words; the most common version is that Desaix, having pulled out his watch, exclaimed:—

> Ah! the battle is lost; still, it is but four o'clock, and we have

time enough to win one.

It is Walter Scott who states that as Bonaparte and Desaix met, the latter said, "The battle is lost. I suppose I can do no more for you than secure your retreat?" to which Bonaparte replied, "By no means. The battle is, I trust, gained. The disordered troops whom you see are my centre and left, whom I will rally in your rear. Push forward your column." (Walter Scott errs when he says that Desaix was shot through the head.)

Here is another point where imagination has been allowed to triumph over reality. We take the evidence of an eyewitness, of Marmont. His eulogy of Desaix leaves no doubt that he entertained friendly regard for his personal and military qualities, consequently that he was not likely to suppress anything to his advantage. Now, Marmont writes that General Desaix preceded by a few minutes the arrival of Boudet's division, and overtook the First Consul. He found the business in a deplorable state, and had formed a bad opinion of it.

A kind of council, in which I assisted, was held on horseback. He (Desaix) said to the First Consul, 'Before attempting a fresh charge, it will be necessary to disconcert the enemy by a brisk fire; without this it will not succeed. It is thus, General, that battles are lost. We need absolutely a vigorous artillery fire.' To Marmont, who was explaining to him how he was going to establish a battery with the pieces that still remained, to which he would add the guns of Boudet's division, Desaix replied, 'Very good. Look here, my dear Marmont, some cannons, some cannons, and make the best possible use of them.'

It is unfortunate that we have no reliable record of all that occurred during this brief conference held on Desaix's arrival. Marmont was present; but he mentions only the few words spoken by Desaix which are recorded above. Respecting all the rest of the discussion he is silent. We are ignorant whether there were or were not voices in favour of a retreat. All our information on that point comes from Bourrienne, who relates that Bonaparte himself was strongly opposed to it.

Most people seem altogether to ignore the presence of the commander-in-chief at this discussion, and accept without questioning General Desaix's spurious words. The legend, in short, makes Desaix settle what fresh turn the action was to take. It is forgotten that Bonaparte naturally presided at the conference, and it is on that account that it is much to be regretted that Marmont did not give the exact words used. It would then have been seen that the idea of resuming the offensive emanated from Bonaparte himself, and from no one else. Marmont simply narrates what referred to himself, the disposition of the artillery.

Marmont took five guns, which still remained in a serviceable condition, five which had been left on the Scrivia, and had only just come on the ground, and eight of Boudet's division —in all eighteen guns, making altogether a very respectable battery.

The reserve always plays a very important role in a battle. It is the reserve that confronts the enemy and checks his advance, whilst it gives prompt aid to the troops which, already hard pressed on some point, are beginning to give way. The reserve rallies the runaways, stays the enemy's pursuit, and, profiting by the enemy's faults, strives to re-establish the contest. It was thus at Marengo, when late in the afternoon all the French line was in retreat. A reserve division, aided by a few regiments of heavy cavalry, stayed the pursuit of the Austrians, attacked their principal column in front and in flank, overlapped it, and compelled most of the troops to lay down their arms.

The arrival of Boudet's division re-established somewhat the equilibrium of the forces. It was the turning-point of the contest, and from that moment the fate of the battle changed. The retreat of the French ceased as if by enchantment, and the troops, which were downcast and all too ready to seek safety in a speedy retreat, turned about and faced the foe. A sudden joy spread over the countenance of every soldier. The stragglers took heart, and, coming back with Desaix, rejoined their regiments.

Desaix took post with the centre on the main road between San Giuliano and Cascina Grossa. Boudet's division was deployed, being partly concealed from view by hedges and a thick belt of vines. The 9th Light occupied the left of the road under General Musnier. The other brigade, consisting of the 30th and 56th Regiments, under General Guénand, was on the right.

Gardanne took part on Desaix's left, facing Cascina Grossa. On the right of Desaix, on a slight elevation, were Marmont and his eighteen guns; next came Kellermann's cavalry, and the little there was of it with Boudet's division. To the right, and a little in the rear of Kellermann's cavalry, was the cavalry of the Consular Guard. Lannes was in the middle of the plain, having the grenadiers of the Consular Guard, led by Major Goulez, on his right: then came Monnier's corps extending towards the Castel Ceriolo-Salé road. Champeaux's brigade and the rest of the cavalry formed the reserve.

Two battalions of the 72nd, which had been held in reserve, co-operated with Desaix's troops in the final advance, though Boudet does not mention the fact. Monnier is loud in then-praise.

By this time the head of the Austrian main column was on a level with Cascina Grossa.

With regard to the actual formation of the troops, we cannot do better than accept Boudet's statement. His words are:—

> I placed on the left of the main road my first brigade, of which a portion was deployed, the other in close column. I likewise ordered my second brigade to assume the same disposition on the right of the road.

The 9th Light Infantry was moved forward to inspire courage to the rest of the troops, and to give time to the other brigade to take post. The artillery was placed in front of Boudet's right brigade to the north of the road. Marmont indicates its position on the right of the road. The eighteen-gun battery occupied one-half of the front of the army.

Desaix led the left brigade; Boudet, by his direction, superintended the action of the right one. Boudet speaks of a retirement by echelon of the left brigade, ordered by Desaix to bring it more abreast with the right, which induced the Austrians to advance with greater confidence, and so caused them great surprise when the French turned and charged. This retirement, at the utmost of 200 paces, ceased, and a general advance then took place.

The left brigade, the 9th Light, had to contend against Zach's first line, composed of Wallis's regiment and the Hungarian grenadiers, who were advancing full of confidence as if victory was already theirs.

Just before resuming the offensive, the French force could not have amounted to very much more than 11,000 infantry, 1,200 cavalry, and 18 guns. The reinforcement Boudet brought up consisted of 4,850 infantry, 120 hussars, 128 *cuirassiers*, and 110 gunners. Bonaparte rode along the front of the troops, speaking encouraging words and spurring them to another effort.

Shortly after 5 p.m., the leading Austrian troops, which Zach had deployed into two lines on approaching Cascina Grossa, unconscious of the danger which menaced them, arrived within range of Marmont's guns. Zach, who had advanced with them, fully convinced that he had only to gather the trophies of victory, and that he was on the point of closing every avenue of retreat to the foe, found himself suddenly received by a powerful discharge of artillery. It was Marmont, who with his guns opened with canister-shot. A thick shower of death-dealing metal fell on the head of the Austrian column; it took the Austrians aback, for they did not anticipate a fresh resistance, being fully convinced that the French were only bent on retiring. This sudden and unlooked-for opposition startled Wallis's men, who, dreading an ambush, fell back.

✶✶✶✶✶✶

> In his report on the battle, Boudet makes some remarks on the fire of the great battery: "A cannonade then opened, in which the enemy by the number of his guns had too marked a superiority over us to make the contest equal. Every instant one saw files of our troops cut down, which increased their impatience to get to close quarters." Marmont is silent on this point. After stating the position the battery occupied on the right of the San Giuliano road, his words are: "A smart and rapid fire made the enemy first hesitate, and then brought him to a standstill.... After about twenty minutes of this artillery fire, the army moved forward." Lauriston says the artillery opened to good purpose and with the greatest effect. When the French resumed the offensive, the Austrian artillery drew back, for fear of their guns being taken and turned against themselves.

✶✶✶✶✶✶

If the French were surprised in the morning, the Austrians got a surprise in the evening, when the French thus unexpectedly resumed the offensive. A surprise is ever more fatal when one side allows itself to make perfectly sure of success.

Zach, however, soon succeeded in restoring order and in checking the advance of the French. The Austrians had by this time recovered from their surprise; the Hungarian grenadiers, having allowed the fugitives to get through their line, advanced slowly, firing on the French, who, in their turn, hesitated and broke. Victory was more doubtful than ever.

Most writers have made the last phase of the battle, the advance of Desaix with Boudet's division, to have been a very speedy affair; but in reality, it was not so. Marmont states that the artillery prepared the action by firing on the Austrians for fully twenty minutes. Then followed the advance of the infantry. Petit states that it took an hour to form up for attack—a terrible hour to pass, he says, seeing how the Austrian artillery was bearing cruelly on the French. But Desaix's men needed a short rest after their hurried march from Rivalta.

On the point of the advance, Boudet writes in his report:—

> All the line got into movement, and advanced at the double; my division was foremost. My left brigade, composed of the 9th Light, had on its front to contend against the Hungarian grenadiers who had been brought together by General Melas so that this chosen corps might pursue with advantage the victory which he considered already as his own. This body of grenadiers was supported by a very large mass of cavalry, which overlapped the wing of my leading brigade; their resistance was obstinate, but rendered void by the valour of the 9th Light. A fortunate charge of our cavalry crowned this attack. . . .
>
> Several times the enemy's cavalry attempted to turn and surround the 9th Light; but it was received in a very discouraging manner.
>
> My second brigade, consisting of the 30th and 59th half-brigades (which I led in person), with really astonishing boldness, strength, and rapidity, pierced the centre of the enemy's army and cut it asunder. This brigade had constantly to defend its front flanks and rear against artillery, musketry, and various bodies of cavalry. The last especially came to the charge several times, with intent of attacking in rear. But the perfect order of the close columns in which our battalions had kept, notwithstanding having to march across vineyards and other obstacles of ground, rendered the attempts of the cavalry not only useless, but also caused them a considerable loss.

The critical moment of the battle had arrived. In their advance the infantry had left some of the guns behind. Marmont, in trying to get two of them and a howitzer forward near the high-road, was about to limber up, when through the clouds of smoke, he beheld a French regiment—the 30th—breaking up, followed by a heavy column of the enemy. Thereupon he speedily poured four rounds of canister on the head of the advancing Austrians; when just at that moment Kellermann and his horsemen dashed forward in front of the guns and made a vigorous charge. Marmont, in his *Mémoires*, states that, having noticed the French battalion waver, he had advanced his guns to avert the impending disaster. This was at the very moment when the Austrians, having fired a last volley, broke into a double to attack the French infantry.

That a regiment gave way, overwhelmed by numbers, and was pursued by the Austrians is a disputed point. Victor makes no mention of any check in the advance of Desaix's column, neither does Boudet. Kellermann, in his report, made on the 15th of June, the day after the battle, writes:—

> I observed that the infantry, which was marching on the left of the Marengo road on a level with Cascina Grossa, was beginning to give way, and that the enemy's grenadiers were charging it at the double.

Marmont writes:—

> All at once, I saw in front of me and to the left the 30th half-brigade in disorder and in flight. ... I perceived, fifty paces from the 30th, in the midst of a mass of thick smoke and dust, a mass in good order. At first, I thought them French, but soon detected that this was the head of a deep column of Austrian grenadiers.

Marmont and Kellermann do not agree; for the 30th was not marching on the left of the Marengo road; as we have seen that the regiment on that side was the 9th. Rocquancourt deplores that such a thing should have been as much as mentioned; nevertheless, here is the evidence of two of the principal actors, and it seems plain that some corps did so retire.

A combat which commenced with such spirit was bound to reach a point in which the least circumstance was likely to be decisive, and this circumstance occurred in Kellermann's timely charge.

Desaix had sent one of his *aides-de-camp*, Savary, to the First Consul to ask that Kellermann with his cavalry might be ordered to support him in his coming attack. Kellermann's brigade was advancing in one line on the right and abreast of Desaix's infantry, his advance being partly concealed by the vines which were trained on the trees. He was on the alert, and anxiously looking for any opening which might present itself. A glance showed him what aid he might render to the infantry, then beginning to give way in the neighbourhood of Cascina Grossa, were he to charge the advancing Austrians.

He seized the favourable moment, wheeled the 2nd and 20th Regiments into column, broke into a gallop, and rushed at the enemy. He thus fell suddenly on the left flank and rear of the Austrians at a moment when their muskets were unloaded, and by this brilliant manoeuvre captured General Zach and 2,000 men.

De Brossier writes:—

Kellermann met sa troupe au galop, depasse rapidement l'ennemi et le charge impétueusement de revers.

Melas states:—

La cavalerie ennemie apparut , les contourna, et mit en désordre complet nôtre cavalerie.

The 2nd Regiment of Cavalry, followed by the 20th, burst through the massive Austrian column; the two regiments then turned about and rode through it a second time. The charge annihilated in a moment three battalions of grenadiers and the whole regiment of Wallis; all were sabred, trampled over, or broken. In this charge, the 2nd Regiment had, out of eleven officers, seven killed or wounded. The regiment captured two standards. It was a trooper of this same regiment, Riche by name, who made Zach prisoner.

Kellermann explains this encounter in the following words:—

I detected that the infantry which marched on the left of the Marengo road, abreast of the Cascina Grossa, was beginning to waver, and that the enemy's grenadiers were charging it at the double. I reflected that there was not a moment to lose, and that a rapid movement might bring victory back to our flag. I halted my line of battle; I ordered platoons to the left and forward. The 2nd and 20th Cavalry found themselves at the head of the column which hurled itself headlong with impetuosity on the flank of the Austrian grenadiers at the moment when they had delivered their fire."

Zach had pushed too far forward; his column having outstripped the rest of the troops, these latter were unable to come to his aid. The grenadiers, attacked in front and on the flanks, heaped together in one mass, were more easily hemmed in, and forced to lay down their arms.

But Kellermann had no sooner directed his charge against the infantry than his eyes fell on Lichtenstein's cavalry, which was marching on the flank of the Austrian infantry to the north of the road about Guasca. He at once halted the rear of his column by ordering platoons to the right; in this way he formed again some 200 troopers into line, and with these he rushed forward to attack the Austrian cavalry and prevent their helping the grenadiers. The enemy's cavalry, stupefied by this resumption of the offensive, had remained rooted to the ground as if paralyzed, witnesses of a disaster which it was in their power to stop at once.

✶✶✶✶✶✶

Marmont writes *à propos* of Kellermann's charge, that a body of 2,000 of the Austrian cavalry only half a cannon-shot away witnessed his attack of Zach's column without taking the slightest step to go in aid of their comrades.

✶✶✶✶✶✶

Kellermann writes:—

> I took the situation in at once, and halting half of my column, wheeled it again into line before it had had time to enter into the midst of the enemy, and carried it in the direction of the cavalry which had been checked by this manoeuvre.

À propos of his famous charge against the Austrian column at Marengo, Kellermann was wont to say, "I made it alone and by inspiration."

It would be difficult to seek in history for a parallel to the audacity of Kellermann's double manoeuvre, to his scorn in weighing the odds, and to the happy inspiration which led him to dare the bold attempt.

Marmont and Kellermann declare the first step taken, when Desaix resumed the offensive, to have been unpromising. The French drew back, and, without the intervention of Kellermann's horsemen, the Austrians might have resumed their march. The instantaneous collapse of Zach's column, due to the charge of the French dragoons, had in it something of the miraculous.

Kellermann's double manoeuvre marks him as a real cavalry leader. The Austrian column on his left he attacks by wheeling into column of troops, hiding the smallness of his numbers by his daring onset. But he espies another enemy on his front. He suddenly changes the formation of the rear half of his small column by wheeling it into line, and charging to the front. There was not a moment to lose. The opportunity would have swiftly passed away; and it was the celerity of the conception and execution which gained the victory for both charges.

A fact difficult to explain is how Kellermann was able to upset a column of 6,000 men with such a handful of cavalry, and at such a small cost. He himself remarks:—

> This astonishing success has not cost me more than twenty men

in killed and wounded.

Were the Austrians spell-bound, that they could not use their bayonets? However, of all who surrendered, only a small portion were made prisoners, for a very large part melted away in the confusion which ensued.

The Austrians were completely taken aback at seeing their career of victory arrested and the battle renewed.

The defeat of the advanced guard of the principal Austrian column infused fresh courage into the French. Their divisions, which only a few moments before had been beaten and driven back, turned about and advanced in the best of order. The whole of the French, in short, rushed forward like one man to the charge, and moved against the enemy, stirred by the inspiring sounds of bugles and drums.

Gardanne's division, which was advancing on Cascina Grossa to drive out O'Reilly's troops, received an unexpected reinforcement as it moved to the attack. A battalion of the 44th half-brigade, which had crossed the Simplon after Béthencourt, reached the field and joined their comrades.

Kellermann rallied his horsemen, still heated by the very lucky charge they had just made, and went in pursuit of Lichtenstein's dragoons. These had thrown themselves on to Pilatti's brigade, bringing with them the inseparable disorder of a flight. Pilatti's brigade, already shaken by the severe handling it had received in the forenoon, seeing Lichtenstein's dragoons withdrawing in disorder, imitated their bad example; the greater part fled to find safety behind Ott's column, some sought protection in rear of the main column.

Lichtenstein's dragoons in their flight fell over the Austrian centre when in progress of deploying, and put it into disorder, thus enabling Lannes, the Consular Guard, and Monnier's troops to dash against it with vigour. The main body of the Austrian Army, overthrown by the cavalry which was to protect it, began to give way; a new group of fugitives, like a rushing torrent, helped to sweep it away. At this same moment Kellermann came up with his cavalry, and began cutting the Austrians up. The disorder increased, and soon reached its maximum; many men fled, and went to seek refuge in the rear.

The mass of fugitives made for Marengo, to get a safe shelter in the village. The confusion became extreme. The officers tried in vain to rally their men behind the Fontanone; but all to no purpose. The men were deaf to their voice, and the mass threw itself tumultuously on the bridgehead. Horsemen, infantry, guns, waggons, in a disordered mob made for the two bridges on the Bormida, all trying as soon as possible to place the river between them and their pursuers.

The rout of Zach's column became a disaster for the whole of the Austrian Army. Well does Lanfrey say of Kellermann's charge:—

> This prodigious and crushing blow changed, in an instant, the whole face of things. Never was a more sudden or complete subversion ever witnessed. (Lanfrey, *Histoire de Napoléon Ier*, vol. ii.)

It was amazement which made the Austrians first give way; they were then seized by an extraordinary panic, and this soon spread to their cavalry, which rode over its infantry till the whole army became a mass of inextricable confusion. Melas's words are:—

> This sudden and terrible change of fortune ended in completely destroying the courage of the troops."

No one was able to account for the flight of the cavalry. Most of the men did not even know for what reason they were flying so precipitately. In their wild career, they went through their principal column, and caused it to waver. Not a few, but a mass of horsemen, overturned Nairn's battalions when in the act of deploying, and before that manoeuvre was completed, carried the men off in their flight. Soon all, cavalry and infantry, were rushing pell-mell along the high-road.

Nothing could stop the fugitives; and though Kellermann had been compelled to slacken the pursuit, to give the infantry time to push forward, the flight continued in disorder in the direction of Marengo. The sight of Weidenfeld's grenadiers, formed up at Spinetta and holding firm, had no effect in restoring confidence. The fugitives had passed them a long way, and still they were flying. Every one hurried on. The only thought in every mind was to escape the imagined danger.

Fear, whether arising from an adequate or inadequate cause, speedily obtains the mastery over every other consideration. The best of troops are liable to a panic; this spreads from one individual to another, and quickly ends in a dishonourable flight. Troops like the Austrians, which had fought with great gallantry all the forenoon and far into the afternoon, notwithstanding the heavy losses they had sustained, cannot have been seized with panic without good cause. Possibly they became demoralized by the toil and fatigue they had endured fighting for hours in the overpowering heat of that brilliant summer day, by the losses caused by the concentrated fire of Marmont's battery, by the resistance they met when making too sure of victory, by the good array in which they found the troops they believed to be in flight. The last of these causes came on them as a surprise, and, as we all know, a surprise has a most unfavourable effect on the morale of soldiers. Terror, first of all, paralyzes the moral and physical faculties, gives rise to hesitation, followed by confusion, and the loss of that well-tempered courage which keeps the ranks together; then a need for looking after one's own safety overcomes everything else.

Kellermann delivered a last charge at the head of 360 mounted Consular Guard and 200 men the remnants of his own brigade and of the dragoons attached to it. He attacked and dispersed the enemy's cavalry.

****

At the moment when the Consular Guard was rushing on the Austrian cavalry, an Austrian soldier, overthrown and bleeding, was seen supplicating the French cavalry not to crush him. "My friends," called out Bessières, "open your ranks and spare that unfortunate."

******

The battle was not over yet, for Weidenfeld and O'Reilly undertook to defend the Fontanone brook, in order to give time to the fugitives to escape. Boudet and Lannes, however, were pressing on with vigour. At dusk, the French carried the village of Marengo, when the Austrians retired to Pedrabona, where they were joined by Ott's corps.

Crossard laments the retreat of the entire Austrian Army, when it was only its centre that had been defeated; he especially censures the left for retiring so placidly. Defeat, with a river on its rear, for the Austrian Army would have been ruin. Fortunately, the return of victory on the French side came late in the evening, after the French troops had expended their strength by many hours of hard fighting.

The retreat was effected with considerable confusion. An unreasonable panic had seized hold of the troops, and such was the general fear, that the drivers of the guns, alarmed lest they should not be able to gain the choked bridges leading to Alessandria quickly enough, plunged with their guns into the Bormida. The day after the battle, fully twenty pieces were brought out from the bed of the river.

Crossard mentions in his *Mémoires* that the first effects of the resumption of the offensive by the French was felt about the important post of Castel Ceriolo at about five in the evening. Of that village he says:—

For some time held by the Austrians, it not only covered their flank, but was the most stable pivot for any manoeuvres that the left of the Austrian Army could undertake.

Ott, preceded by a numerous body of cavalry, had followed the retiring French in the direction of San Giuliano Novo and the Villa Ghilina. Whilst on the march some runaway cavalry apprised him of the misfortune which had overtaken the right wing, and how Zach and Kahn had been completely overthrown. On the receipt of the unexpected news, and dismayed by so complete a change of fortune, Ott sought how best he could repair the blow. He halted his column, and with his centre battalions formed line to his right, with the intention of falling on the flank of the French, who were advancing on Marengo. This manoeuvre, which naturally would have suggested itself to any other commander, was no longer possible, for the main Austrian column had withdrawn with such rapidity that the opportune moment passed by very quickly.

Besides, not only had Lannes and Monnier resumed the offensive, but the French cavalry was beginning to show itself on the Salé road. As Ott's mission was to hold in check a strong French column which the Austrian staff supposed to be advancing from that side, the presence of Rivaud's cavalry brigade about Piovera seemed to indicate its coming, and Ott, warned by the cannonade at Marengo, and the 9th Light being about to carry the village, had to look after his own safety.

Jean Rivaud's brigade consisted of the 12th Hussars and the 21st Chasseurs. These troops were eager to join in the fray; they marched along the Salé road and rushed at the Austrians.

Ott withdrew his forces in good order, making for Castel Ceriolo. Much to his astonishment, when nearing that village, he found that it was already in possession of the enemy. This point has never been properly explained.

★★★★★★

The officers of Carra Saint Cyr's brigade stated that after the brigade had retired from Castel Ceriolo, from an hour and a quarter to an hour and a half, isolated from the rest of the army, it was met by an A.D.C. bearing an order for all the troops he fell in with to resume the offensive. The brigade accordingly faced about, and arrived at the village of Castel Ceriolo by sunset.

★★★★★★

Everything tends to show that Castel Ceriolo was abandoned by Carra Saint Cyr's brigade late in the afternoon; possibly it was reoccupied by some stray parties of the French during Ott's retreat. This is not at all improbable, for any party of men might have during the retreat sought refuge in any houses or farms in the plain, and have sallied forth as soon as they found the ground around them was clear. The ease with which Ott apparently brushed the occupants of Castel Ceriolo aside would lead one to believe that they were only a small body.

Night was coming on when Ott ordered General Vogelsang to capture the village. A passage was thus opened by main force, and this obstacle being fortunately cleared away, Ott's column pushed on, and regained the bridgehead. In this attack General Vogelsang was severely wounded.

The day was rapidly closing, and the Austrian Army, so unexpectedly defeated in the midst of its success, was hurrying in chaotic disorder to seek safety on the left bank of the Bormida. Galloping squadrons trampled over broken battalions without a thought save of precipitate flight. The infantry were not in a much better plight, as their morale was completely shaken by the desertion of the cavalry. The whole army presented a scene of wild terror and confusion.

Petit states that the clock at Marengo was striking ten as he and his comrades were returning slowly towards San Giuliano. At that hour, the sounds of the strife were silenced, and the exhausted French took up their cheerless bivouacs. The ground was thickly strewn with the corpses of the combatants. Gardanne was again at Pedrabona, holding the position from which he had been driven out in the morning by overpowering forces.

A deadly silence reigned over the plain, broken at intervals by the groans of the wounded who had not yet been removed, and for whose succour the means were none too plentiful.

During the night of the 14-15th of June, Bonaparte took steps to follow the advantages he had obtained over the Austrians. At break of day, Gardanne's advanced guard moved on the bridgehead, driving back O'Reilly's advanced posts.

As Major Count de Neupperg appeared beyond the bridgehead, the firing ceased. The count was conducted to Torre di Garofoli to ask for forty-eight hours' armistice. Bonaparte agreed to this on condition that the Austrians should retire to the left bank of the Bormida, a point which Melas conceded. General Skal went later on, at noon, to the French headquarters, to open a negotiation with the First Consul.

Melas, having sought the advice of a council of war, after mature deliberation, adopted the alternative of evacuating Piedmont, all Genoese territory, and the largest portion of Lombardy. His army marched out with the honours of war, retaining its arms, cannon, and baggage, and retired by the shortest way behind the Mincio. The fortresses of Tortona, Alessandria, Turin, Coni, Ceva, Genova, Savona, Santa Maria, the Duchy of Parma, including Piacenza, and the citadels of Milan, Arona, and Pizzighettone, were handed over to the French.

One of the results of having scattered his forces broadcast all over Lombardy was that Bonaparte felt himself compelled to let the Austrian Army go free after Marengo. Had he engaged with the greatest portion of his forces, there can be no doubt that a simple evacuation would not have satisfied him. With more troops he would have wrung a peace from the emperor in the month of June.

The battle was no sooner over than Captain Viviaud, attached to General Dupont, chief of the staff, was hastening to Piacenza to call up part of the troops left in reserve on the Po. On the 15th of June, he writes from Piacenza to intimate that the object of his mission has been attained. By noon Loison had quitted his cantonments at San Giovanni, and would be at Voghera at a very early hour. Duhesme would set out with his division at night, due to arrive at Voghera the following day. But all fear of the Austrians resuming the offensive had been put an end to for the present, in virtue of the convention concluded.

On the 16th, two days after the battle, Dalton reports that Boudet's division was encamped on the battlefield, surrounded by the corpses of the dead, and had no picks or spades with which to bury them, he declares:—

> Soon, the place will not be fit for occupation. The air already smells of infection.

Berthier writes to the First Consul that he purposes establishing his headquarters at Torre di Garofoli, on account of the infection caused by the corpses which cover the entire plain of Marengo.

In a few days the French Army was concentrated around Piacenza, with headquarters at Pavia. A division had been detached to Bologna. The total of the army was 48,932 men, with 5,748 horses, 51 guns, and 13 howitzers.

CHAPTER 7

Observations

The last phase of the battle was the happy combination of several fortunate circumstances. An ammunition-waggon blown up by the fire of Marmont's guns shakes the enemy. Desaix drives Boudet's division with great impetus on the head of the heavy Austrian column, which is being swept by the fire of Marmont's guns; and by this action gives to his soldiers that impulse which is so highly inspiriting when in the height of a movement of attack. The amazed Austrian column hesitates and stops, and at that very moment Kellermann rushes on its left flank with a portion of his brigade, whilst with the rest he attacks the Austrian cavalry which is to protect it.

The result of Kellermann's charge was that one half of the Austrian column was sabred or captured, whilst the other half was thrown into disorder by the fugitives, and, seized by panic, offered no resistance to the French.

This in itself was a signal success. But a more momentous one was the capture of the general who was at that moment commanding the Austrian Army.

The enemy's column found itself cut off, and unable to take another step, either for advancing or for retiring. Having lost all hope of safety in flight, it submitted to dire necessity, and laid down its arms.

Thus, it was the combined action of Desaix, Marmont, and Kellermann which decided the fate of the battle. But this attack on the left would not have been of half so much consequence had the rest of the troops, which for hours had contended against superior forces, not resumed the offensive, and rushed at the enemy. We must not forget who it was that restored confidence in these troops, fatigued by a lengthy and hopeless combat, and worn out by heat and exhaustion; that it was their general, Bonaparte, who restored confidence in these dejected soldiers; that it was his magnetic influence which urged them to renew the fight, and to secure victory.

On the Austrian side, the commander-in-chief had deserted his troops; and there can be no doubt that a change of direction had an injurious effect on the operations. The Austrian account admits this in the following words:—

> This sudden withdrawal of the general-in-chief certainly produced a bad effect; the change of leadership occasioned a certain amount of hesitation in the original dispositions.

A great commander has generally been found at the post of the greatest danger. At Marengo, at the critical moment, there was no unity of command, and to this much of the Austrian defeat must undoubtedly be attributed.

Incidents that take but a moment to occur should take but a moment to relate. For all that, such was the consequence of Kellermann's charge that much has been said and written on the subject.

In his *Mémoires*, Marmont observes regarding the attack of Zach's column by Kellermann:—

> If the charge had been delivered three minutes later, our guns would have been taken and withdrawn; and possibly, not being any longer under the influence of the surprise engendered by the volleys of case-shot, the enemy's column might have been better prepared to receive the cavalry. It might have been the same if the charge had preceded the discharge. Therefore, it needed this precise combination to insure such a complete and, it must be said, unhoped-for success. Never did fortune intervene in a more decisive manner. Never did any general show more insight, more vigour, and more apposite promptitude than Kellermann in this instance.

Writers have not paid sufficient attention to the happy combination of the three arms. The influence of the cavalry charge on the result of the battle is incontestable. In extolling Kellermann's promptness, due credit has, however, been withheld from Marmont. He never demanded it. Still, his share in the final defeat is found in his own words—that, but for "the influence of the surprise engendered by the volley of case-shot, the enemy's column might have been better prepared to receive the cavalry."

There is no question that Boudet's artillery and that of the reserve were the first to stay the advance of the Austrians, the first to have some effect on the pursuing columns. (Melas writes in his report, "After a violent and rapid fire which dismounted our artillery, the troops, which up to that moment had remained victorious, commenced to hesitate.")

Kellermann's charge was a spontaneous movement. There was no time for anyone to give the order for the charge. Such an order could only emanate from the officer who was in actual command of the cavalry. The idea of asking for the assistance of the cavalry would naturally have suggested itself to Desaix, and we have Kellermann's own testimony that Savary rode up to him near San Giuliano and delivered an order to that effect.

★★★★★★

See *Réfutation de M. le Duc de Rovigo, ou La Vérité sur la Bataille de Marengo*. Marmont also relates that Savary, who was bearing orders for Kellermann, rode up to the great battery and asked him where that general was likely to be found.

★★★★★★

The order was to march on a level with General Desaix's corps, and to support him in the new conflict which was about to take place. Savary states that the First Consul's words were:—

You will tell him to charge, without considering the cost, as soon as Desaix will unmask his attack. (*Mémoires du Duc de Rovigo, tom.* i.)

This latter version is as fanciful as several other statements found in the *Mémoires du Duc de Rovigo*. It does not accord with Kellermann's own words:—

This decisive and unforeseen onset was neither prepared nor combined. It took less time to perform than to tell.

Kellermann did his best, but he could hardly have calculated on all the effect his charge would have. In any case, his success raised the spirits of the French. Lannes's and Victor's men, encouraged by the result of his charge, advanced, and the Austrian cavalry, fleeing from Kellermann's dragoons, rode over their own infantry, until the whole maddened and panic-stricken mass fled in wild disorder towards Marengo and the bridges beyond it. The Austrians, who had fought bravely during the day, appear to have lost confidence in their leaders, and in the luck of their own side.

It may be pleaded for the Austrian soldiers that they had been under arms before daybreak, that they were oppressed by fatigue, and had fought through the great heat of the day. But what applies to the Austrians applies just as much to their opponents.

This battle brought forward prominently the marked superiority in fighting qualities of the French over the Austrians. Imagination plays a considerable part in French soldiers, and any idea of superiority and strength acts on them, and renders them blind to all horrors, odds, and danger. The superiority of the French had been already established during Massena's operations in the neighbourhood of Genova, and in Suchet's advance from the Var. Only at Marengo it stood out still more conspicuously. In Massena's operations to recover his lost communications with France in the past April, 1,400 men kept 10,000 Austrians in countenance for eight hours. The idea that they were about to be supported by a second battalion of grenadiers, that Sacquelen's column was speeding to their aid, and that in the mean while Soult was turning the enemy, made the French soldiers on that occasion perform prodigies of valour.

The Austrians had shown conspicuous bravery and perseverance in the fighting on the banks of the Fontanone and in the capture of Marengo. But they were wanting in staying qualities. Their deportment in the evening was very different from what it had been in the forenoon. With all his good qualities, the Austrian soldier lacked the fire and the pertinacity of the French troops. All through the fighting in 1800, the same charges can be brought against the Austrian generals. They showed conspicuous lack of enterprise; and they did not seem to know how to turn to account the first advantages gained.

At Marengo, the French soldiers shone to great advantage. Their stubborn resistance against great odds, when mowed down by a powerful artillery fire, was equalled by their brilliant dash in the final phase of the contest. The French, who had been fighting ever since morning, exposed to cruel losses, tired, hungry, and thirsty, nevertheless resumed the offensive as if by inspiration, and carried it out with extraordinary vigour.

Le coq français est le coq de la gloire;
Par les revets il n'est point abattu.

Favart.

The cavalry, which had missed its proper role of exploring and keeping touch with the enemy, fully made up for it by its gallant conduct during the battle; especially when the enemy was driven back into Alessandria.

The artillery had rendered good service, but was overpowered by the greatly superior artillery of the enemy. Almost all the French pieces had been dismounted, and during the retreat there remained not more than five fit to fire.

Nothing was ever so remarkable as the rapidity with which the French resumed the offensive, and swept the Austrians clean off the plain. Mad with joy at seeing victory returning to their standards, they stepped boldly forward, their faces beaming with what the Romans called *gaudia certaminis*, the excitement of the contest. Such instantaneous outburst of *élan* was thoroughly in keeping with the national character, for no nation is so swift to pass from the depths of despair to the brightest of hopes, and *vice versâ*.

The disorder which reigned in the ranks of the Austrians was only too patent. The French dashed forward, and in less than an hour crossed the plain which it had taken the Austrians eight hours to conquer. (Jomini, *Histoire des Guerres de la Révolution, tom.* xiii.) The charge of the French defies description. French impetuosity was opposed to the methodical tactics of the Austrians, and the latter were not allowed time to rally.

What told much in favour of the French was that, after they had once resumed the offensive, they did not waste any time in securing their prisoners; they left them behind, and only occupied themselves in pressing back the adversary with vigour.

In the evening the Austrians defended Marengo with an obstinacy quite equal to what the French had shown in the forenoon. Nevertheless, they had to yield before the impetuosity of Boudet's, Victor's, and Lannes's troops, whose ardour so many hours of hard fighting had not been able to quench.

In his report, General Boudet states:—

> The enemy's resistance, in certain positions, was terrible. It would have been useless toying to have driven him off by musketry. Only bayonet charges were able to dislodge him, and these were executed with unexampled quickness and intrepidity. In truth, it is impossible to bestow sufficient praise on this brigade (Guénand's brigade), partly composed of conscripts, who in courage and firmness have rivalled the oldest soldiers.

Another, though an indirect cause of the victory, was the bearing of the French troops since the opening days of the campaign. Massena and Suchet certainly were not present at Marengo, nevertheless, they had prepared the way for victory by destroying much of the morale of the Austrian Army. The tough daily combats under the walls of Genova, and in the retreat to the Var, cannot but have seriously shaken the self-confidence of the Austrian soldiers.

Bülow attributes the loss of the battle to the slowness of the Austrian movements, and to the uncertainty which marked their resolutions. (Bülow offers many suggestions as to the plan the Austrians might have followed, but says very little indeed of the tactics of the battle.) Their generals had neglected to make any dispositions which could ensure victory, or, if not that, which could at all events render their defeat less disastrous.

The Austrians fought the Battle of Marengo with a river at their back, and a river over which there was virtually but one point of passage. It was this last fact that brought about such a very long delay in getting their troops to the right bank of the Bormida and in deploying. In the incertitude of success, all the rules of prudence enjoin having several bridges laid down over the river, and employing simultaneously every road which is adapted for troops, so as to shorten the time required for reaching their ground and deploying. There was nothing to prevent the Austrians laying bridges above and below the existing bridgehead of Alessandria; had this been done their action against Victor's and Lannes's troops would have probably been decided before Bonaparte's arrival on the battlefield, and long before Desaix could have arrived from Rivalta.

Dampierre, writing to General Mathieu Dumas, 16th of June, states that Melas himself had given orders to the second line to fire on any one in the first line who should dare to forget his duty. This statement, if true, does not speak well for the Austrian Army. The necessity for such an order would tend to show that it was not animated by the best spirit.

★★★★★★

In a letter from Suchet to Bonaparte, written from Nice on the 30th of May, occurs the following passage: "Amongst the enemy's troops is a corps of Hungarian grenadiers, the pick of the enemy's army. Ordinarily it attacks with impetuosity, but these columns are so disgusted that as soon as they are beaten by you, you will get quit of them cheaply. They march always united, and number from 3,000 to 3,500 men."—De Cugnac, *Campagne de l'Armée de Réserve en 1800*, vol. ii.

★★★★★★

Others, however, say quite the reverse, and show what a thrilling effect the decision taken by Melas to cut his way through the French Army had on the Austrian soldiery. The Austrian account expresses itself thus:—

> A very forcible order of the day explained to the Austrians the full gravity of the dangers by which they were surrounded; but likewise, the glory which attended them should they conquer. The army was full of courage, and the words of the commander-in-chief had still further increased the excellent spirit by which these troops, accustomed to victory, were animated.

On this point we have the evidence of Crossard who relates how General Vogelsang on the 14th drew his attention to the gaiety of the troops.

Dampierre had already made an accusation against the spirit of the Austrian troops. Writing to General Gardanne on the 11th of June, he says:—

> The people of the country assert that it is difficult to form an adequate idea of the disorder in which the last (Austrian) troops retired on the night of the 20th (9th of June, the night of the Battle of Montebello). There are very good grounds for believing that, if night and a few squadrons of cavalry had not concealed their disorder, we should have made from 2,000 to 3,000 prisoners—men belonging to disheartened corps who wished for nothing better than to surrender. On this point almost all the deserters and prisoners agree.

There were favourable chances for Melas, for the composition of Bonaparte's army was not of the best. The greater part of the troops he led to Marengo had no experience of the manoeuvres performed in a pitched battle.

It was remarkable how very slow the Austrians were in turning their first advantages to account—a neglect which in the end told greatly against them, as it gave time to Desaix to appear on the field. All the chances of success in the battle were in their favour; and this Bonaparte himself conceded. What must we think of the commanders and staff who were not able to turn these advantages to good profit? From noon up to three o'clock, and even later, victory went with the Austrians. But they did not overpower their adversaries by their fire, no more did they succeed in capturing a single battalion. During those hours, whilst the Austrians held the superiority over the French, they made only 1,100 prisoners, of whom 25 belonged to the Consular Guard.

There were no brilliant movements to carry their efforts in gigantic strides from one part of the field to another. On the Fontanone they had experienced great losses because they had neglected to press on Gardanne as he was compelled to yield ground. And for what reason? To attend to their deployment—a manoeuvre which might have been left to be executed as soon as they had got beyond Marengo. Here was a waste of time in performing a processional evolution, when they should have pressed the enemy sword in hand.

If Bonaparte had committed a fault in scattering his corps too much, Melas had made a greater one in unduly deploying his wings in the battle.

When Desaix and Kellermann attacked, the Austrian Army was in a long deep column; a formation which is not only unwieldy, but also labours under the disadvantage of offering a wide mark to the fire of the enemy's artillery. A comparison of the efforts made by the two armies is remarkably instructive. The French grasped their opportunity, and turned to account the slowness and disunion which they discerned to be reigning amongst their opponents. Lannes, with some 8,000 combatants, had for three hours kept in check from 18,000 to 20,000 of the enemy—a thing which could have never occurred had the Austrians attacked boldly at noon. Crossard was in the Austrian left flank; he states most distinctly that where he was there was no energy and no enterprise.

In the "*Bulletin de l'Armée de Réserve*" issued at Milan on the 17th of June, occurs the following passage:—

> *Un général autrichien de beaucoup de mérite disait ait quartier général:*
> *'Nous n'aurons de repos et de bonheur sur le continent que lorsque,*
> *d'un concours unanime, nous en interdirons l'accès à cette nation venale*
> *et mercantile, qui calcule sur notre sang pour l'accroissement de son*
> *commerce.'*

This officer and others may have said whatever they pleased against England, but they overlooked the fact that the war had been undertaken against the advice of their best general, the Archduke Charles, and that England had nothing to do with the management of the campaign nor with the behaviour of the Austrian troops on the battlefield. Never, possibly, in any battle was a victorious army so quickly put to flight, nor did one so quickly abandon every advantage it had gained by hours of hard fighting. Nothing availed to re-establish order; nothing could bring the Austrian soldier back to his sense of duty. Had the Austrians displayed more staying power, their victory would have made the above observation unnecessary.

A favourite plea of the Austrians after a defeat was to throw all the blame on England. Mack did this after Ulm, and the Emperor Francis after his defeat at Austerlitz.

Chevalier Cavour accuses the Austrians of not having drawn full advantage from their superiority in artillery when attacking farm buildings and barns. Such buildings, he states, were carried by the infantry with musketry and bayonet, and this was the cause of much bloodshed.

Not only did the Austrian commander show little judgment and audacity, but his employment of the cavalry was faulty in every sense. His first false step was the withdrawing from the battlefield of one-third of it to go and observe Suchet, who was quite out of reach of taking part in the contest. That in itself was bad enough; for had the seventeen squadrons so detached been present to charge Victor's retiring troops, they might have completed their defeat early in the day. The remaining two-thirds of the cavalry were dispersed all over his line of battle in place of being kept in hand as a powerful reserve to be launched forth so as to strike a decisive blow at a propitious moment.

Pilatti's force was set to undertake a risky operation in which it suffered heavily, and the rest of the Austrian cavalry engaged in partial charges and in securing prisoners when it should have come irresistibly forward to crush the French. Commandant Picard very justly observes of the Austrian cavalry engaged, that after having bravely seconded the attack from the beginning and contributed largely in making the French withdraw, it did not know either how to push back the infantry, when very little was required to convert the retreat into a rout, nor how to resist the French cavalry when Bonaparte resumed the offensive. More than once it even declined to cross swords with the enemy.

The Austrian cavalry was admirably mounted, and skilled in all the manoeuvres of war; but Melas evidently did not understand its employment in large masses. None of the Austrian cavalry leaders, when the battle was going all in favour of their side, showed a particle of the boldness and enterprise displayed by Kellermann when the day was going dead against the French, working with horses that had not partaken of oats for several days. (Duvignan's report. See De Cugnac, vol. ii.)

Up to Marengo, if the Austrian cavalry had not exactly done all it should have done, nevertheless its prestige had not been lowered by defeat. It was feared by the French cavalry, and more so by their infantry, which had so often been disconcerted by its attacks.

The officers and men of the Austrian infantry, on the whole, did their duty manfully. It does not speak well for them, however, that they allowed the 200 men of Kellermann to capture some thousands of their number when they had their bayonets to rely upon. It has also been remarked that many more lives were lost during the advance than during the retreat— a fact which would be tantamount to a proof that the retirement was not carried out with all the stubbornness desired.

Wellington once declared that Napoleon had won most of his battles by the power of artillery. He certainly did not do so at Marengo, where that arm was meanly represented. De Cugnac, indeed, believes that the want of artillery was one of the reasons which made Bonaparte accept Melas's capitulation.

In Chapter 1, it has been seen that from the very commencement of the campaign the French officers were disturbed by the scarcity of ammunition, and that the limited number of rounds in the men's pouches formed a subject of constant complaint. (Just before the Battle of Montebello, on the 6th of June, Victor wrote to the general-in-chief, adding the following postscript: "*Los cartouches se brûleront bien tôt; nos soldats en ont bien peu.*")

On the French side, the Battle of Marengo was conspicuous for the dearth of ammunition. According to Lauriston, the French had no more of it than was sufficient for five or six hours' fighting. Dampierre had a gun rendered useless, and incapable of firing a shot, simply for want of ammunition. Ismert complains that his people were without guns or ammunition. Victor and Lannes fell short of the latter. Victor states that the troops were compelled to retire through want of ammunition, after having lost a large number of men. Quiot adds that the artillery had fallen short of cartridges, and the infantry had expended all theirs.

The day following the battle, the soldiers of Boudet's division refilled their pouches out of those which the enemy had left on the ground.

The battle was won, but the heroic Desaix had gained the victory at the price of his life.

Marshal Victor, Duc de Bellune, begins a work, *Extraits d'un Histoire inédite des Guerres de la Republique et de l'Émpire,* with the following exclamation:—

Hoche died! ...
At the news, the whole of France uttered a piercing cry of anguish; and all Paris, in the midst of the whirlwind of its intrigues and of its pleasures, of a sudden paused to weep.

******

The *peace-maker* died as they were celebrating in Paris the anniversary of the foundation of the Republic. Championnet, in his funeral oration at the grave, said: "A great man never dies. He may descend into the tomb; but there immortality begins." To Hoche's honour it is related that he had been confined in the *Conciergerie*, by order of Saint Just, for some weeks. He was there when Saint Just entered that prison the day before his execution. Instead of heaping reproaches on his fallen enemy, Hoche, with true magnanimity, pressed his hand and made way to let him pass.

******

With far greater reason the gay and restless capital could suspend its cares and its joys to shed bitter tears for the loss of the brave and gifted Desaix.

Pleurez, pleurez fils de la gloire,
Il n'est plus, le brave Desaix.
M. Maury.

Thiers' eulogy was short but exact:—

Sa mort priva l'armée d'un excellent général, et la France d'un de ses plus vertueux citoyens.

Unfortunate Desaix! how many utterances historians and others discovered for your expiring lips! A writer has justly said that history, like love, is apt to surround her heroes with an atmosphere of imaginary brightness; and for many the romantic has a greater charm than truth. The words attributed to Desaix, that he died regretting that he had done nothing to deserve that his name should be handed down to posterity, are pure fiction. The words are given in the bulletin of the 15th of June, and sound grand. Nevertheless, Bonaparte in this

TOMB OF GENERAL DESAIX.

instance, evidently prompted by a desire to immortalise his friend's last moments, seems not to have been able to refrain from romancing.

Thiers says that, hit in the chest, Desaix told General Boudet, who commanded the division which he was leading, to hide his fall from the troops, lest the news might tend to unsteady them. This is what Boudet writes in his report:—

> Death came and carried this great captain away from his comrades. In his last words he commanded that his fate might be hidden, lest the news should give rise to an alarm which might be detrimental to the army.

A report, attributed to Lauriston, declares that Desaix uttered to Lefebvre-Desnouettes the single word, "*Dead;*" (the writer states that Desaix fell at the commencement of the charge of the 9th Light; that he turned round and saw him fall), that, as he had no distinctive uniform, his fall was not observed by the soldiers, and that Lefebvre had his body removed. By all accounts Desaix's fall was not noticed, and the statement of some writers (Mathieu Dumas, Jomini, etc.), that the troops were irritated by the death of their general, is without foundation.

That Lefebvre had the body removed cannot be reconciled with Savary's assertion. The latter is silent on Desaix's last moments, for the simple reason that he was not at the side of his general. Desaix was struck during the absence of Savary, who had been sent to ask Bonaparte that Kellermann might be ordered to co-operate in the forthcoming attack.

Later in the evening Savary learnt from the colonel of the 9th that his general was no more. Looking all over the field for him amongst the heaps left by the battle's surges, he found his body near the place where he had last seen him, under a pile of slain, naked but for his shirt. (From Boudet's description of the battle formation assumed by his division, it results that Desaix must have fallen in the fields of Vigna Santa, on the left of the Tortona road.) He could identify him only by his abundant hair, and by the wounds he had received at Lauterbourg and at the crossing of the Neus. The *aide-de-camp* had his general's body wrapped in the cloak of one of the hussars which he found at hand, placed it on his horse, and then conveyed it to headquarters at Torre di Garofoli.

★★★★★★

Through respect for Desaix, and owing to Bourrienne's solicitation, the First Consul took Savary and Rapp on his staff as *aides-de-camp*. They served him to the last with zeal and fidelity. Rapp had an Alsatian frankness which did not quite please his master.

✶✶✶✶✶✶

In the *Mémorial du Depôt Général de la Guerre, tom.* iv., Desaix is stated to have died instantly:—

> *Il est mort sour le coup.*

The narrative adds:—

> *Il n'a eu que le temps de dire au jeune Lebrun* (the son of the Third Consul) *qui etait avec lui: 'Allez dire au Premier Consul que je meurs avec le regret de n'avoir pas assez fait pour vivre dans la postérité.'*

The two statements are quite at variance. Bourrienne gives the lie to the words contained in the famous bulletin, which he declares Bonaparte made him put down, when engaged in drafting it. He also denies that it was in the arms of Lebrun that Desaix died, or that he uttered one single word. According to him, Desaix fell a short distance from Lefebvre-Desnouettes. He adds:—

After all, the onset in which he succumbed was so brief, the disorder so instantaneous, the change of fortune so sudden, that it is not in the least astonishing if, in the midst of such confusion, the circumstances of his death were not verified in a more positive manner.

Marmont is quite certain that Desaix never pronounced the fine words which have been placed in his mouth: he was pierced by a bullet through the heart, and fell down rigid, without uttering a single word. (*Mémoires du Duc de Raguse, livre v.*) Corréard, in his biography of Desaix, (*Biographie de Louis Charles Antoine Desaix*), states:—

He is no sooner in presence of the enemy than he is struck by a bullet, and falls without uttering a word.

Gourgaud (*Relation de la Bataille de Marengo, Extraite de Mémoires de Sainte Hélène*), writes:—

> *Mais comme il marchait à la tête de deux cent éclaireurs de la neuvième légère, il fut frappé d'une balle au coeur et tomba roide mort au moment où il venait d'ordonner la charge.* (See *Mémorial, tom.* iv.)

Desaix was remarkably unostentatious; at Marengo he wore no

distinctive mark of rank by which his body might be identified. Not like Nelson, who wore all his orders when he went into action at Trafalgar.

******

The comparison between these two officers may be considered immoderate but it is not so when looking at Desaix's age, for he was only thirty-two when he fell at Marengo. What might not a man of his talent have done had he been spared? Mahan declares that Nelson's page in history covers a little more than twelve years—from February, 1793, to October, 1805. He consequently did not begin to be eminent before he had attained the age of thirty-five.

A writer states that Desaix was struck in the back by an accidental shot from one of his own men, the bullet passing through the heart. De Cayrol, however, in his critique of Sir Walter Scott's *History of Napoleon*, asserts that in his official capacity he had occasion to examine Desaix's body the day after the battle, and that he could positively declare that the bullet had pierced the heart, coming out at the back.

******

At all times Napoleon, like even the greatest of mortals, was not devoid of a certain weakness. He would never acknowledge himself under an obligation to anyone. He was not as ready as Jourdan, Hoche, Kléber, and Moreau in acknowledging the services of those who had fought under his orders. After Marengo he insisted that all the credit of the victory should be assigned to himself. In this and other instances, he displayed bitter jealousy of any general who appeared by his deeds to undermine his reputation. On this point he was meanness itself.

Much has been said about the cool remark with which Bonaparte greeted Kellermann when that officer appeared at his supper-table on the night of the battle. "You made rather a good charge today."

******

Bourrienne relates that Kellermann, from provisions acquired from the Convent del Bosco, furnished supper for Bonaparte and his staff, who were famishing. The army, he declares, was in a destitute state.

******

We should bear in mind, however, that this meeting occurred very few hours after the event, when Bonaparte was elated by the good fortune which had befallen, him, and when, possibly, the full importance of Kellermann's charge had not been thoroughly estimated. Many officers who have taken part in a general action may have noticed how in the first flush of victory it is anything but easy to grasp the full extent of the various incidents of the contest. Some writers seem to believe that this is what actually happened to Bonaparte, that he had not at the moment when he spoke grasped all the importance of Kellermann's charge. And what does Boudet write?

> The cavalry has likewise contributed to it (the victory) with a good deal of promptitude and courage.

> He also had not taken in all the result of the charge.

Bourrienne relates what Bonaparte told him, apparently when they were alone at a later hour of the night.

> Little Kellermann made a lucky charge. He did it just at the right moment. We are much indebted to him. You see what trifling circumstances decide these affairs.

So, he thought the charge decisive, though he attributes it to luck, and not to judgment in seizing the opportunity.

At Marengo the incidents were so confused, the events were so extraordinary, that it was impossible to write a clear narrative of the battle. Bonaparte tried in vain to give to his account a certain sequence and order which were far from being found in the events. The official reports do not credit Kellermann with the preponderating role of the victory.

Capefigue states on this point:—

> The account of the Battle of Marengo was controverted (*defiguré*) by the *Moniteur*. Bonaparte has not given due credit to Kellermann, he has grasped all. (Kellermann's boast, "It is I who placed the crown on that man's head," was not in good taste. It showed singular want of tact.)

There are noted instances in which Napoleon was unjust to his officers. He was so to Kellermann, and he was so later to Montbrun; and thus, two of his best cavalry officers, for diverse reasons, fell under his displeasure.

Evidently the officers were not unanimous in assigning the credit for the victory to Kellermann. Crossard, who writes with too evident animosity, tries to deprive Bonaparte of any credit. His words are:—

> Desaix prompted the action which decided the Battle of Marengo,

and Kellermann carried it into effect.

The baron seems to have overlooked the fact that Desaix's action would not have been possible had Bonaparte withheld his consent, and how very impatient the First Consul had been for the arrival of the column from Rivalta.

The day following the battle, Crossard had an interview with Dupont, who, pointing to Boudet, said, "It was he who gave you the finishing blow." Lauriston, writing on the 19th of June, extols Boudet as having saved the army. ("*Vous serez bien aise d'apprendre que la division Boudet à eté regarée comme ayant sauvé l'armée.*") There were others, therefore, besides Bonaparte, who, very soon after the battle had been fought, did not accord the principal credit to Kellermann.

Boudet's words are quite worthy of notice. They are:—

> The remarkable advantages which were gained on the left, and above all the capture of the artillery and prisoners, were absolutely due to the bearing and acts of valour of this corps (9th Light). The cavalry has equally contributed to it by its timely action and courage."

Mathieu Dumas assigns to Kellermann a great share of the success in the second battle, but he credits Desaix with the most prominent part.

It was nothing but gross exaggeration to place Kellermann's name above that of Bonaparte in the events of Marengo. Abroad this was done to lower Bonaparte's reputation, and by the Army of the Rhine out of pure jealousy. A few seconds of enterprise, an extremely able seizure of a fleeting opportunity, were set against all the incidents favourable and unfavourable of that eventful day. That Kellermann put the finishing stroke to the battle in a very brilliant exploit no one will ever deny. He followed the principle which should guide every cavalry leader, that the incidents of the fight should make them form their plans of action on the spot, almost intuitively. But to pretend that he could bring forward any exclusive claim to the honours of that day, in which the French on all sides had fought so bravely, is nothing but wilful exaggeration.

Possibly many writers have made Kellermann the saviour of the French Army at Marengo as a reproach to Bonaparte for having said so little of Kellermann's exploit.

In Murat's report General Kellermann is mentioned three times:—

General Kellermann, placed on the left, supported the retreat of General Victor's division with the greatest courage. . . .

I must, above all, speak to you of General Kellermann, who by his timely charge has known how to clinch the victory, as yet wavering, and to capture for you 5,000 or 6,000 prisoners. . . General Kellermann has particularly distinguished himself.

For all that, Kellermann's name does not figure amongst those proposed by Murat for promotion, nor was he promoted general of division on the battlefield. But he was promoted very soon after, on the 6th of the following month.

Might not Bonaparte's coolness towards Kellermann have had its origin in the ungenerous way in which the Directory tried in 1796, to impose the elder Kellermann on him as a colleague, so as to serve as a check to his already rising ambition? May not the name have carried with it some painful recollections?

War does not always reward a man according to his deserts. This poor appreciation of Kellermann's services is a very good illustration of the French saying, "*A moi la peine; aux illustres le profit.*" Many of us, in a much humbler sphere, have had a somewhat similar experience, in propping up an incapable chief, who enjoyed an unmerited reputation.

A well-contested battle is ordinarily lost two or three times before it is over. The last moment is the supreme one; it is the end of the game, and at this instant the conqueror has almost always employed all his resources.

The Austrians seem to have wasted their troops. Dampierre, who at the commencement of the battle had not, by his own showing, more than 300 men, all told, succumbed in the evening to an attack from six guns or howitzers, a complete regiment of hussars, and several regiments of infantry. When he capitulated, of his 300 men 194 had been injured, and all his ammunition was expended.

The presence of Boudet's division on the field of Marengo from early morning would, possibly, not have had the same results as its appearance in the declining hours of the day. Then it possessed all the elements of a surprise, which told on the enemy because he had made too sure of victory, and was not in the least expecting a resumption of the offensive.

In every battle, certain episodes of the very greatest consequence occur—episodes which turn the scale in favour of one side when taken advantage of in a skilful manner. A well-directed and timely charge, the overwhelming fire from a number of batteries, a determined headlong advance, have often exercised a determining influence on the fate of the contest. Any such fortunate event cannot deprive the general of any credit in the general direction of the battle.

It is absurd to say that Bonaparte was saved from a ruinous defeat by two of his generals acting without orders; for are generals in the field never to act on their own responsibility? Bonaparte's detractors—those who claim the victory for Desaix or for Kellermann—seem to ignore the fact that in war it is the bounden duty of all ranks alike to assist the commander-in-chief to the *fullest extent of their abilities*. A battle would be a very tame affair were everyone to await a command, and were any of the fleeting opportunities which frequently occur to be allowed to pass for want of an order.

The return of Boudet's division was not an accident. It might have been thought providential, had not Bonaparte, as soon as he saw the extent of the Austrian attack, sent orders for its speedy return. No one has ever denied his great concern for the arrival of Desaix; and why did Bonaparte so long for his arrival on the battlefield, but because he had pinned his faith on Desaix's troops, and intended with them to retrieve the waning fortunes of the day?

General Boudet in his report on the battle, and Marmont in his *Mémoires*, speak of a council held by Bonaparte, Desaix, and other generals under a brisk artillery fire, to make dispositions for a movement which should be capable of insuring victory. Taking into account Bonaparte's imperious nature, we should not be far wrong in assuming that he it was who issued the necessary orders to his subordinates.

Is no credit due to Bonaparte, who, knowing that Desaix could not appear on the battlefield before a late hour in the afternoon, bravely faced the situation, and not only fought a restraining action against superior numbers, but advanced boldly to attack the enemy at Castel Ceriolo? The efforts of Carra Saint Cyr and the Consular Guard were unsuccessful, but no one will assert that in the direction of the contest Bonaparte failed to show his high qualities as a general.

The action of those bodies, which occupied the enemy's attention on the right, was undertaken by his direction. And this manoeuvre afforded Desaix time to arrive. The situation in which the French were placed made his coming up a matter of the supremest importance; and contriving to find time for it was the move that secured the victory. Bonaparte re-established the fight on the right, and by his good dispositions and proper employment of his reserves won the battle. He has been generally known to perform miracles in the battlefield.

It would appear absurd to believe that, had fortune gone against Bonaparte at Marengo, the fate of the entire campaign would have been sealed.

Had Desaix not come up, the Stradella road was open, and Bonaparte had bridges in rear covered by batteries, by which he could have crossed the Po. Besides, as we have seen, the Austrians were tired out, and were not in a condition to undertake a vigorous pursuit, so that the French would have soon pulled themselves together. A single victory does not decide a war, and in Lombardy Bonaparte had many thousand fresh troops, which, added to his own, would have formed a respectable force, sufficient to destroy the Austrians as they attempted to cross the Po in pursuit.

★★★★★★

At a late hour on the evening of the 14th, Lapoype's division reached Voghera. This would have been the first reserve Bonaparte would have met had he been compelled to retire.

By drawing to himself the troops of Duhesme, Moncey, and Chabran, he would have had from 35,000 to 40,000 combatants on the line of the Ticino.

★★★★★★

Besides all this, the skill he had displayed as a general in 1796 showed that he was quite capable of retrieving a lost battle, and in a most brilliant manner. He was a breaker of rules; but with his genius he could run the risk, for his genius made him revert to measures other than those in common use.

That the French Army was saved from defeat by a series of extraordinary circumstances, possibly no one will dispute. The same, however, may be said of all great military events. But if the dispositions just before and during the battle are open to well-merited criticism, the same cannot be said of the campaign, which, on the whole, was a most brilliant one. Nor can we quite agree with the dictum that Fortune, being a woman, reserves her favour for the young, for the result here was due to something beyond pure luck.

The march across the Alps and his subsequent seizure of the Austrian communications was one of the greatest conceptions of Bonaparte's military genius, and well deserved the crowning triumph of Marengo.

Thiers, in summing up, so completely accords with our views that we cannot refrain from quoting him.

In this world, nevertheless, the voice of the people has always adjudged the glory; and this voice of the people has proclaimed as the conqueror of Marengo the man who discovered, with the glance of genius, the advantage to be derived from the high Alps to issue on the rear of the Austrians; who, for three months had deceived their vigilance; created an army which did not exist; rendered this creation incredible to the whole of Europe; crossed the Saint Bernard without a beaten road; dashed suddenly into the middle of Italy; bewildered with astonishment, and hemmed in his unfortunate adversary with a marvellous art; and gave him a decisive battle, lost in the morning, regained in the evening, and certainly to have been regained on the morrow if it had not been so that very day.

To show what the soldiers thought of Bonaparte, what implicit confidence they reposed on him, we have simply to turn to the battle-field, and to see how concerned they were, lest by heedlessly exposing himself to danger, as he did, he should meet his death.

Professor Seeley says, (*A Short History of Napoleon the First*), with regard to Marengo, that Bonaparte was raised from the brink of absolute ignominious ruin to the very pinnacle of glory. This is a very poor conception of genius. Frederick the Great lost several battles, nevertheless he soon eclipsed these defeats by brilliant victories. And who will ever believe that Bonaparte was likely to be ruined by a single battle—that a defeat on the field of Marengo would have brought about the collapse of the entire campaign?

Though the emperor always dwelt with pleasure on the recollection of the Battle of Marengo, still he was outnumbered and nearly defeated. Of the battle Jomini (*Histoire des Guerres de la Révolution, tom.* xiii), writes:—

> Cependant, de toutes les batailles gagnées par Bonaparte, il n'en est pas dont il doit moins s'enorgueillir que celle de Marengo. Assailli ici à l'improviste comme à Eylau, il fut sauvé dans l'une et l'autre de ces journées par un corps détaché à plusieurs lieues du champ de bataille."

Bonaparte laid himself open to a reverse by the undue dispersion of his troops, and he conquered in the end more through the inaptitude of his adversaries than through his own dispositions. There can be no question that the same results might certainly have been gained without incurring anything like the same risks. It may appear an anomaly, still it is a fact, that it was just because Marengo was won after having been nearly lost that it attained such a dazzling fame.

The battle stands forth as a brilliant example of a commander intercepting his adversary's communications without compromising his own. Marengo was the old, old story of failure turned into success—a success so unexpected, so little looked for, that it made a man immortal.

The Austrians had persisted in disbelieving an invasion which the French announced with such clamour. They paid dearly for this excess of obstinacy and want of foresight. What meagre consolation it was to say that Bonaparte no doubt had won the battle, but that he had done so against all recognised rules of war!

The movements which place the aggressor in the rear of an army must commence from afar. The enemy must be surprised, all his suspicions must be lulled, and the manoeuvre executed with great rapidity by forced marches well hidden from sight. Bonaparte brought his army to the rear of the Austrians in this campaign by very rapid marches and movements full of brilliant audacity and ability.

The difficulty in such operations lies in this, that the aggressor is very liable to lose his own communications. Here we have a case in point. Having entered Piedmont, Bonaparte recognised how the road he had followed in coming over the Alps was not adapted for a line of retreat or a line of supplies. He had consequently to proceed to Milan, join Moncey, and change his line of operations, adopting the better one of the Saint Gothard.

With a great and noble aim in view, a general must be prepared to run some risks. Besides, the danger of certain operations ceases when they are kept from coming to the knowledge of the adversary. They are then akin to a surprise, inasmuch as they leave no time to the enemy to prepare the proper dispositions for facing them.

Most writers appear to have overlooked an important point. This is that, if the weakening of his army by detaching one of his best divisions in the direction of Rivalta and Novi was imprudent—so imprudent that it has remained as the principal blot in that marvellous campaign—it is strange that such a capable leader as Desaix should have complied without any remonstrance.

Bonaparte had a great regard for Desaix and for his ability, and did not fear an ambitious competitor in him; and we may reasonably imagine that he would have freely discussed the situation with him.

Surely Rapp or Savary, who were Desaix's A.D.C.'s, would have mentioned in their *Mémoires* any objections Desaix might have raised against this dangerous dispersion of forces, if for no other purpose than to extol the glory and credit of their chief. Boudet, Auguste Colbert, and others who were by his side on the 13th and 14th of June, should have known the general's opinions. But on this point, all have remained silent. Neither did anything come to light in the very free discussions which always follow a campaign.

Mathieu Dumas states that on reaching Torre di Garofoli Bonaparte received from Rivalta and from the side of the Po information which made him foresee the resolution taken by General Melas, and the impending battle; that it was this information (and not the swelling of the Scrivia, as stated in the account of the battle given by Berthier and by others) which decided him to spend the night there, so as to make his dispositions. What dispositions he made that night are not apparent, for even Bruyère, who was sent to recall Desaix, only started late on the forenoon of the 14th. There is no record whatever of the dispositions the author says were made with regard to Lannes, Carra Saint Cyr, or the Consular Guard.

A good indication of what might be expected was to be found in the noise of movement the Austrians made in front of the French posts on the night of the 13th. If this warned Victor of an impending attack, surely, he should not have neglected to have reported at once the fact either to Berthier or to Bonaparte.

Those who try to extol Desaix's or Kellermann's share in the victory have failed to look at a very important fact. Looking at the desperate state the French Army was in at 5 p.m. on the 14th, at the considerable duration of the struggle, carried out as it had been under a powerful sun, and at the lateness of the hour, it was but natural that a commander would have used the division Desaix brought up from Rivalta to cover his retreat. Bonaparte, on the other hand, had detected that the only hope he had of saving himself from an ignominious defeat was by attacking with Desaix's troops, and he had the audacity to turn them to account to renew the contest and to overcome the enemy. This was, no doubt, a desperate venture. But Bonaparte had the courage to risk it, and in doing this he repaired several of his errors. It is in the last phase of the hard-fought field of Marengo that the conqueror of Italy showed his insight and the range of his military ability.

The principal merit which does so much honour to Bonaparte was the great conception of the plan of campaign, the very improbability of which misled his adversaries and made them blind to their danger. The plan was entirely his work, and has always been considered one of the most splendid that his brilliant master-mind ever conceived. Fortune helped him, no doubt; but, being a master of the art of war, he knew how best to turn fortune to account.

★★★★★★

"An unexpected movement," writes Jomini, on the subject of the Battle of Mösskirch, "may change a defeat into a victory, like that of Desaix at Marengo; but it is only likely to produce great results when these are prepared by the original combinations of the general plan of operations."

★★★★★★

The opening paragraph of Berthier's report to the First Consul, written on the evening of the 14th on the battlefield, runs thus:—"I have to give you. Citizen Consul, an account of the Battle of San Giuliano, where you have fixed victory after it had remained undecided for thirteen hours of obstinate fighting."

This was very fulsome flattery, only surpassed by a subsequent paragraph in which he describes Bonaparte as leading Desaix's troops to the attack!

Shortly after the battle, Bonaparte spoke his mind to Bourrienne:—

Onwards, onwards, still some great events like this campaign, and I may go down to posterity. (Bourrienne, *Mémoires*, tom. iv.)

Up to his last days Napoleon was proud of the Battle of Marengo. Madame de Rémusat (*Mémoires, tom.* iii), relates how on his return from Tilsit he said:—

I am, and shall always be, for the French much more the man of Marengo than that of Jena and of Friedland.

In looking at all the results which followed the victory, and to the prestige he acquired from the campaign, he was right. It was only the military critic who did not set the same value on his dispositions for the great battle, and who could not hold him absolved for incurring the risks he ran in the event that made him—that put the imperial diadem on his brow.

★★★★★★

On the 5th of May, 1821, Napoleon's body, dressed in the uniform of the Chasseurs de la Garde, was laid on a modest little bed, and his companions in captivity laid over all the blue cloth overcoat which the emperor had worn at Marengo.

******

The battle changed the fortunes of Europe and of the conqueror. The officers most deserving of praise were Victor, who had tenaciously defended Marengo and defeated Haddick's and Kaim's onslaught; Lannes, who with no more than 8,000 combatants held from 18,000 to 20,000 victorious troops in check for three hours; Carra Saint Cyr, who captured Castel Ceriolo; Boudet, for having broken the impetus of the Hungarian column; and Kellermann, who dared to launch his slender body of horsemen against the formidable column of Austrian infantry—a column which from its very weight looked as if it would step over anything which would dare to stand in its way.

Indirectly, also, much was due to Massena and Suchet, who fought so bravely for the honour of the Army of Italy. Both had inflicted very severe losses on the Austrian Army, which at the period of the battle was nothing in morale like what it had been at the beginning of the campaign.

Kellermann was not only conspicuous in the brilliancy and opportunity of his charge against Zach's column. All through the day, he had borne down on the Austrians whenever an opportunity offered. His destruction of Pilatti's cavalry, the effective aid he gave to Victor by leading on charge after charge in ceaseless succession, and his masterly covering of the retreat by keeping up a menacing attitude, were admirable. That Berthier should not accord him a lion's share in the victory is not astonishing. A prepossessed officer like Berthier quickly perceives how any such acknowledgments are liable to detract from the glory of the commander-in-chief.

How noble was the spirit which fought only for glory, and was not animated by more sordid aims! In a battle which decided the fate of the world for many years, Murat mentions in his report a dozen officers, and no more.

One of the principal causes of the successes obtained during the Revolution was that the generals were full of youth and ambition, and were generously prodigal of their lives and blood to acquire fame. They were not restrained by that caution which creeps in with age, and they could give free scope to their daring. They may have often committed faults against the rules of strategy and tactics; but, as their impetuosity was generally crowned with success, no one took much notice of their errors.

Jomini states that the possession of the whole of Northern Italy as far as Mantua and the Mincio, the cession of twelve fortresses with 1,500 cannon and immense stores of provisions, were the results of Desaix's attack and of Kellermann's daring charge delivered at a most opportune moment.

A few battalions and 600 cavalry decided the fate of the Peninsula.

This is not fair to the gallant soldiers who, against great odds and heavy artillery fire, held the Fontanone brook; to the Consular Guard and Monnier's division, which stayed the advance of the Austrian left; nor to the men who held the ground for hours, thus gaining time for Desaix's battalions to reach the battlefield.

For a long spell of years fortune certainly befriended Bonaparte. But for the swelling of the Scrivia, on the 13th of June, Boudet's division would have been so far on its way to Novi as not to have been able to reach the field of Marengo even at as late an hour as it did.

The divisions of Boudet and Monnier were, on the 14th, to have been one at Novi, the other at Voghera. But the swelling of the Scrivia compelled them to bivouac half a day's march from Marengo, and owing to this fortuitous accident both were able to reach the battlefield in time.

The complete success of his expedition, the conquest of one-half of Italy, a difficult enterprise brought to a most satisfactory conclusion in sixty days, was enough to dazzle, to fascinate all men.

Marengo raised Bonaparte to the pinnacle of power. The most clear-sighted people were not long in discovering what distance that victory had placed between Bonaparte and them. Before the battle, he was held in high estimation by the French, but an important result of that event was to increase this feeling to such an extent as to lead the French to deem it their bounden duty to obey him. Whilst this feeling grew and waxed strong at home, his enemies abroad learnt to fear and respect him.

Bonaparte could well exclaim, "In one day we have recovered Italy." The sudden victory of Marengo rendered useless all the work of a long time, and robbed the Austrians of all the conquests they had made in 1799. How much precious blood had been spilt in that and the few previous years to no purpose!

Fault has been found with Melas for agreeing to the armistice the day following the battle. He has been credited with having been strong enough to have been able to break through the French. Bülow particularly censures him on this point. We must, however, bear in mind the last phase of the Battle of Marengo; that a panic had seized the cavalry, that no effort was made to meet the offensive return of the French, and how easily the advantages gained during the day had been surrendered. The Austrian Army had lost heavily, its best men were strewn over the battlefield; for the bold men, the fighting cream, are those who lead the way, and they lose heavily.

The morale of the Austrian Army was undermined. Of late the troops had been beaten in every encounter. And this may have made Melas reluctant to have recourse so soon to another trial of strength. And that consideration may have suggested his regaining his communications at the price of the fortresses of Piedmont as the safest plan to pursue.

It might be pleaded in Melas's favour that his government had obstinately assured him of the non-existence of the Army of Reserve. But when the facts showed him that he had been deceived on this point, he did not concentrate his troops sufficiently soon, nor was his concentration sufficiently complete, for he had left many garrisons in Piedmont.

What decided Melas to capitulate was a desire to save the survivors of the battlefield and the garrisons in Piedmont, so as to concentrate a fine body of 60,000 men about Mantua with whom to continue the campaign. Jomini relates that he was pushed to it by the old generals, who had been separated from their stores and other property when the baggage of the army had been directed on Parma. All this was now at the mercy of the enemy, and the officers were keen to save their property. Jomini explains in a footnote how he obtained this information; but he evidently was not quite certain of the accusation he was bringing.

Crossard states that, on the evening of the battle, Prince Charles de Bohan arrived at Alessandria with 9,000 men drawn from Mondovi, Coni, and Ceva; that there were besides 1,500 men who had not taken any part in the battle, and had remained in Alessandria; and that 11,000 might in twenty-four hours have come from Genova, had the British sailors undertaken to hold that city till a further effort was made to decide the fate of Italy at Alessandria. (Crossard, *Mémoires Militaires et Historiques pour servir à l'Histoire de la Guerre depuis 1792 jusqu'en 1815, tom.* ii.)

These assertions of Crossard seem to show that on the third day after the Battle of Marengo Melas would have been more formidable than the First Consul. Neupperg's words to him whilst treating were:—

> Do not believe that you have annihilated us; you will see us, if you like, reappear possibly stronger than when we began the battle. We have lead, powder, bayonets, and cannons; break off negotiations, attack us, and you will render us a service. (*Crossard, tom. ii.*)

Bonaparte showed his wisdom when he consented to accept the terms proposed by Melas. It was prudent to do so, for the Austrians were still very strong.

The surrender of Genova was the hardest condition of all, the same post as carried the news of its capture having taken those of its restitution.

Hohenzollern surrendered the city to Suchet, acting as he deemed loyally by the Convention of Alessandria. With regard to Genova, this convention did not quite cover the case, for the English had shared in the siege and by a vigorous blockade of the port had conduced largely to Massena's evacuation. They had, therefore, every right to hold a city which their allies were forced to give up, and Hohenzollern was not at liberty to dispose of it.

The English pointed to the terms stipulated in their convention with Austria, the second article of which ran thus:—

> The contracting parties agree not to make during the duration of this convention any separate peace with France without the reciprocal consent of each other; not to treat with the enemy, and not to receive overtures of a peace particular or general, without communicating mutually and to act in perfect harmony.

The Austrian commander paid no attention to their protest.

Before the fate of the day had been decided, Melas, as we have related in Chapter 6, had despatched a staff officer to Vienna to report prematurely to his imperial master how victory had sided with the Austrian Army at Marengo. Something, but in the opposite sense, occurred in Paris. The first news which reached the city foretold a disaster. The hearer had quitted the field before Desaix's arrival turned the scale, and reported that at 5 p.m. the battle was going against the Consular Army, which was retreating. This news, accepted too readily, overwhelmed the citizens with consternation. It was only on the following day that the express with the news of the victory arrived; then the gloom and despair of the people were turned into universal intoxication.

On his entry into Milan after Marengo, Bonaparte was received in triumph as befitted a mighty conqueror. Adulation had no limits; every term of praise was used. *"Unico uomo!" "Eroe straordinario!" "Modello impareggiabile!"* People went out of their way to invent a title which seemed to be sufficiently comprehensive.

A year after his accession to the empire, in 1805, Napoleon went to Italy in order to be crowned with the iron crown. He visited Marengo on the 14th of June, the anniversary of his famous victory, and commanded in a sham fight in which the various episodes of the battle were reproduced. On that occasion Berthier, then minister of war, presented His Majesty with a descriptive narrative of the battle. This brief sketch, for it only comprised some sixty pages, was afterwards printed in Paris for distribution.

In this narrative there are no details of the passage of the Alps nor of the cheek at Fort Bard. It should not surprise anyone, considering the occasion on which it was presented and the position Bonaparte had then attained, to find Berthier attributing all the honour and glory of the eventful 14th of June to his imperial master. The arrival of Desaix and the effect of his advance does not receive all the *éclat* it deserves. One single paragraph disposes of Kellermann's brilliant charge, in which no mention whatever is made of that general's initiative. Nevertheless, coming from Bonaparte's chief of the staff, and written when the events were still fresh, it forms a valuable record.

The Duke of Ragusa adds a note to his *Mémoires*, in which he relates that the official news of the Battle of Marengo published in the bulletins was sufficiently true. Napoleon had given instructions to the War Department to amplify this narrative and to add to it some maps. Five years later he sent for the work. It did not please him; he erased it, and dictated a fresh one (of which hardly one-half was true), and ordered the Depot to prepare for the *Mémorial* a narrative on these lines. Lastly, after three more years, the emperor became again desirous to see this work. It displeased him, and experienced the same fate as the first. In the end he drew up a third, in which all the facts are false. A geographical engineer having put aside the first and second narratives, published them at the time of the *Restauration*; and all three are to be found in the same volume of the *Mémorial*, with plans. (*Mémoires du Maréchal Marmont, Duc de Raguse, tom.* ii.)

Lieutenant J. Campana, *Marengo étude Raisonnée des Opérations Militaires, etc.: d'apres la Correspondanee et les Mémoires de Napoléon*, quotes long passages from the *Mémoires*. The emperor's evidence as to certain facts in his campaigns would be invaluable, were it not that he gave us the facts very much as he wished them to be believed, and this makes us very diffident in accepting them.

Lord Rosebery (*Napoleon, the Last Phase*) says:—

Napoleon at Saint Helena was, as it were, making the best case for himself, just as he was in the habit of doing in his bulletins. His bulletins represented what Napoleon desired to be believed. So did the *Mémoires*." This want of veracity Lord Rosebery extends to others besides Napoleon. Of all the Longwood publications, he says, there are none wholly reliable. "There seems to have been something in the air of Saint Helena that blighted exact truth. (*Ibid.*)

The First Consul entered Milan on the 17th of June, and was received by the acclamations of the people. Though he had written a letter from the battlefield to the Emperor of Austria— a letter full of wisdom and amicable protestations, counselling Austria to break off with England and ally itself to the French Republic—still he had no sooner reached Milan than he took measures for the prosecution of the war.

On the 18th, he went in great ceremony to the Cathedral to assist at the solemn *Te Deum* of thanksgiving for the saving of the Republic and the glory of the French arms. The music was that of the best composers in Italy. The ceremony was superb and imposing,

Bonaparte did not tarry in the capital of Lombardy long, for he arrived in Paris on the 2nd of July. It was in the middle of the night that he alighted from his travelling carriage, but on the following day he was received with every demonstration of joy. On the 14th of that month, the victory of Marengo was celebrated in Paris by a festival. There was a surprise in store for the good people of Paris, for just as the games were about to commence, the *wall of granite*, the Consular Guard, marched into the field. They managed to keep their ranks while the parade lasted, but their presence had roused the enthusiasm of the people to such a pitch, that, as they marched away, parents, brothers, sisters, sweethearts, and friends rushed forward, and felt only happy in the embrace of these weather-beaten heroes.

It was after his return to Paris that Bonaparte received overtures from Louis XVIII. and other members of the royal family.

Thugut was strongly opposed to the breaking of the treaty recently and solemnly entered into with England; nevertheless, the Austrian Cabinet resolved to gain time, and, if they could not obtain tolerable terms of peace, run all the hazards of a renewal of the war. Count Saint Julien appeared in Paris as plenipotentiary on the part of Austria, and bearing a letter from the Emperor Francis. In this letter occurred the following passage:—

> You can rely in everything which Count Saint Julien will say on my behalf, and I shall ratify whatever he will do.

The preliminaries of peace were soon arranged; but the Cabinet of Vienna evaded the ratification of the preliminary articles, recalled Saint Julien, and intimated that it could only enter into negotiations with the concurrence of Great Britain.

Bonaparte was highly indignant at Austria's refusal to ratify the preliminaries, and immediately gave notice that the armistice would cease on the 10th of September. Macdonald, with 15,000 men of the 2nd Army Reserve organised at Dijon, was sent to Switzerland to form a connecting link between the armies of Italy and of Germany, and to succour either according to necessity.

******

Ranald, the Chief of Clanranald, had been out with the prince in 1745-46, with him was Neil MacEachim of the Uist branch of the family, who followed James II. to France. He was father of Stephen James Macdonald, Duke of Taranto. This distinguished soldier sided with the Revolution, entered the army, and rapidly rose to high rank. Though he rendered very important services to Bonaparte on the 18th *Brumaire*, he lost his favour by his honest support of the cause of Moreau. He was only reconciled with the emperor on the field of Wagram, where he most highly distinguished himself. He held many commands in Spain, in Russia, in Germany, and made desperate efforts against the Allies in 1814. When he felt convinced that further resistance was hopeless, he advised Napoleon to abdicate. On the Emperor's return from Elba, he left Paris with Louis XVIII., and refused to serve during the Hundred Days. He lived till 1840, upholding in the Chamber of Peers the principles of constitutional liberty.

******

Augereau, with 18,000 men, was to come from Holland and take up a position on the Lahn, so as to co-operate with the extreme left of Moreau's army.

By the month of September, France had more than 200,000 picked troops in the field.

Negotiations went on with England for a naval armistice, but the British would not be imposed on by Bonaparte and subscribe to his unfair demands. When the First Consul saw that England would not give in, he ordered Carnot to lose no time in putting the armies on a proper footing for resuming hostilities.

On quitting the field in Italy, Bonaparte did not leave all danger behind him, for soon conspiracies were set on foot with the intent of killing him. What had deeply offended a batch of desperate men was his assumption of power and the excessively vigorous measures he had put in force against the old Jacobin party. The police were very active, and some of the discovered conspiracies lay a good deal in the imagination and officiousness of the police-agents. A plot to assassinate him at the opera was discovered by the police.

Ceracchi, the only one of the conspirators, was found in the saloon, but unarmed. According to Lanfrey, the whole plot had been concocted by a blackguard, Harel, a police-agent. All that those accused at that time had been guilty of was loud and seditious talk at their clubs or workshops—an exaggerated freedom of speech often indulged in by men with excitable imaginations. Harel had done all, and his deposition, full of gross contradictions and improbabilities, was willingly accepted by a timid jury.

CHAPTER 8

Hohenlinden

It was only a fortnight since the opening of the campaign, and Kray had been compelled to seek refuge and protection behind the ramparts of Ulm. The Austrian Army was disheartened by two lost battles and five or six excessive marches. This had undermined the morale of the troops; in Ulm, however, it would find the rest it needed, with ample supplies to satisfy its wants.

Notwithstanding the recent defeats, Kray was still in command of a powerful army. The Austrians alone numbered 56,000, of whom 13,000 were cavalry and 4,000 artillery. He had besides 20,000 allies, which brought up the number of combatants to 76,200. The Prince of Reuss was in the Tyrol with 25,000 men, and there was also a division on the Main.

The intrenched camp of Ulm had been traced with great skill and forethought by the Archduke Charles. The works were of such an extent as to render all idea of a regular blockade out of the question. The camp occupied both banks of the Danube. The town and bridgehead were armed with 140 guns; the advanced works were also well armed with artillery. The magazines were ample and well stocked. Ulm covered the Austrian line of retreat by Donauwörth and Ratisbon. (When, in 1805, Ulm fell into Napoleon's hands, he ordered the fortifications to be levelled to the ground. He was anxious that the place might not in future afford a point of support to the Austrians.)

There, in his own good time, Kray could wait for reinforcements, repair his losses, raise the spirits of his troops, and by a judicious employment of his immense resources, obliterate the last effects of Moreau's manoeuvre.

The French experienced the greatest difficulty in ousting the Austrians from this formidable position, and employed six weeks in various attempts to dislodge Kray's army, but all in vain. Nor could Moreau dream of marching on, leaving 80,000 men in his rear: this would for certain have led to an attack on his communications with France.

On hearing that Moreau, by order of his government, had detached Moncey's force to Italy, the Austrians seem to have persuaded themselves that he was going to be reduced to a purely defensive attitude. Nevertheless, it was at that very time that he contemplated his enterprise against Augsburg in Bavaria, conceived, no doubt, as much with the intention of drawing Kray from Ulm, as of profiting by the resources of that wealthy city.

After the departure of Moncey's contingent for Italy, on the 11th, 12th, and 13th of May, there remained to Moreau 72,000 combatants; there were besides the division in Switzerland, the several garrisons and the convalescents soon likely to come out of hospital.

Several of the senior officers had been strongly urging Moreau to carry Ulm by force; but he would not risk a direct attack, as in case of a defeat he would have had to retire, compromising not only the fate of his campaign in Germany, but also of that of the Army of Reserve in Italy. He much preferred getting what he desired by manoeuvring, and hoped that by moving the bulk of his troops in the direction of Augsburg and Munich, he would ultimately succeed in enticing Kray out of Ulm.

His dispositions were not of the very best, and were calculated to invite an attack. On setting out, he left Sainte Suzanne alone on the left bank of the Danube, on which river he had no bridge. Saint Cyr was his nearest support, and he was stationed on the right bank, at the confluence of the Danube and the Iller. Such a disposition of the forces left to observe the entrenched camp of Ulm could not but tempt Kray to attack, and, had he done this with all his forces, Sainte Suzanne must have been thoroughly defeated.

Judging that the distance of the French right wing and centre from the left precluded Moreau from affording any effectual support to his left wing, Kray sallied forth on the 16th of May and attacked Sainte Suzanne at Erbach. The Austrians advanced with a very numerous body of cavalry, which was commanded by the Archduke Ferdinand. After the cavalry followed several columns of infantry.

The left attacked Legrand's division at Ringingen and Erbach; the centre attacked Papelau; and the right Souham, at Gerhausen and Asch, near Blaubeüren. In the combat which ensued Sainte Suzanne was hard pressed, and the French troops were driven back in disorder for several miles. Nothing but the presence of mind and brilliant valour of their general saved them.

Seriously alarmed by the violence of the cannonade, which showed how fast the French left wing was losing ground, Saint Cyr thought it necessary to come to the rescue. He sent *aide-de-camp* after *aide-de-camp* to recall the troops from the banks, of the Iller to those of the Danube. To do this without wasting time, they were ordered not to wait for the outposts to be drawn in. Stationed on the bridge of Unterkirchberg on the Iller, Saint Cyr himself kept despatching the troops to the Danube as fast as they came up.

Fearing that Saint Cyr might be looking for a ford or a repairable bridge, the Austrians lined the left bank of the Danube, and opened a brisk cannonade, to which Saint Cyr replied. This cannonade across the mighty river had a strange result, for it alarmed the Austrians about their own line of retreat, and caused them to draw back. The first step back was a fortunate opportunity for the French. It inspired the soldiers with fresh ardour. The divisions of one accord rushed forward, and drove the Austrians back under the protection of the cannon of Ulm.

After the first engagements of the campaign, the Austrian soldiers were greatly depressed, and had given clear indications that they were quite incapable of sustaining any serious encounter with the French. The warlike qualities of the latter were being demonstrated in almost every action. Legrand's division, in this instance, being the nearest one to the river, was severely handled by the enemy, who strove to prevent its being reinforced from the right bank. At one moment a numerous body of cavalry rushed on the French. Adjutant-General Levasseur, who had already been dismounted in a charge, seized hold of a riderless horse, and galloped up to the 10th Cavalry, then on the point of quitting the field. He brought the regiment back, charged the Austrian horsemen, though fully ten times as strong, and stayed their march. Nor did the rest of Sainte Suzanne's troops show less spirit; after many hours' hard fighting, all they demanded was to be led against the enemy.

What was about to happen at Marengo within a few days occurred in this fight at Erbach. The French, inferior in numbers, were driven back at all points; but a well-directed charge of cavalry and a harmless cannonade changed the situation entirely. French elasticity prevailed, and the French, who had been fighting since early morning, rushed forward and with unresisting force drove back their numerous foes.

Starray attacked without vigour, and showed considerable indecision. He allowed Prince Ferdinand to bear the entire weight of the attack. Had he supported him with the main body, even the stubborn resistance of the French would have been undoubtedly overcome.

Moreau, who was not thoroughly well informed, once believed that Kray contemplated retiring behind the Lech so as to form a junction with the Prince of Reuss. But the combat at Erbach showed him that the Austrian forces lay concentrated on the left bank of the Danube. Moreau then approached Ulm to see if Kray would quit it through fear of being attacked.

After the affair of the 16th of May, he made a demonstration to reconnoitre the strength of the new works.

The approach of the six French divisions between Erbach and Blaubeüren had no influence on the Austrian general's decisions. Whatever intentions of a retreat he may have at one time entertained with the object of drawing closer to the Prince of Reuss and covering Bavaria, he now dropped them and stuck to Ulm.

An attack of the intrenched camp was full of danger. Seeing all the risks, Moreau decided to extend to his right, to manoeuvre on the Austrian line of communications, and to obtain by means of demonstrations made on the enemy's line of retreat what he could not obtain by force. He determined to direct Lecourbe to march on Augsburg, hoping that Kray would lead his forces on the Iller to attack the French left; which would pave the way to a decisive battle on a field so favourable for the French infantry.

Lecourbe was simply to show himself on the Lech, and at once to fall back on the centre, when the French Army would be in a favourable condition for fighting.

On the 20th, Moreau crossed to the right bank of the Danube with Saint Cyr's troops and the left wing, and took post between the Danube and the Iller. On the 22nd, Kray bid the Archduke Ferdinand to issue forth from the camp of Ulm with 10,000 men, to acquire positive news of the French Army, and to crush, if he could, the corps which the French might have left to observe the place. This led to a partial combat at Achstellen and Dellmensingen, which served to give a further proof, if any were wanted, of the stubbornness of the Republican forces.

The French, however, at this time began to experience difficulties in providing for their subsistence. Their prolonged stay around Ulm had exhausted the local resources, and their difficulties increased from day to day. There had been glaring abuses, and Moreau had to remedy them by taking vigorous measures. The commissary Pommier was tried and shot; and two generals who had fallen under suspicion of having countenanced dilapidation were dismissed.

The Prince of Reuss now tried to do something to show enterprise on the Rhine valley, by pushing detachments in the direction of Ragaz and of Bregenz. But Molitor easily drove him out of the latter city on the 24th, and the Austrian troops fell back from Ragaz.

Moreau's mind was fixed on Augsburg, with the aim of enticing Kray away from his intrenchments and of obtaining a more ample supply for his army, which felt the pinch of want, being, as it was, denuded of magazines and confined in the narrow space between the lake of Constance and Ulm. Augsburg, being a wealthy city, promised to relieve his wants.

Supported by Hautpoul, Lecourbe crossed the Lech at Landsberg on the 27th of May. Gudin, with the advanced guard, appeared before the bridge, and crossed over with the last of the enemy before the Austrians had time to break the bridge. The following day Montrichard and Hautpoul joined forces at Schwabmünchen, and without any obstacle entered Augsburg.

Kray, having become aware of the dispositions of the French, resolved to do something to attack the troops between the Danube and the Iller. During the night of the 5th of June, he sent 30,000 men out of Ulm to concentrate on the right of the Danube, to assail these troops, whilst other 26,000 men, posted between the Iller and the Kamlach, were to hold the French Army in countenance.

Moreau had foreseen such a movement. In fact, he had provoked it. Lecourbe had received, on the 3rd, orders to evacuate Augsburg, to return to the Wertach and to Buckloe. The centre and the reserve speedily approached the Iller, which Grenier crossed in all haste with Ney's division to come to Richepanse's aid.

Richepanse's troops were somewhat scattered, and the Austrians at first were able to score a success. Everything went in their favour till Ney came into action, and fell on the daring Austrians at the head of Bonnet's brigade on the plateau of Kirchberg. The Austrians gave way before this impetuous attack, and regained both, leaving many prisoners in the enemy's hands.

Emboldened by this success, Richepanse assumed the offensive, and, after a severe contest, chased Kray from Beuren. Ney's success at Kirchberg, and the arrival of Delmas's brigade which appeared on the field at the fall of the day, coming from Kelmuntz towards Guttenzell, left Kray no chance of victory. Seeing every effort fruitless, he ordered his army to retire to Ulm.

It was towards the end of June that Moreau ordered an attack to be made on all the Austrian detachments that still remained on the right bank of the Danube. Grenier attacked what there was of Giulay's, or Gyulai's, and Starray's corps between Günzburg and Burgau. Lecourbe's advanced guard attacked those between Burgau and Dillingen. The result of these attacks was that Giulay took up a position between Albeck and Riedhausen; Starray withdrew beyond the Brenz, leaning on Gundelfingen. Grenier and Lecourbe were then ordered to make false attacks on Günzburg and Dillingen.

Starray, who had demanded and obtained from Kray reinforcements with which to watch the banks of the Danube between Günzburg and Donauwörth, had sent the greater portion of the troops back to Ulm, keeping eight battalions and five squadrons only round Gundelfingen. General Devaux had taken five battalions and three squadrons to Donauwörth. This was all that was employed to guard a line some twelve leagues in extent, which would have needed at the very least 10,000. Kray, with the rest of the army, remained inactive in Ulm.

Moreau had resolved to make a wide turning movement, so as to gain the Lower Danube and threaten Kray's communications. But the weather broke, and on account of the heavy rains his designs could not be put into effect till the 10th of June. Lecourbe then made himself master of Schöngau and Landsberg, and on the 12th he reoccupied Augsburg. The French centre and right conformed in this wheel of the army; the first descended the Kamlach and the Gunz, and made for Krambach, driving Starray's posts before them; the left advanced in the valley of the Both and of the Iller on Weissenhorn and Vohringen.

The crossing of the Danube by the French was rendered difficult by more than one impediment. The Austrians patrolled the left bank, and kept careful watch. They had besides broken all the bridges over the Danube up to Donauwörth—a serious embarrassment for the French, who had neither pontoon-trains nor barges for crossing rivers. However, fortune helped them, for some of the destructions had been carelessly carried out. The reports brought in by the advanced guards showed that the bridges of Kremheim and of Blemheim had suffered the least. It was on these reports that it was decided to cross at those points, and, with that object, a large number of stout planks and beams were collected.

Grenier and Lecourbe had been directed to make false attacks on Günzburg and Dillingen. Ney's attempt at Dillingen and Grenier's at

Leipheim had failed. Still, these failures were not without advantage, inasmuch as they served to impose on the enemy. Starray was mystified as to the intended point of passage; he was perplexed, and kept his troops scattered.

Starray's action had helped Lecourbe greatly in crossing the Danube. He had turned to no account whatsoever the reinforcements he had received from Kray after such earnest demands. Instead of watching the course of the river from some central point between Günzburg and Donauwörth, he had sent back to Ulm the greater portion of his troops. Kray, if possible, had done even worse, for he had kept the rest of his army in absolute inactivity.

Moreau, taking advantage of Kray's supineness, and having succeeded in distracting the attention of his troops, now made dispositions for crossing. On the night of the 18-19th, Lecourbe took the divisions of Montrichard and Gudin, with Hautpoul's cavalry reserve, and concealed them in rear of the woods which line the Danube opposite Blemheim and Kremheim—a locality selected with great skill.

These villages, between which the Danube makes a sudden detour, are only about a thousand yards from each other, and separated by a stream called the Nebel-Bach. The left bank of the river is here higher than the right, but the slope is very gentle, and the plain between Hochstadt and Schwenningen is very suitable for the deployment of cavalry and the manoeuvring of troops.

At break of day on the 19th, Lecourbe opened with his guns on Kremheim and Blemheim, and cleared the Austrians from the banks of the river. After a while eighty expert swimmers, led by Captain Dogometry, swam across the Danube; they were followed by two boats conveying supports and loaded with clothing and arms. On setting foot on the left bank these intrepid soldiers seized their arms, and, naked as they were, fell upon the Austrians, who were simply astonished by such daring. This detachment captured two guns, and took possession of Kremheim. Some ladders placed across the ruins of the bridge enabled a few gunners to cross to serve the captured guns.

The pioneers set to and began at once to repair the bridge; this was done so speedily that soon one half-brigade got across and occupied the two villages with the intention of keeping the enemy at a distance till the repairs had got so far forward as to allow the crossing of all the arms.

The alarm rapidly spread all along the Austrian posts; there was no longer any doubt as to where the veritable point of attack would be. The Austrians were gathering from all sides; their commanders at Dillingen and at Donauwörth were hurrying forward all the troops they could get together. These might have had time to overcome the leading French troops and destroy the hastily repaired bridge, had not Lecourbe taken steps to prevent a junction of such troops as were certain soon to appear on the field.

Lecourbe had foreseen that he might very soon expect the Austrians to come up from Donauwörth, and to descend the Danube from their positions of Gundelfingen, Günzburg, and Ulm. Having made a personal inspection of the neighbourhood, and having recognised that it was by Schwenningen on the Donauwörth road that any Austrian troops ascending the Danube would appear, he ordered his infantry and a few platoons of cavalry to occupy that village. The moment was critical, and on holding Schwenningen depended the success of this bold enterprise.

The wisdom of his dispositions was soon apparent, for it was not long before an Austrian force of 4,000 infantry, 500 cavalry, and six guns appeared in sight. General Devaux, who commanded at Donauwörth, marched on Schwenningen as quickly as possible, and attacked it.

The village was attacked, captured, and recaptured several times in the space of two hours. The numerical superiority of the Austrians was on the point of telling, when Lecourbe brought a timely reinforcement to Puthod's brigade, some squadrons of *carabineers*, and his own escort of the 8th Hussars. All the available cavalry then rushed on the Austrian infantry, which was widespread in the open ground about the river. A vigorous and timely charge overthrew the Austrians, who abandoned the field, leaving their guns and 2,000 prisoners in the enemy's hands. Two battalions of the Würtemberg contingent attempted to resist by forming square. They fought desperately, but nothing availed; they were broken, their colours were taken, and their colonel was captured. In fact, they did not fare any better than the rest.

Thus, the Austrians marching up the Danube were disposed of and pursued by Laval's brigade along the Donauwörth road. Still, it was to be expected that others might be soon coming from the opposite direction—from Dillingen, Gundelfingen, and Ulm. By this time the bridges of Kremheim and Blemheim had been fortunately repaired, so that the other divisions were able to get across the river.

When Laval had been well started in Devaux's pursuit, Lecourbe marched in the direction of Hochstadt with the divisions of Gudin

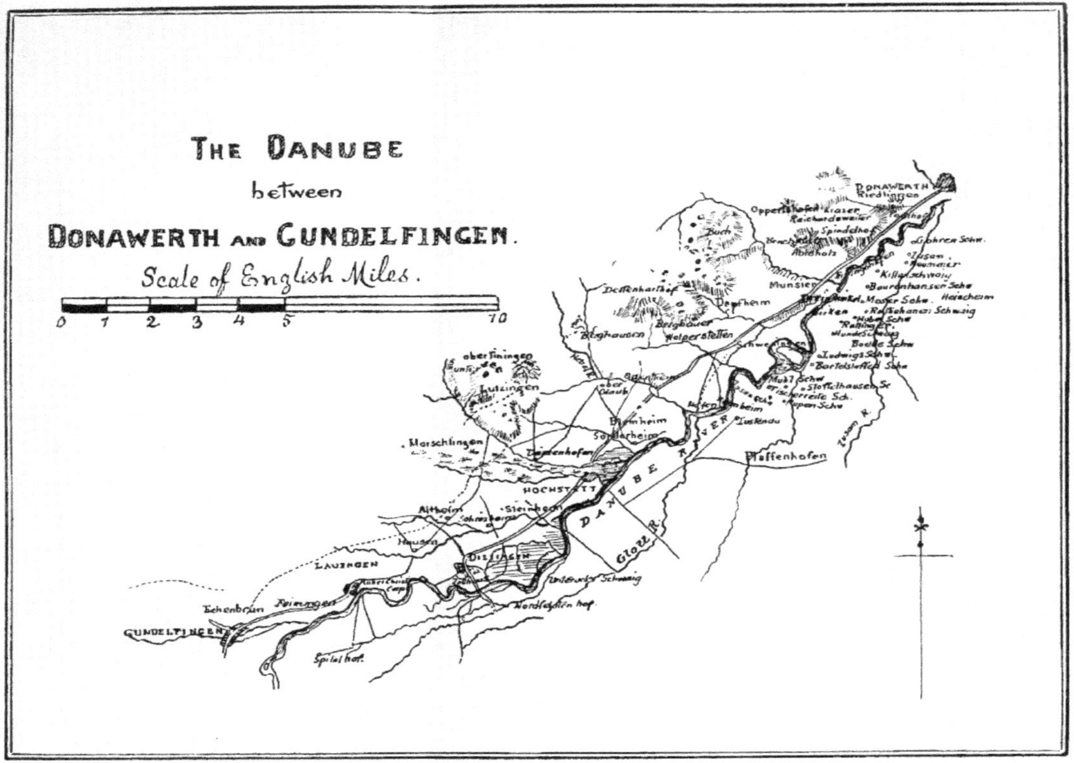
THE DANUBE
between
DONAWERTH AND GUNDELFINGEN.
Scale of English Miles.
0 1 2 3 4 5 10
DONAWERTH
Riedlingen
Lohren Schw.
Killerschwaig
Bourenhauser Schw.
Moser Schw.
Heischeim
Munster
Dettenhartshof
Buch
Schweningen
Ludwigs Schw.
Bortelsleffed Schw.
Stoffelhausen Sc.
Pfaffenhofen
Weilperstellen
Blindheim
Sonderheim
oberFiningen
Lutzingen
Morschlingen
HOCHSTATT
Steinheim
Altheim
DANUBE RIVER
Glotz R.
DILLINGEN
Unterhofer Schwaig
Nordfelden hof.
Hausen
LAUINGEN
Echenbrün
Faimingen
GUNDELFINGEN
Spielhof.

and Montrichard's and d'Hautpoul's reserves.

Starray, warned by the distant cannonade, had collected some 3,000 or 4,000 men at Hochstadt, some five or six miles below Dillingen. He had besides asked for reinforcements, but deeming himself unequal to a contest with the French, kept falling back on Dillingen, where he had left three battalions in reserve. The 37th half-brigade and a squadron of the 9th Hussars followed him step by step.

Lecourbe came round the left of the village of Schrezheim at the head of two regiments of *carabineers* and *cuirassiers*, the 6th and 9th Cavalry and the 9th Hussars, sixteen squadrons in all. The French were in a plain, separated from the enemy only by the Egge, a small stream on the banks of which stood the village of Schrezheim. Lecourbe crossed the village at speed, and on emerging on the other side deployed into line and charged the Austrian cavalry. Surprised by such a determined onset, the Austrian horsemen retired in disorder, leaving uncovered the infantry they should have protected.

The Austrian infantry just managed to enter Dillingen, where it only kept together for an instant, notwithstanding the cover afforded by the walls and ditches of the place. Attacked again from the side of Altheim, from which Lecourbe was issuing at a gallop, it had to cross the plain of Lauingen in serried masses, leaving to the enemy over a thousand prisoners—men who, to resist the attack of the French squadrons, were still holding to the protection afforded by the ditches and gardens of Dillingen.

On the previous evening 2,000 *cuirassiers* under De Klinglin with De Kospoth's infantry brigade had arrived at Gundelfingen on the Brenz, sent by Kray to support Starray. These troops had remained inactive, and only served to rally the remnants of Starray's corps. They had some slight advantage over Lecourbe's cavalry at first, but they soon found that they could not hold their own against the ever-increasing forces of the French.

Moreau, informed that a considerable body of cavalry was approaching Medlingen, imagined, and with good reason, that the cavalry would be closely followed by Kray's main body. He consequently determined to overthrow these horsemen before there was any chance of their being supported. With this object he strengthened Lecourbe's cavalry by four regiments of light cavalry, and by a portion of the cavalry of Decaen's division. These troops he launched against Klinglin's squadrons, whilst Montrichard was directed to lead the 37th on Gundelfingen.

The two combats of the morning had been decided by the dash of the French cavalry, and here was an occasion for gathering fresh laurels. Lecourbe had left his infantry in Lauingen whilst he deployed all his horsemen on the plain. The Austrian cavalry at that time enjoyed the highest reputation in Europe for general excellence and manoeuvring qualities, and here was a fair opportunity for putting its mettle to the test.

Their first line advanced boldly at a gallop and drove before it the 2nd regiment of Carabineers and a few squadrons of hussars which had joined it in the charge. The French *cuirassiers*, aided by the *carabineers* and hussars, who had quickly rallied, then fell on the Austrians and drove them back in their turn. It was now time for the second Austrian line to advance and close with the French, who had got rather scattered in their charge. Borne on with great impetus, they compelled the French to withdraw in hot haste. The latter had still the 9th Hussars in reserve; this regiment, adroitly led, boldly takes the enemy's cavalry in flank, surprises it by its dashing onset, overthrows it, and thus gains possession of the battlefield for the French.

The result of the fight was greater than could be gathered by the execution done. At Schwenningen, at Schrezheim, and at Lauingen, the French cavalry had incontestably established their superiority over the Austrians, and the same had occurred at Marengo a few days before. This ascendency was not soon lost, and was to become a very formidable element in the coming wars.

A fresh battle followed the overthrow of the Austrian cavalry. A severe contest was maintained till eleven at night, when Montrichard, at the head of the 37th half-brigade, entered Gundelfingen, and all the positions on the plain remained in the hands of Moreau.

The result of this hard-fought contest was that 20 guns, 4,000 prisoners, and four standards fell into the hands of the French. Beyond these trophies the day was glorious for Moreau and for Lecourbe. It had also raised the prestige of the French, and, above all, of the cavalry, which, up to that time, had been considered inferior to that of their adversaries.

The French were very much elated by their victory of Hochstadt, for it made amends for the great battle lost in the same locality on the 13th of August, 1704. Marlborough and Prince Eugene then defeated Tallard, Marsin, and the Elector of Bavaria. This second battle was not on the same scale, nevertheless it led to very important results.

On the field of Hochstadt a faulty employment of the Austrian cavalry was again seen. Where some 50 squadrons properly employed on the plains of Dillingen might have made the crossing of the Danube slow and very uncertain for the French, these troops were kept idling around an intrenched camp, where they could cause only embarrassment.

From the direction of the enemy's march, it was impossible for Kray not to have foreseen Moreau's intention. A little more enterprise on his part would have enabled him to fall on the French left; in default of which he might have quitted Ulm, and have concentrated some 50,000 combatants between Günzburg and Donauwörth.

It was on the 19th of June that the French found themselves securely established on the left bank of the Danube. Kray had detained Moreau in the neighbourhood of Ulm, and so prevented his striking a decisive blow at any vital part of the empire. The concentration of most of the enemy's troops on his line of retreat awoke him into activity, and no sooner had he gauged the danger which threatened him than he decided to march out of Ulm.

Having left Pétrasch in Ulm with 10,000 men for its protection, he started during the night for Aalen with his great artillery park of 160 guns with 800 waggons. His cavalry on the Brenz was to cover his movements. The troops set out in three columns, and marched on the 21st to Heidenheim by difficult roads. After two or three hours' rest, they continued the march to Neresheim, which was reached at midnight of the 22nd. Notwithstanding all the hardships of the previous day's march, the troops were again in motion for Nordlingen on the following day. Kray marched in very bad weather, and the heavy rains had made the roads almost impassable.

Still, the rapidity of his retreat was such that he reached Neresheim in twenty-four hours. It was a rapid march that the Austrian Army executed on the 21st and 22nd of June, and it got them out of their difficulties at a cost of a severe strain. The army was extricated from a dangerous position by the ability of its commander, in whom the perils which surrounded him had infused singular energy.

Moreau, not informed in time of Kray's march, lost a fine opportunity. Though hampered by a convoy of nearly a thousand vehicles, the Austrians carried out their march with considerable expedition, and chiefly during the night. They moved in a semicircle of which the French occupied the base. Had Moreau executed a flank attack on the 21st and 22nd, there can be no doubt that he would have cut the Austrian Army in two, and that a great portion of their park would, in that case, have fallen into his hands.

Bonaparte accused Moreau of having shown in this instance an excess of circumspection; but this criticism was not merited, for the circumstances were not at all favourable for vigorous action. To begin with, Moreau was not informed in good time of Kray's retreat—a most important point—for Richepanse only became aware of it as the last Austrian detachments were about quitting Ulm. Secondly, the rain had spoilt the roads, in a country entirely devoid of solid causeways, and to such an extent that moving an army had become a matter of very serious difficulty. Thirdly, Moreau was afraid lest he should be enticed too far from the river and from his communications on the right bank. His inaction, therefore, can justly be attributed to a wise consideration of circumstances.

Kray had halted on the 24th at Nordlingen, to give some rest to his troops after their excessive fatigues. Their despondency was so great that he dreaded the result of a serious engagement, judging by the ardour displayed the preceding day by Lecourbe's and Ney's columns.

Alive to the necessity for cheering his troops and rousing their flagging spirit, he spread a report to the effect that a suspension of hostilities was being signed in Italy, that it was evident that it would be soon extended to Germany, and that before long peace must ensue.

Moreau reached Nordlingen; but, unaware of the state of disarray reigning in the enemy's army, fearing that he might be led into an endless pursuit, and foreseeing that, on account of the wretched state of the roads, he was not at all likely to overtake the Austrians, he ordered a halt. What might not have followed a battle lost under such circumstances!

At this time, Kray sent him an envoy to announce that it had come to his knowledge that the French and Austrian armies in Italy had concluded an armistice. The news of the brilliant events which had led to this armistice he very carefully withheld; and this made Moreau suspicious. He saw in Kray's proposal only an artifice to gain time, and consequently refused to take any notice of it.

Moreau now resolved to recross the Danube, leaving Richepanse to carry out the investment of the principal strongholds on that river. Having reinforced Decaen's division, he ordered that general to proceed by forced marches by Augsburg and Dachau on Munich. The main body of the French Army was directed on the capital of Bavaria. By this move it was intended to lay Bavaria under contribution, and to sever still further the communications between Kray's army and that of the Prince of Reuss in the Tyrol. Bavaria would be detached from the coalition, and the French would be able to subsist on the local resources.

Kray, having recrossed the Danube at Neuburg on the evening of the 26th, seriously threatened Decaen; but the danger had been foreseen betimes at the French headquarters, and on the same day Lecourbe, who had recrossed the Danube at Donauwörth and the Lech at Gonderkingen, arrived at Rain. He was followed by the rest of the army, and only Richepanse was left before Ulm.

On the 27th the French right wing continued its march on Neuburg, hoping to out-march the enemy. Gudin marched in the direction of Pottmes; Montrichard followed the road of Unterhausen; the centre was to replace him at Rain; lastly, the left, leaving Legrand's division at Donauwörth, pushed Ney's as far as Lopsingen and Wembdingen and Baraguay-d'Hilliers between Harburg and Monheim. The French evidently did not expect to be attacked, or they would not have occupied this disjointed position. Kray, informed of their approach, of the weakness of their forces, and allured by the prospect of overpowering a portion of the French in their scattered state, marched to meet them.

The right and centre of his first line were the first engaged, they fell on d'Espagne's brigade near Unterhausen; another Austrian corps held back Gudin about Chiliarch. Accustomed to victory, the French were not prepared to yield easily; nevertheless, the disproportion between the two contending sides was too great. Montrichard called up Schiner's brigade to support d'Espagne, but with no good results; the troops were overpowered, and, being turned on the heights of Sinning, were vigorously pushed back. The Austrians, satisfied with this slight advantage, allowed them to rally behind Oberhausen, without striving to push them further back.

Warned by the sound of the guns, Lecourbe hurried to the scene of action. He had demanded to be supported by Grandjean's division, which was directed on Strass. The reinforcements arrived just in time to save Montrichard. The French resumed the offensive, and dashed at the enemy with rare bravery. At eight in the evening, Oberhausen and the heights were carried, notwithstanding all the efforts of the Austrian squadrons who dashed at the attacking columns the moment they showed. The combat ceased, and Kray, seeing no prospect of overwhelming a portion of the French Army, profited by the night to evacuate Neuburg, after which he destroyed the bridge over the Danube.

Fatigue and continuous hard work had by this time reduced Kray's troops to a most deplorable state. Satisfied with having contended against a victorious adversary with some degree of equality, he continued, on the 28th, his march to Ingolstadt, where he left a garrison. His army crossed the Danube at Vohburg, and camped at Siegenburg. On the 1st of July, he took up a position at Landshut, his army being in a most pitiable state.

Decaen's division entered Munich on the 28th of June, after which Moreau, with his left, invested Ingolstadt.

In this part of the theatre of war, nothing of any real importance occurred during the rest of the summer. Moreau turned his attention to the Prince of Reuss; the principal event being the conquest of Feldkirch, which fell into the hands of the French on the 14th of July. Its fall brought about the occupation of the Grisons, and opened a fresh line of communication with the Army of Italy. It was at this time that the operations were suspended by the armistice of Parsdorf, which was signed on the 15th of July.

For four months several schemes of adjustment between Austria and France had been discussed, but to no purpose. Austria still possessed sufficient means of resistance, and England was ready with her gold. The emperor was not loth to temporise further, and to continue the armistice till the commencement of the rainy season would have rendered military operations impossible. This would have given him time to recruit his army. But Bonaparte, who detected his object, ordered his generals to resume hostilities. During these four months neither Austria nor France had been idle, and their preparations had been carried out with increased activity.

The Cabinet of Vienna conceived that to restore confidence in the army nothing could be better than to change the commander-in-chief, and Kray was at once relegated to his possessions. The general deserved all pity, for he was never left a free hand in the campaign. The emperor had placed at his side M. de Lehrback, who overrode all his dispositions, every day reminding him that he was not to risk a decisive action.

★★★★★★

Kray had already foreseen all the ill-feeling he was likely to incur in replacing the Archduke Charles, and he had petitioned the emperor to recall his nomination, but in vain, so he felt compelled to obey.

★★★★★★

The Austrian Army numbered 120,000 men, and was commanded by the Archduke John, a young officer, who was guided by Lauer, the grand master of the artillery. This army was divided as follows: Klenau, with about 25,000 men, held Ratisbon and the Palatinate. The main body, from 60,000 to 65,000 combatants, lined the course of the Inn from Braunau to Rosenheim. Of these, 9,000 men garrisoned the bridgeheads of Mühldorf, Wasserburg, Rosenheim, and Braunau. General Hiller commanded the extreme left, the Austrian Tyrol corps. He had under him 20,000 men, with some Tyrolese rifle regiments.

Moreau had an army of 100,000 men, not including the garrisons of the places surrendered. Bonaparte had reinforced his army with a division under Macdonald, about 14,000 men, which left Dijon in July to take post on Lecourbe's right, between Coire and Feldkirch. Another division, commanded by Augereau, replaced Sainte Suzanne's corps on the Main, leaving this last to form the extreme left of Moreau's army.

Lecourbe commanded the right wing, and, with a portion of his army, watched the issues of the Vorarlberg and the Tyrol between Feldkirch and the Isar. Gudin's and Montrichard's divisions of his wing were on the Rosenheim road in front of Hoffendorf.

The centre, the divisions of Decaen, Richepanse, Grandjean, and d'Hautpoul's cavalry reserve, were concentrated between Munich and Haag.

The left, commanded by General Grenier, comprising the divisions of Ney, Hardy, and Legrand, extended from Hohenlinden towards Hoertkofen, watching the valley of the Isen and its issues.

Two divisions of the extreme left, under the orders of Sainte Suzanne, had been ordered to proceed from the borders of Altmühl to the right bank of the Danube.

Moreau had formulated an able plan. Whilst a Franco-Bavarian force covered his flank, he was to continue operating by the right bank of the Danube. The Army of Italy, reinforced by Macdonald's corps, which had now in reality become its left wing, was to cross the Adige above Verona, and then to advance on Vienna by the Noric Alps. For the execution of this plan, Macdonald had to cross the Rhaetian Alps in the depth of winter, and this in the face of Hiller's superior forces.

No sooner had measures been taken to carry this plan into effect than more important events came to prevent its execution. The Austrian Army, in its position behind the Inn, had every prospect of being able to withstand Moreau's efforts. Every consideration made it advisable that it should there await the enemy.

No other line could have afforded a greater resistance to the invader. This river, the most important Alpine affluent of the Danube, has a great volume of water, and flows with great impetuosity. In the Tyrol, as far as Kufstein, its waters run between inaccessible mountains, the sides of which are covered by pine forests. From Kufstein to Mühldorf it flows in a deep bed cut by the vehemence of its waters through solid rock. Both banks present a series of steep precipices, excepting only in a few places, and these were strongly fortified and held. This powerful line was supported, on the right, by the fortress of Braunau; on the left, by that of Kufstein. It was almost impossible to force the centre of this line, defended as it was by 80,000 good troops; and to attempt to turn it either by the Tyrol or by Bohemia would have been equally perilous.

But whether it was distasteful to a young commander in his first opportunity, and with superior forces, to restrict himself to a purely defensive role, or whether his advisers deemed the initiative to offer a more sure and more brilliant prospect of success, it was decided to abandon the defensive, and, by a swift march, to gain the left flank of the French Army, its most vulnerable point.

Klenau was to issue from Ratisbon, and at the same time the principal part of the army was to cross the Inn at Braunau and Mühldorf, and to advance in echelon from the right between Erding and Landshut. When this operation was completed, the army, pivoting on its left, was to wheel to its left, on the important position of Dachau, and cut off the French from their principal line of communication.

This manoeuvre to meet with success required more than ordinary speed in the execution. But this was impossible in the middle of winter on marshy ground which was crossed only by heavy and broken roads.

The French, who had during the armistice diligently studied the ground occupied by the Austrians, had come to recognise all the extent of the danger involved in a direct attack of the line of the Inn. They had accordingly arranged to simulate a certain timidity, which might induce the enemy to quit its strong position, and advance through the forest of Ebersberg, where their numerous cavalry would find it impossible to act. This plan was based on the supposition that the Austrians intended to remain on the defensive; for Moreau, alive to all the advantages the Austrians would derive by keeping strictly on the defensive, did not for a moment dream that they would take the initiative.

The resumption of hostilities was notified to take place on the 28th of November. On the previous day the Austrians, notwithstanding the heavy rains of the past days, had commenced the execution of their plan. The weather considerably retarded the march of their columns; their advanced guard reached Landshut only on the 29th. The wretched state of the roads already cast heavy doubts on the possibility of the undertaking. To this mischance was added the reported presence of Sainte Suzanne on the right bank of the Danube, as well as the news of Moreau's movement on Ampfing and Mühldorf. All the Austrian plans were thus upset, and their authors had to look for some practical alternative. The one they adopted was to stop the advance, and to fall back on their left towards Ampfing and Dorfen. This movement, performed amid torrents of rain, and on dreadful roads, completed the exhaustion of the Austrian troops.

On the 28th, the different French divisions had set out in the direction of the Inn. Grenier took the road leading to Haag and Dorfen: Richepanse and Decaen followed that of Wasserburg; and Montrichard marched in the direction of Rosenheim. They were in utter ignorance as to the archduke's designs. Informed of his danger by a reconnaissance made on the evening of the 30th, Moreau decided to fall back on his former positions.

The Austrian march in the first instance towards Landshut, and next in the direction of Ampfing (which was totally unknown to Moreau), had put the French left, 25,000 men under Grenier, in great danger; for fully 60,000 of the enemy were ready to fall on them. The Austrians had crossed the Inn at Oetting. As Grenier was leisurely making for Ampfing, he was suddenly assailed by vast masses of the enemy which advanced against him in admirable order. He was speedily overcome and put to the rout. Ney, with his division and with Hardy's, came up in support, but after a brief resistance he also was driven back; and a similar fate was shared by Grandjean when he hurried up to Ney's assistance. Legrand had a sharp conflict in the valley of the Isen; but he likewise was beaten and compelled to retire to the neighbourhood of Dorfen.

The Austrians were everywhere successful; the attack on Grenier had spread the alarm right through the whole of the French Army. But the Austrian staff attached to their victory more importance than was due. On account of the extent of front occupied by the French, and of the presence in the field of the commander-in-chief and his staff, they hastily concluded that they had had to contend against the entire

French Army, whilst in reality only three divisions had been engaged. Their fatal confidence was still further augmented by the French continuing their retreat on the following day, the 2nd of December.

This brilliant commencement was highly encouraging. But, like other successes in war, this one demanded to be followed up with vigour; and it was here that the Austrian commander-in-chief failed. Intoxicated by this first success, he was unable to appreciate the immense advantage of this combat, and how it behoved him to force the beaten French back without intermission on to the columns which would surely be coming up to their support. The Archduke, satisfied with his first result, allowed Moreau a respite, and made no move on the following day. Consequently, that skilful general was allowed time to retire through the forest of Hohenlinden, to the ground which he had quite lately occupied, and had carefully studied; for he had foreseen how it would be a very probable field for a decisive battle.

The forest of Hohenlinden lies between the Isar and the Inn. Parallel to the course of these two rivers, it measures from six to seven leagues in length, and from one league to a league and a half in depth. The thickness of the pine trees, which grow very close together, not only gives a gloomy appearance to the forest, but also obstructs the passage of cavalry and artillery. Two great roads traverse the forest; one leads from Munich by Hohenlinden to Mühldorf, the other also from Munich by Ebersberg to Wasserburg.

On the Munich side of the principal defile lies the village of Hohenlinden. A stretch of open ground extends to some distance on the south of it; at the other extremity of the defile, on the Mühldorf side of the forest, lies Mattenpoet. Exception made of the two main roads leading to Mühldorf and Wasserburg, the forest, broken and uneven, is crossed only by country paths which, Alison states, are almost impracticable during the storms of winter even for foot-passengers.

Everything portended an approaching battle; and Moreau, who had carefully reconnoitred the ground, had determined, on the advice of Dessoles and Grenier, to arrest the Austrians in front of Hohenlinden. It happened that, during a discussion on the proper dispositions to be taken, a Bavarian officer of the engineers attached to the French staff remarked on the existence of a cross-road between the roads of Wasserburg and of Mühldorf, which led to Mattenpoet at the northern entrance of the Hohenlinden defile. Moreau determined to turn this information to advantage. He thereupon arranged to stop the Archduke at the opposite issue from the forest, and for the divisions

General Moreau in front of Hohenlinden

of Decaen and of Richepanse, sent from Ebersberg and Zornotting, to fall on his rear.

On the 3rd of December, the Austrian Army was to march on Ebersberg, Hohenlinden, Preisendorf, and Harthofen. It had been divided into four principal columns, besides which there was an advanced guard and two detached corps. The orders were for these columns to meet in the plain of Amzing, and to close on Munich the same day; so little did the Austrian staff foresee any opposition.

The army comprised 50 battalions and 140 squadrons. Kienmayer was in command of the column on the right; next came Baillet Latour, who had command of the right wing, 25,000 strong; Kollowrath commanded the third column; and Riesch the fourth, about 10,000 strong. Of these columns the third, the one detailed to march on Hohenlinden, was the strongest. It numbered 40,000 men, and it was the only one that marched on a metalled road. It was under the personal direction of the archduke. With this column also marched the greater portion of the artillery, for the columns on the flanks had to advance by inferior roads, principally used by woodcutters. In marching, the infantry came first, then followed a long train of artillery and waggons, and last came all the cavalry.

The success of the preceding days had raised the spirits of the Austrians. The enemy was deemed to be in full retreat, and no resistance was expected before the imperial forces would deploy in battle array in the clearing on the Munich side of the forest.

Moreau had made very able dispositions. He strove, as much as his plan and many obstacles of the theatre of operations permitted, to close up his troops, and to hold them in hand so that they should be thoroughly able to render each other mutual support. On the 3rd, at break of day, Richepanse and Decaen's divisions moved off. Montrichard was directed to replace them with his division, and to support them on the Wasserburg road. Grouchy, who had received the command of Grandjean's division, was posted at the opening of the defile in the clearing in front of Hohenlinden, his right resting on the forest, his left on the road.

Ney occupied the border of the Krainacker wood, to the left of Hohenlinden. The remainder of Grenier's corps, composed of Bastoul's and Legrand's divisions, were extended as far as Hörlkofen, watching the defiles of Isen and of Langdorf. In rear of Hohenlinden, partly on the right and partly on the left of the road, was posted d'Hautpoul's cavalry.

Collaud, with that portion of Sainte Suzanne's corps which was on the right of the Danube, had been ordered to abandon the direction of Landshut, and to come by forced marches by Freising to Erding, where some companies of Legrand's division and d'Espagne's brigade were awaiting him. But the Austrian attack was so unforeseen that one-third of Moreau's army could take no part in the action. Neither Lecourbe nor Sainte Suzanne could close up in time. The French were in the minority; with less than 60,000 men they fought against more than 70,000.

The Austrians were marching as fast as they could, as men who knew the value of time in a season when the day, either for marching or for fighting, was the shortest. The confidence imparted by the advantage gained at Ampfing, and the belief that the French Army had beaten a retreat, made them negligent in the matter of scouting, and the centre column, marching on a good metalled road, outstripped the others. The archduke was ignorant of the dispositions that Moreau had made, and was elated by his success of the 1st of December. He was young, and had seen in retreat this formidable Army of the Rhine—an army which, for a long time, the very best Austrian generals had appeared unable to stop.

The four Austrian columns had for rendezvous the open ground which lies between Hohenlinden and Harthofen, but there was little prospect of their arriving simultaneously. They were marching at a considerable distance from each other, and through a dense forest. The conditions were bad, but they were made worse by the weather, which was simply awful. The centre column alone approached the point of destination at the time when all four ought to have been ready for action. The flank columns lagged far behind.

During the night there was a change of wind, and the heavy rain of the preceding days turned into snow. Snow was falling in large flakes when the battle began at about nine o'clock in the morning. Soon the forest presented a uniform white surface on which it was impossible to distinguish the beaten track.

The first efforts of the Austrians were made against Grouchy. Eight choice battalions tried to turn his right, by stealing round the wood which served him as a support. Grouchy rushed on them, stopped them, and beat them back, capturing the general who commanded them. Other attacks directed on the front of the division did not meet with much better success. The conflict was as obstinate and bloody as any the French had sustained.

Battle of Hohenlinden

The action at this period simply consisted in holding the central Austrian column in check, so as to gain time for Richepanse to complete his movement on Mattenpoet.

Baillet Latour's troops were already nearing the border of the wood of Krainacker; the battle was becoming more spirited, and extending towards the left. Moreau, in the meanwhile, had been able to detect signs of uneasiness and hesitation in the Austrian forces, which made him suppose that Richepanse was commencing to bear on the Austrian rear. Whether he was likely to be successful or not, it was desirable to deliver some master stroke, if for nothing else, to disengage him. Moreau ordered Ney's and Grouchy's divisions to move forward —an order for which the troops had been impatiently waiting. Ney fell on the enemy, overthrew him in the defile, and captured 1,000 men and 10 guns.

Moreau had issued orders for Decaen's and Richepanse's divisions to move up along the forest as the Austrians came down, and once having reached Mattenpoet by way of Saint Christophe, to work back in the direction of Hohenlinden on the rear of the Archduke's principal column.

The manoeuvre was bold and simple, and was, moreover, confided to an officer who possessed ample ability to carry it to a successful termination.

Richepanse, as we have already seen, had taken the direction of Mattenpoet before daybreak. But whilst his division, blinded by the snow, was labouring in the tortuous and difficult lanes indicated by the Bavarian staff officer, Riesch's column had reached Saint Christophe, and penetrated between his first and second brigades.

Any other officer would possibly have halted to re-establish the connection between the two brigades, and reunite his division. But Richepanse knew too well the full importance of the rule which had been assigned to him to do so. He continued his march with all possible rapidity, and with only two half-brigades and the 1st Regiment of Chasseurs he boldly entered into Mattenpoet. He counted on Decaen to disentangle his second brigade and to come to his help.

Falling suddenly on the Nassau *cuirassiers*, which he found dismounted, he captured a large portion, and the rest he dispersed. A large body of cavalry was coming up from Haag; against this he directed Walther, whilst, turning to the left, he threw himself impetuously into the narrow defile. The great park of the army was at that moment following on the traces of Kollowrath. In beholding such a rich prize

The chasseurs at the Battle of Hohenlinden

the French forgot their fatigues, and discarded all thought of danger, and, attacking, spread terror and death in every direction. A battery and three battalions were sent back by Kollowrath to stop them; but in vain, for in spite of the canister, the French closed on them with the bayonet and put the Austrians to flight. This was the last effort of the Austrians; and after this Richepanse met Ney's victorious troops, which were bearing on the Austrians from the opposite direction.

★★★★★★

Michael Ney. In the year 1766 (17th of January) was born at Sarrelouis Michael Ney. At the age of sixteen, much against the desire of his father, he enlisted in a regiment of hussars, in which he was a non-commissioned officer at the outbreak of the Revolution. A man possessed of such extreme intrepidity and rare coolness in danger was bound to become conspicuous in those days of hard fighting. His comrades, soon recognising his eminent talent in the field, voted for his advancement in their regiment. He was next appointed *aide-de-camp* to General de Lallemand, and was adjutant-general to Kléber. For the capture of Mannheim by a *coup de main* in 1799, he was promoted general of division.

It was only after the campaign of 1800, that Bonaparte, wishing to conciliate some of the Republican leaders of the Army of the Rhine, appointed Ney to be Inspector-General of Cavalry. He was afterwards created Marshal of France, Duke of Elchingen, and Prince de la Moskowa. But his greatest award was the title of *the bravest of the brave*, not an empty title when bestowed by the great Napoleon, who could count brave men by the thousand in his army.

★★★★★★

The confusion Richepanse's onset had occasioned in the rear spread rapidly to the van. This enormous column, the hope of the Austrians, was no more. For the French skirmishers had speedily extended along the flanks of the road, and caused the enemy severe losses. The road, not long before covered by thousands of soldiers moving in martial array, was now strewn with corpses, full of riderless horses, and clogged by an immense train of vehicles, gun-waggons, and guns. But Richepanse, not forgetful of Walther whom he had left to deal with the cavalry coming from Haag, retraced his steps. Walther had been seriously wounded; but Montbrun, at the head of the *chasseurs*, was still holding his own against very superior forces. Richepanse arrived on the scene, threw his infantry right and left into the forest, and placed himself at the head of the cavalry. He led a charge along the road, and compelled the enemy to beat a hasty retreat. He was here rejoined by his second brigade, which Decaen had succeeded in disengaging.

The Austrian main column no longer existed. But the wings had not yet taken part in the action, for the archduke had omitted to take into calculation the bad nature and state of the roads. Owing to this oversight, the columns of Kienmayer and of Baillet Latour only reached the battlefield as the fate of the battle was being decided on the main road. As they appeared at Preisendorf and Buch, they were attacked by Grenier, who was ready to meet them with Bastoul's and Legrand's divisions supported by one of Ney's brigades and the cavalry reserve. The Austrians were twice as numerous; but, elated by the report of the success obtained in the centre, Grenier did not hesitate to assume the offensive. The fight was stubborn, the same positions were carried and retaken several times, and for a long while the result remained uncertain. At last Legrand drove the Austrians back on Langdorf, whilst Bonnet, at the head of one of Bastoul's brigades, drove the troops opposed to him back on Isen.

Baillet Latour still persevered in his efforts against Bastoul's centre. Bastoul was nearly overcome, and had had to fall back on his right, when d'Hautpoul came to his aid, and charged the Austrians. These, however, still held their ground firmly, until the arrival of Joba's brigade, which threatened their left at an opportune moment, and made Latour nervous about his retreat, which he hastened to effect.

On the Austrian left, Riesch, notwithstanding the fight in the morning, had not given up all hope of arriving at the rendezvous, and was marching in the direction of Hohenlinden. Decaen, keen to support Richepanse, who was marching on Mattenpoet, had not driven this column as far away as he should have done; so when, on his arrival at Mattenpoet, he heard from Grouchy of Richepanse's success in the defile, he turned about and, in all haste, marched the Polish legion of Kniasewicz back to Saint Christophe, whilst Durutte's brigade was directed on Albaching. The Poles at first had to sustain all the weight of the Austrian column, but Durutte soon appeared on the enemy's right and rear, and made them retire along the Wasserburg road.

The battle was over; Moreau had conquered. One hundred guns, many flags, and 11,000 prisoners were the harvest of the victors. An immediate advance into the valley of the Isen, where the whole of the enemy's right was crowded, would have made the victory still more complete.

Moreau's retreat with the object of getting the Austrians entangled in the forest of Hohenlinden, was a master-stroke. He has, however, been severely criticized for the risky manoeuvre by which he bore on the enemy's rear. Critics remark that such a manoeuvre, performed by an isolated corps without support, exposed to a thousand chances of miscarriage, must always be extremely hazardous. (In this case, the general detailed to carry it out was remarkable for his intelligence and energy. This matchless officer, after having rendered such distinguished services to the Republic, met with a miserable end in Guadaloupe. Attacked by yellow fever, he was soon laid in his grave.)

He weighed the safety of one of his brigades against the importance of the special task assigned to him, and he decided to attack with the small number of troops he had, trusting that Decaen would succeed in shaking the enemy off. But what might not have occurred had the Austrians been more numerous at Saint Christophe to bar the way to Richepanse—if they had hastened on the venturesome general's traces as he marched on Mattenpoet? The idea of intercepting the enemy was brilliant; but the plan might have failed for the simple reason that the troops detailed for this manoeuvre were not sufficient. It would not have been too much if two divisions had been detailed for it. Napoleon said of Hohenlinden that:—

> It was one of those great triumphs that are brought about by chance, and obtained without plan.

In this he was not just to Moreau. Nor are those who hold that the march to Mattenpoet was a sudden inspiration of Richepanse; for the official report and other documents found at the Depot de la Guerre prove most distinctly that it was not so.

Moreau's combinations were full of simplicity and greatness. He had foreseen all, and guarded against all possible surprise. His tact, his steadiness during the action, his calm, showed off his military genius, which developed into greater proportions every day.

Alison states:—

> The whole arrangements of the French general were defensive; he merely wished to gain time, in order to enable his right and left wings, under Lecourbe and Sainte Suzanne, to arrive and take part in the action.

But the orders given to Richepanse, though only general ones, could but be interpreted in one sense, and Richepanse viewed them in the right sense. Guided by a miserable and low hatred which is supposed to have originated in Moreau's too open disapproval of some of the measures which followed the 18th *Brumaire*, and more so in his rejection of the plan of campaign, Napoleon wrote some unworthy strictures on the Battle of Hohenlinden, and principally on the action taken by Richepanse.

✶✶✶✶✶✶

Lanfrey directs attention to the *Mémorial du Depot de la Guerre, tom. iv.*, in which Moreau's orders to Richepanse were; "*Combattre l'ennemi après son débouché décidé sur Hohenlinden.*"

✶✶✶✶✶✶

As in the case of Massena, these criticisms were penned after the events. When announcing the victory to the Corps Législatif, he made use of these words:—

This victory has resounded over the whole of Europe; it will be classed in history among those memorable days which have been rendered illustrious by French valour.

Writing to Moreau, he said:—

I refrain from telling you all the interest that I have taken in your fine and skilful manoeuvres; in this campaign you have surpassed yourself.

Bourrienne relates that when the First Consul received the intelligence of the victory of Hohenlinden, on Saturday, the 6th of December, he had just returned from the theatre; that he literally danced with joy, for he had not expected so important a result from the movements of the Army of the Rhine.

To secure all the advantages which the Battle of Hohenlinden offered, it was indispensable to occupy Salzburg as soon as possible. From that point, the Austrian corps then occupying the upper valley of the Inn and the Tyrol could be taken in reverse. The direct road leading from Vienna to Italy could be menaced; and if the French, victorious on the banks of the Adige, pursued vigorously the enemies they had beaten on that river, there would be no refuge for them but in the depths of Hungary. In the valley of the Danube the hereditary states were quite open, without any fortresses for their protection which might present a barrier and arrest the march of a successful invader. This constituted the real weakness on that side.

The French crossed the Inn without much opposition. The Austrian Army, already considerably disorganised, became more so from the impression produced by this passage. In an excellent position in front of Salzburg, where the Saal and Salza meet, their staff had succeeded in rallying about 30,000 infantry and 10,000 cavalry.

On the 14th of December, Lecourbe, under cover of a dense fog, plunged into the midst of the enemy's squadrons. Thanks to the distance at which the Austrian infantry were stationed, and to the mutual help eagerly given by the regiments engaged, no unfortunate result followed Lecourbe's rashness.

The centre crossed the Salza at Laufen. Moreau detached Decaen's division to go to the support of the engaged wing. It advanced against the right of the position, making a great noise with the artillery. The Austrians became alarmed for their communications, and hastily retired. Decaen was the first to enter into Salzburg, where he was speedily joined by Lecourbe. Grenier and Sainte Suzanne were advancing on the left in echelon. Grenier crossed the Salza partly at Laufen and partly at Tittmoning, moving on the Traun by way of Ried. Ney's division was detailed to invest Burghausen. Sainte Suzanne scouted the course of the Danube, keeping a column on the left bank to keep up communications with Augereau.

The Austrians strove to turn to account the many excellent positions which exist in the country between the Salza and the Enns; but what could a disorganised army accomplish? Richepanse, with his division, had been thrown as an advanced guard on the Voklabruck road. The general did not lose sight of the enemy for a moment, and boldly attacked them without thinking of awaiting the coming up of Grouchy and Decaen, who followed in second line to support him. The Austrians endeavoured to hold the positions of Frankmarkt, of Voklabruck, and of Schwauenstadt, but they were speedily turned out and put to flight. In all these combats (all the glory of which belongs to Richepanse and his brave troops) the French captured 6,000 prisoners, 25 guns, and several thousands of covered waggons and carriages.

On the evening of the 20th of December, the entire French Army was deployed, the principal portion of it being on the far side of the Traun. Little troubled by the presence of Hiller on his right, or of Klenau on his left, Moreau was preparing to march on Vienna, and to dictate peace in the capital.

Austria paid dearly for not having followed the advice of the Archduke Charles. He had retired to Bohemia, and it was there that the news of the Austrian reverses reached him and caused him sore distress. Now when the reverses which his wisdom had foreseen had reduced the empire to dire extremities, the emperor, alarmed by the dread of a Franco-Russian alliance, restored him to the command of the army. But it was far too late. The Austrian Army had been too severely beaten, and the Archduke saw no other way open for saving Vienna from the conqueror who was approaching, than to sue for peace. He forthwith sent to propose a suspension of arms.

At no period in their history, not even in the early part of Maria Theresa's reign, was the situation of the Austrian monarchy in a more critical juncture. The French, after the signal victory of Hohenlinden, had crossed the Inn and the Ipps, and, arriving at Steyer, in Upper Austria, were within seventeen leagues of Vienna. The Gallo-Batavian Army at the same time were advancing along the Danube. Macdonald, in possession of the mountains of the Tyrol, had the option of descending into Italy or Germany, while Brune, after taking 15,000 prisoners in twenty days, was ready to penetrate into the mountains of Carinthia. (V. Arnault, C. L. F. Panckoucke, and others, *Memoirs of the Public and Private Life of Napoleon Bonaparte*, vol. i.)

General Grune presented himself at Moreau's headquarters with full powers to conclude an armistice. This demand was backed by an assurance from the archduke to the French commander-in-chief that the Emperor of Austria was determined to make peace with or without the consent of his allies. A more ambitious general might have insisted on dictating his terms within the walls of Vienna; but Moreau disdained the empty honour of a triumphal entry into the Austrian capital. He had done, he thought, enough for his glory.

The resumption of hostilities dated only from the 28th of November, and in the course of about twenty days the French Army had won a decisive battle, had conquered some eighty leagues of territory, had forced the Inn, the Salza, the Traun, and the Enns, one and all of them formidable barriers. It had reached a point not twenty leagues distant from the capital of the Austrian empire. Its trophies were immense. Of the Austrians more than 45,000 had fallen in battle, or had laid down their arms; 147 field-pieces, 400 waggons, and about 800 army vehicles had been captured. In Rocquancourt's words:—

The annals of war show few examples of a more extraordinary pursuit, more fruitful and better directed. (J. Roequancourt,

Cours Complet d'Art et d'Histoire Militaires, tom ii.)

In Volume 1, we have remarked how a victory obtained in Italy could never have had the same results as one gained on the Danube. The truth of this observation was proved by the different results which followed the battles of Marengo and Hohenlinden. Not only was the latter one of the finest battles fought in the eighteenth century, but it was decisive. Though the results of Marengo were not to be despised, that victory of itself was not sufficient to inspire terror in the minds of the Austrian Government; the battle had been fought too far from the centre of the empire. It was only after Hohenlinden, when the French were almost at the gates of the capital, that the Cabinet of Vienna seriously entertained overtures of peace.

The eighteenth century closed with two important battles—Marengo and Hohenlinden. These were the last battles of the First Republic, and in both French valour prevailed. In two distinct theatres of war, Germany and Italy, the French had established their reputation as the foremost soldiers on the continent of Europe—a reputation which they were to uphold in many hard-fought fields under Napoleon.

For some soldiers, Hohenlinden, the last of the Republican victories, eclipsed Marengo; but though it led to greater results, for it forced Austria to sue for peace, and was richer in fine manoeuvres and in trophies, it has not been accorded the same measure of renown. True enough, the victory of Marengo was not quite as momentous in its consequences, but the already brilliant career of the victor, his name already in everybody's mouth, his position as First Consul at the head of the nation, and, more than all, the boldness of his enterprise, had captivated the French.

During these last hundred years to most men the passage of the Great Saint Bernard, followed so quickly by the triumph of Marengo, has formed an object of the very highest interest. Moreau trusted for success more to skilful combinations and to methodical arrangements than to fortune, and his deeds lacked that daring which so easily captivates the minds of men.

Bonaparte had an *entourage*—men who had come to believe in his star, and were too ready to fall in adoration before him. These men took great care to magnify his deeds, and to rank them above all others.

When the First Consul assumed the reins of government, he had promised the people victory and peace. In less than a year after that date, in the sunlit fields in front of Alessandria and in the dense forest of Hohenlinden, French arms had inflicted two severe defeats on the most determined of their antagonists. Now that these had been thoroughly humiliated, what remained to be done was to bind them by a solemn treaty of peace. On the 9th of February, 1801, this treaty was signed, and the news excited the most enthusiastic joy when it reached the French capital. Bonaparte announced it to the people of Paris in the following words:—

A glorious peace has terminated the Continental War.

The Peace of Luneville was the fruit of Marengo and Hohenlinden. It restored France to the honourable position it had held before the disasters of 1799.

The First Consul, who did not relish having a competitor, above all a successful soldier, left Moreau unemployed, and the latter soon retired to his property of Grosbois. (The property of Grosbois had belonged to Barras. Moreau bought it from him, and the First Consul bought it from Moreau, when he was sent into exile, and bestowed it on Berthier.) Work in the field for the soldier was now over, for the whole of the Continent was at peace with France. She had leisure to breathe till 1805, by which time Moreau, accused of having conspired against the life of Bonaparte, had been arrested (15th of February, 1804), tried, and banished from France for two years.

★★★★★★

Everyone must deeply regret that such an able and soldierly commander as Moreau should have fallen at Dresden bearing arms against his countrymen. He might have pleaded as an excuse for this, that he had yielded to his ambitious wife's counsel—that in fighting Napoleon he was not fighting France. But in what greater estimation his memory would now be held in his country, had he rejected, as he should, his wife's silly advice and the allurements of the Allies!

★★★★★★

Bonaparte had delivered France from the domination of the sections, from the tyranny of the Directory, and from the attacks of foreign foes; his influence increased from day to day, until nothing could satisfy the people but that the government of the country should be made hereditary in the family of the First Consul. The happiness of France, her glory, her prosperity, all seemed to require it; and the nation would not be contented until the conqueror of Marengo became absolute master of its destinies as Emperor of the French people.

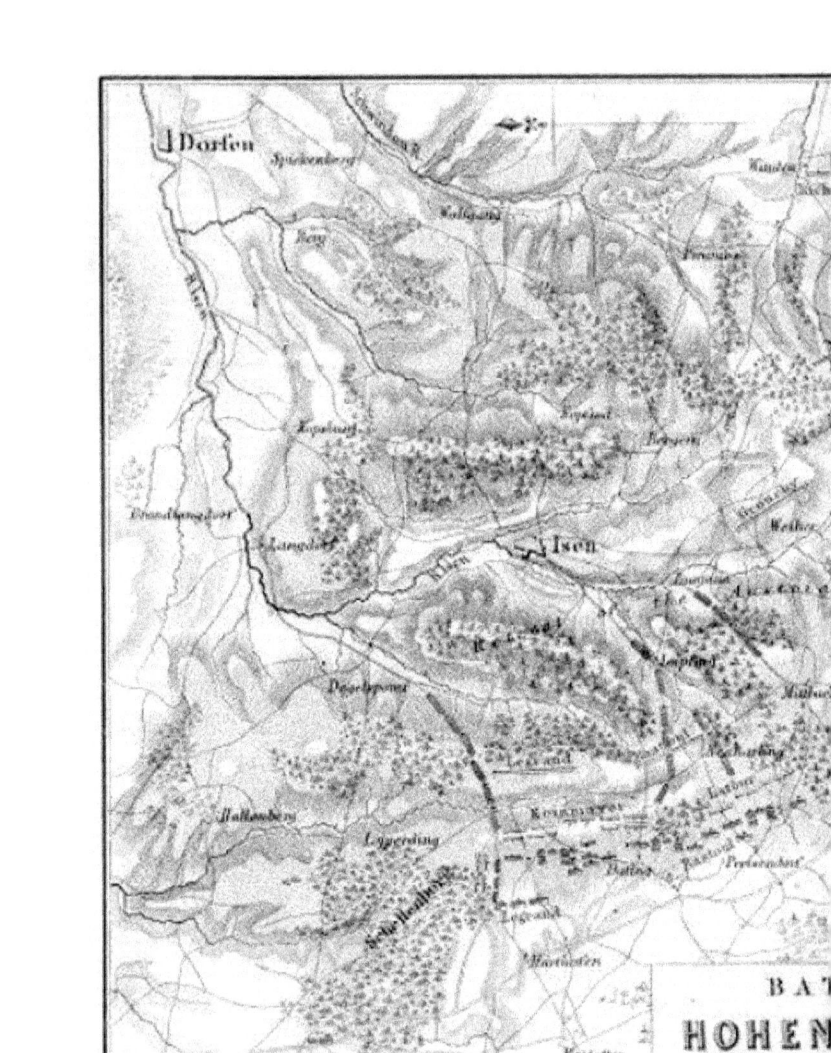

ALSO FROM LEONAUR
AVAILABLE IN SOFTCOVER OR HARDCOVER WITH DUST JACKET

THE FALL OF THE MOGHUL EMPIRE OF HINDUSTAN *by H. G. Keene*—By the beginning of the nineteenth century, as British and Indian armies under Lake and Wellesley dominated the scene, a little over half a century of conflict brought the Moghul Empire to its knees.

LADY SALE'S AFGHANISTAN *by Florentia Sale*—An Indomitable Victorian Lady's Account of the Retreat from Kabul During the First Afghan War.

THE CAMPAIGN OF MAGENTA AND SOLFERINO 1859 *by Harold Carmichael Wylly*—The Decisive Conflict for the Unification of Italy.

FRENCH'S CAVALRY CAMPAIGN *by J. G. Maydon*—A Special Correspondent's View of British Army Mounted Troops During the Boer War.

CAVALRY AT WATERLOO *by Sir Evelyn Wood*—British Mounted Troops During the Campaign of 1815.

THE SUBALTERN *by George Robert Gleig*—The Experiences of an Officer of the 85th Light Infantry During the Peninsular War.

NAPOLEON AT BAY, 1814 *by F. Loraine Petre*—The Campaigns to the Fall of the First Empire.

NAPOLEON AND THE CAMPAIGN OF 1806 *by Colonel Vachée*—The Napoleonic Method of Organisation and Command to the Battles of Jena & Auerstädt.

THE COMPLETE ADVENTURES IN THE CONNAUGHT RANGERS *by William Grattan*—The 88th Regiment during the Napoleonic Wars by a Serving Officer.

BUGLER AND OFFICER OF THE RIFLES *by William Green & Harry Smith*—With the 95th (Rifles) during the Peninsular & Waterloo Campaigns of the Napoleonic Wars.

NAPOLEONIC WAR STORIES *by Sir Arthur Quiller-Couch*—Tales of soldiers, spies, battles & sieges from the Peninsular & Waterloo campaingns.

CAPTAIN OF THE 95TH (RIFLES) *by Jonathan Leach*—An officer of Wellington's sharpshooters during the Peninsular, South of France and Waterloo campaigns of the Napoleonic wars.

RIFLEMAN COSTELLO *by Edward Costello*—The adventures of a soldier of the 95th (Rifles) in the Peninsular & Waterloo Campaigns of the Napoleonic wars.

AVAILABLE ONLINE AT **www.leonaur.com**
AND FROM ALL GOOD BOOK STORES

ALSO FROM LEONAUR
AVAILABLE IN SOFTCOVER OR HARDCOVER WITH DUST JACKET

AFGHANISTAN: THE BELEAGUERED BRIGADE by G. R. Gleig—An Account of Sale's Brigade During the First Afghan War.

IN THE RANKS OF THE C. I. V by Erskine Childers—With the City Imperial Volunteer Battery (Honourable Artillery Company) in the Second Boer War.

THE BENGAL NATIVE ARMY by F. G. Cardew—An Invaluable Reference Resource.

THE 7TH (QUEEN'S OWN) HUSSARS: Volume 4—1688-1914 by C. R. B. Barrett—Uniforms, Equipment, Weapons, Traditions, the Services of Notable Officers and Men & the Appendices to All Volumes—Volume 4: 1688-1914.

THE SWORD OF THE CROWN by Eric W. Sheppard—A History of the British Army to 1914.

THE 7TH (QUEEN'S OWN) HUSSARS: Volume 3—1818-1914 by C. R. B. Barrett—On Campaign During the Canadian Rebellion, the Indian Mutiny, the Sudan, Matabeleland, Mashonaland and the Boer War Volume 3: 1818-1914.

THE KHARTOUM CAMPAIGN by Bennet Burleigh—A Special Correspondent's View of the Reconquest of the Sudan by British and Egyptian Forces under Kitchener—1898.

EL PUCHERO by Richard McSherry—The Letters of a Surgeon of Volunteers During Scott's Campaign of the American-Mexican War 1847-1848.

RIFLEMAN SAHIB by E. Maude—The Recollections of an Officer of the Bombay Rifles During the Southern Mahratta Campaign, Second Sikh War, Persian Campaign and Indian Mutiny.

THE KING'S HUSSAR by Edwin Mole—The Recollections of a 14th (King's) Hussar During the Victorian Era.

JOHN COMPANY'S CAVALRYMAN by William Johnson—The Experiences of a British Soldier in the Crimea, the Persian Campaign and the Indian Mutiny.

COLENSO & DURNFORD'S ZULU WAR by Frances E. Colenso & Edward Durnford—The first and possibly the most important history of the Zulu War.

U. S. DRAGOON by Samuel E. Chamberlain—Experiences in the Mexican War 1846-48 and on the South Western Frontier.

AVAILABLE ONLINE AT **www.leonaur.com**
AND FROM ALL GOOD BOOK STORES

ALSO FROM LEONAUR
AVAILABLE IN SOFTCOVER OR HARDCOVER WITH DUST JACKET

THE 9TH—THE KING'S (LIVERPOOL REGIMENT) IN THE GREAT WAR 1914 - 1918 *by Enos H. G. Roberts*—Mersey to mud—war and Liverpool men.

THE GAMBARDIER *by Mark Severn*—The experiences of a battery of Heavy artillery on the Western Front during the First World War.

FROM MESSINES TO THIRD YPRES *by Thomas Floyd*—A personal account of the First World War on the Western front by a 2/5th Lancashire Fusilier.

THE IRISH GUARDS IN THE GREAT WAR - VOLUME 1 *by Rudyard Kipling*—Edited and Compiled from Their Diaries and Papers—The First Battalion.

THE IRISH GUARDS IN THE GREAT WAR - VOLUME 1 *by Rudyard Kipling*—Edited and Compiled from Their Diaries and Papers—The Second Battalion.

ARMOURED CARS IN EDEN *by K. Roosevelt*—An American President's son serving in Rolls Royce armoured cars with the British in Mesopatamia & with the American Artillery in France during the First World War.

CHASSEUR OF 1914 *by Marcel Dupont*—Experiences of the twilight of the French Light Cavalry by a young officer during the early battles of the great war in Europe.

TROOP HORSE & TRENCH *by R.A. Lloyd*—The experiences of a British Lifeguardsman of the household cavalry fighting on the western front during the First World War 1914-18.

THE EAST AFRICAN MOUNTED RIFLES *by C.J. Wilson*—Experiences of the campaign in the East African bush during the First World War.

THE LONG PATROL *by George Berrie*—A Novel of Light Horsemen from Gallipoli to the Palestine campaign of the First World War.

THE FIGHTING CAMELIERS *by Frank Reid*—The exploits of the Imperial Camel Corps in the desert and Palestine campaigns of the First World War.

STEEL CHARIOTS IN THE DESERT *by S. C. Rolls*—The first world war experiences of a Rolls Royce armoured car driver with the Duke of Westminster in Libya and in Arabia with T.E. Lawrence.

WITH THE IMPERIAL CAMEL CORPS IN THE GREAT WAR *by Geoffrey Inchbald*—The story of a serving officer with the British 2nd battalion against the Senussi and during the Palestine campaign.

AVAILABLE ONLINE AT **www.leonaur.com**
AND FROM ALL GOOD BOOK STORES

www.ingramcontent.com/pod-product-compliance
Lightning Source LLC
Chambersburg PA
CBHW031623160426
43196CB00006B/256